DEFENCE AND THE MEDIA
IN TIME OF LIMITED WAR

DEFENCE
AND THE
MEDIA
IN TIME OF
LIMITED WAR

Edited by
PETER R. YOUNG

FRANK CASS

First published 1992 in Great Britain by
FRANK CASS & CO. LTD
Gainsborough House, Gainsborough Road,
London E11 1RS, England

and in the United States of America by
FRANK CASS
c/o International Specialized Book Services, Inc.,
5602 N.E. Hassalo Street,
Portland, Oregon 97213

Copyright © 1992

British Library Cataloguing in Publication Data

Defence and the media in time of limited war.
I. Young, Peter
070.44935502

ISBN 0-7146-34786
ISBN 0-7146-40859 pbk

Library of Congress Cataloging-in-Publication Data

Defence and the media in time of limited war / edited by Peter R.
Young.
    p.   cm.
    "This group of studies first appeared in a special issue on
Defence and the media in time of limited wars of Small wars and
insurgencies vol. 2"—T.p. verso.
    Includes bibliographical references and index.
        ISBN 0-7146-3478-G(HB). — ISBN 0-7146-4085-9 (PB)
    1. Press and politics—History—20th century—Congresses.
2. Freedom and the press—20th century—Congresses. 3. Government
and the press—20th century—Congresses. 4. War in the press–
–History—20th century—Congresses. 5. Armed Forces and mass media–
–History—20th century—Congresses. I. Young, Peter R.
PN4751.D43   1992
323.44'5—dc20   91-46217
                                                            CIP

This group of studies first appeared in a Special Issue on 'Defence and the
Media in Time of Limited War' of *Small Wars & Insurgencies*, Vol. 2, No.
3 (Dec. 1991), published by Frank Cass & Co. Ltd.

Typeset by Regent Typesetting
Printed in Great Britain by
Antony Rowe Ltd, Chippenham

Contents

III. THE AUSTRALIAN EXPERIENCE

Notes on the Contributors

Bill Hayden has been Governor-General of the Commonwealth of Australia since February 1989. He sat in the Queensland State House of Representatives from 1961 to 1984. A minister in the Whitlam government, he led the Australian Labor Party in opposition 1977–83 while also acting as the party's defence spokesman. He was Minister of Foreign Affairs 1983–84 in the first Hawke government.

Peter Gration (General and Chief of the Australian Defence Force since April 1987). He holds a Civil Engineering honours degree from Melbourne University as well as a BA and B.Econ. degrees from Queensland University. Commissioned in 1952 into the Royal Australian Engineers, his service has included Malaysia, Papua New Guinea and Vietnam (CO of 1st Australian Civil Affairs Unit, 1969–70). In 1977 he was the first Australian International Fellow at the US Army War College. GOC Logistic Command 1979–81, General Gration has since held Army or Defence Force staff posts including Chief of the General Staff 1984–87.

Stewart Woodman is Senior Research Fellow at the Strategic and Defence Studies Centre, Research School of Pacific Studies, at the Australian National University (ANU). He holds a BA from Sydney University and a Ph.D. from ANU.

Clem Lloyd is Foundation Professor of the School of Journalism at Wollongong University, New South Wales. He holds BA and B.Econ. degrees from Sydney University, a B.Leg. from Macquarrie University and further degrees (MA and Ph.D.) from Australian National University.

Peter R. Young is Senior Research Fellow in Defence Media Studies at the School of Media and Journalism, Queensland University of Technology. He retired from the Australian Army with the rank of Major after service including Vietnam. He founded the influential Australian Defence Journal *Pacific Defence Reporter* in 1974 (published ten times a year). He was also defence and foreign affairs editor with Australian Network 10 Television. He holds BA (Deaking

University, Geelong) and M.Def.Stud. (New South Wales) degrees and is currently completing his D.Phil.

Carlyle A. Thayer III is Associate Professor in the Department of Politics, Australian Defence Force Academy. He holds AB (Brown), MA (Yale) and Ph.D. (ANU) degrees. He published *War By Other Means: National Liberation and Revolution in Vietnam* (Sydney and Boston: Allen & Unwin) in 1989.

Michael McKinley is Lecturer in International Relations and Strategy at the Australian National University where he received his Ph.D. His published work has appeared in the *RUSI Journal*.

Sir Jeremy Moore (Major-General, RM, Retd.) was a regular Royal Marine Commando Officer from 1947 until 1983. He won the MC in 1952 (Malayan Emergency) and a Bar in the Brunei Revolt of 1962. His commands included No. 42 Commando in Northern Ireland (1972–73), a Joint International Brigade and 3rd Commando Brigade from 1977. As Major-General, Commando Forces, Royal Marines from 1979, he became Land Forces Commander in the recapture of the Falklands Islands during May–June 1982.

Kevin Foster is a Lecturer in the Department of English and Communication Studies, University of New England, Armidale, New South Wales. He took his Ph.D. at Monash University, Melbourne. His MA was taken at Saskatchewan University.

J. Metcalf III (Vice Admiral, USN, Retd.) commanded the 1983 US intervention in Grenada.

Michael J. Dugan (General, USAF, Retd.) was USAF Chief of Staff until his dismissal for a plainspoken interview with the Press during the Gulf crisis in September 1990.

David H. Hackworth (Colonel, US Army, Retd.) is Contributory Editor for *Newsweek* magazine and author of the international bestseller *About Face* (1989), his Cold War memoirs. In 1971 he resigned from the US Army in protest at the Vietnam War's mismanagement. Since then he has covered eight wars as a war correspondent.

Ian McAllister is Head of the Department of Politics, Australian Defence Force Academy. He holds MSC and Ph.D. degrees from Strathclyde University, Glasgow. He has helped conduct studies of the 1987 and 1990 Australian elections as well as co-authoring *Australian Political Facts* (Melbourne: Longman Cheshire, 1990).

Toni Makkai is a member of the Department of Law in the Research School of Social Sciences, Australian National University.

Allan J. Behm is First Assistant Secretary in the Security Division of the Federal Attorney-General's Department, Canberra. He holds a Dip.Phil.

Terry O'Connor is Defence Correspondent of the Australian Associated Press and was an Accredited Australian War Correspondent during the Gulf War.

Adrian D'Hagé (Brigadier, Australian Army) has been Director General of Public Information, Australian Defence Force since December 1990. As a colonel he was Director of Joint Operations during the 1987 Fiji Crisis. Brigadier D'Hagé was commissioned in 1967 and won the MC in Vietnam (1969) with 6th Battalion, The Royal Australian Regiment, a unit he commanded in 1984–85.

Introduction

Events in the Gulf Crisis of 1990–91 have highlighted the importance
of the increasingly complex and difficult relations between Defence
and the Media in time of War – especially in time of limited conflict
when the well-being – let alone the security – of the home nation may
not be affected. This problem has become especially acute given the
growth of the new high technology media and its global spread and
immediacy.

The question of how to reconcile the competing demands for secrecy
on the one hand and the public's right to know on the other is fast
emerging as a major question of our times. It is a question made all the
more acute when we consider that the media now caters to one of the
most sophisticated global audiences that, in Western liberal democracies, has come to expect to have both sides of every argument
presented to them as a right.

How long even the most patriotic of nations would accept any
limitation on that right – or even if they would be prepared to cede it at
all, is an area that has yet to be resolved.

In Brisbane during 3–5 April 1991, there was held what is believed to
be the first ever *International Conference* on the topic of *Defence and
the Media in Time of Limited Conflict* to look at this and other issues
stemming from the problem.

Jointly funded by the Queensland University of Technology and the
Australian Department of Defence, the three-day Conference was a
major success, attracting 160 delegates from Great Britain, the United
States, Zambia, Papua New Guinea, Brunei, New Zealand, France,
Indonesia and, of course, Australia.

This volume publishes nearly all the papers delivered at this conference whose main focus was on post-1945 limited wars especially
Vietnam, Northern Ireland, the Falklands, Grenada and the Gulf; all
of which receive detailed analysis. Most of the contributors had
practical experience of one side or other in the Defence/Media
relationship; several had experienced both roles.

1

PART I
DEFINING THE PROBLEM

Opening Address

HIS EXCELLENCY
THE HONOURABLE BILL HAYDEN
Governor-General of the Commonwealth of Australia

Thank you for the welcome. I am delighted to join you today and to open officially this first international conference on Defence and the Media in Time of Limited Conflict. I am not sure whether you have invited me because, as Governor-General, I hold the Command-in-Chief of the Australian Defence Force; or whether, after 30 years of public life, I have managed to survive my share of battles with the media. Like the veterans of Agincourt, I can strip my sleeve and show my scars with the rest of them.

Whatever the reason, it is a pleasure to be here and to welcome so many distinguished visitors to this conference. For your topic is of profound importance for every citizen of a liberal democracy – a society, that is, whose very lifeblood depends on the free flow of public information and opinion. And yet in time of war, when whole populations may be involved in the conflict – whether the campaign is considered to be 'limited' or not – how do you reconcile the competing demands for the open exchange of information on the one hand, with the self-evident needs for military security and secrecy on the other?

Are there any limitations to what is often called the public's 'right to know'? And if so, who should set them? Politicians? The defence forces? Or does one trust to the media's own good judgement and well-known sense of self-restraint? These are questions that have been argued since the first modern war correspondents, William Russell and Edwin Godkin, sent their hand-written dispatches to the London press from the battlefields of the Crimea in 1854.

What gives them greater relevance today is the immediacy of global telecommunications – as anyone can attest who saw on their television sets the night skies of the Middle East alight with missile attacks even as they were happening. I hesitate to call any war fortuitous. But there is no doubt that the experiences of the Gulf War – the way in which the release of information was handled by the Allied forces, the media's response to it, and the impact of contemporary technology – put the issues to be discussed in a clear and timely perspective.

You may not necessarily reach agreement. The 'friction' (if I may borrow a term from von Clausewitz to describe the unpredictable confusion of war) will always exist between the military and the media – and on the whole I think it a healthy thing that this should be so.

Only by constant challenge, testing and debate do the institutions of a free society retain their vigour and commitment to the wider interest – and hence the significance of this conference. I would like to make some comments shortly on the nature of this 'friction' between the military and the media – each with differing perceptions of their roles and responsibilities – as they have changed over the past few decades.

But it is worth spending a few moments to consider what is meant by the term 'limited' conflict, since it does seem to circumscribe the topic – as though the defence/media relationship would be qualitatively different at times of 'unlimited' or general global warfare when, presumably, the imposition of much tighter censorship would be adopted. 'Limited' conflict is one of those flexible terms about which opinions may differ. The programme notes for this conference say that in such a conflict the 'well-being, let alone the security of the home nation may not be affected'. But every territorial war involves *some-body's* homeland. And those who wrote on the doctrine of 'limited' conflict in the recently published Royal Australian Air Force (RAAF) *Air Power Manual* said: 'Normally, such conflicts would be limited geographically to a single theatre, or operationally in the weapons employed, although they may include the use of tactical nuclear weapons'.[1] Moreover, it goes on, 'the term limited war embraces a host of threats and hostile acts which may confront a nation, from terrorism to full-scale national invasion'. Acts of aggression, that is, that can range in scale from low, to medium, to high intensity conflict.

In these terms, all major wars since the Second World War – Korea, Vietnam, the Falklands and, no doubt, the Gulf War – are considered 'limited' by the *Air Power Manual*. Certainly they were all wars where one or other of the countries represented here were involved – and wars in which there was a high degree of interest by the respective national media. Case studies on most of these conflicts will be discussed during the conference.

The important issue is the extent to which the military's control of the information flow has changed from the quite open, unfettered

news coverage of Vietnam, to the far more restricted media management, if I may so put it, of the Falklands or the Gulf. That, and the
extent to which such changes might be considered justifiable from a
military point of view. Most commentators have seen Vietnam as
something of a watershed. Most journalists had little trouble gaining
accreditation. They could travel relatively freely, often with combat
troops, sending back graphic accounts and, especially, television
pictures of the human tragedy of war in all its bloody horror. The speed
of communications were such, even then, that I have been told of field
commanders having to respond to hostile criticisms in the media back
home on the conduct of a battle, when the action had scarcely ended.

One can only speculate, with the late Brigadier Richard Simpkin in
his book *Race to the Swift*, on 'how far television coverage was directly
responsible for the collapse of American popular support for the
Vietnam War'.[2] 'What does seem certain', Simpkin writes, 'is that
television coverage of armed conflict turns world opinion as a whole
fairly rapidly against the war covered, and more slowly against the use
of armed force to settle disputes'. I think this is a proposition you could
well debate. To the extent that television *did* affect opinion about
Vietnam, it was only after some time. Remember that the United
States forces, and the accompanying television crews, were there for
over a decade and the Australians for somewhat less. I believe that any
discussion of the reasons for the shift of public opinion about Vietnam
would also need to consider the effect of conscription in both countries
as more and more people had family members directly involved. There
was the nature of the civil war itself; the impact of incidents such as the
My Lai massacre; and growing realisation, over time, of the disparity
between official optimism and reports of what was actually happening.

These are things that, ultimately, cannot be disguised in an open
community, however one might try to influence the media. Nor, for
that matter, can they be hidden forever from the people even in a
closed society. However that may be, the cumulative effect of the
Vietnam experience seems to have significantly altered the approach
of the defence forces in many western nations to the dissemination of
news to the media during times of tension and conflict.

As we saw during the Gulf War, far more restrictions were placed on
the media's ability to travel freely in the area of operations, or to report
directly from the combat zone. Rather, the emphasis was on the use of
limited 'pools' of reporters and cameraman, and on briefings by
officers well versed in the art of saying very little at considerable

length. Only accredited correspondents were given access to commanders or were able to make accompanied visits to the war front, but then
rarely during actual operations. Correspondents had to sign an undertaking to comply with security guidelines, and have copy submitted to
review for security breaches, and so on. From the point of view of the
media – which, after all, thrives on action and drama, colour and
movement – the war reporting was not only controlled, it was also
curiously disembodied, if I may be pardoned the term.

A number of commentators noted that after the first few days, once
initial astonishment at the 'smart' bombs had faded and the fear of
chemical warfare, thankfully, did not materialise, instant global television threatened to fall victim to the besetting media sin of boredom –
until pictures of corpses from the Baghdad air raid shelter 'put the
whole dreadful business in perspective', as Peter McFarlane expressed
it in the *Sunday Age*.[3] It was, after all, a war in which people were being
killed. Many journalists accepted the restrictions, in order to report
what news they could. For others, however, it sometimes seemed to
newspaper readers that the real opponents were the combined staffs of
the coalition forces. Alan Moir had a cartoon in the *Sydney Morning
Herald* depicting General H. Norman Schwarzkopf pointing to a board
labelled '... Reporter, Photographer, Cameraman, Interviewer.'[4]
Malcolm Browne, of the *New York Times*, in a critical article on
defence/media relations written at the end of the war, quoted an air
force operational commander as saying: 'I suppose the press has its
purpose. But one thing is certain: you can't do me any good, and you
sure as hell can do me harm'.[5]

There was the ridicule of the military euphemisms for death and
destruction: 'collateral damage' has entered the lexicon, although I
notice it was first used in Vietnam. There was criticism of the blandness
of many media briefings. Peter Stephens in *The Age* had a Pentagon
spokesman saying: 'We just don't discuss that capability. I can't tell
you why we don't discuss it because then I'd be discussing it'.[6]

To inject a little historical perspective in this continuing 'friction'
between media and government, I have before me a cartoon first
published by Herblock in the *Washington Post* in 1957, at the height of
East-West tensions. It depicts a committee room in the State department, a large map with arrows showing Russian penetration of the
Middle East, and an official saying to the assembly: 'However, we've
been pretty successful in keeping American newspapermen out of
China'.[7]

Now, I mention these things because they do bring us to the central dilemma facing this conference – nicely expressed by Peter Stephens in *The Age* where he wrote:

> War, perhaps more than any other time, brings the public right to know and the public interest into conflict. Does the public have the right to know of every battle, every decision, every casualty immediately? Or does the public interest – including the combat troops – limit this right? It obviously must, and the real question is by how much?

From the point of view of the military, the public interest has a number of elements. One factor, clearly, concerns the safety of the forces under their command and the overall security of operations to ensure the advantages of secrecy and surprise. It does not seem to me unreasonable to require clearance before reports are published or broadcast on strategic or tactical deployments, military intelligence, force levels, casualties, logistics, reinforcements, weapons systems, potential weaknesses, and the like.

I think this is generally acknowledged. Even Robert Fisk of the British *Independent* newspaper, who wrote critically of the Allied involvement in the Gulf War and the media reporting of it, accepted that correspondents 'willingly comply with all the security guidelines, which preclude the reporting of military details that could be of use to Iraq'.[8] The question is, who should set the guidelines? On the whole, I think the public generally believes this ought to be a matter for the military – provided that it does not brazenly concoct statements, that it accepts the valid principle of the right to know where possible, and acknowledges that where facts are withheld unreasonably the media will speculate, accurately or not.

Let me interpose to say that, while I have been talking about limitations on information from the theatre of operations, we will all be aware that the speculations of many unrestricted 'expert' commentators back home on the likely duration of the Gulf War, projected Allied casualty rates, the stability of the coalition and so on, fortunately turned out to be quite erroneous.

It is one thing for high-minded journalists to maintain that 'free people need to know what is happening'.[9] But the truth is that journalists are not always in a position to best judge the likely course of events or, in the field, to know what snippet of information may be useful to an enemy. In any case, the pressures of competition to be the first with the latest are such that potentially damaging effects can be of secondary concern to the journalist. The premature disclosure of an intended attack on Goose Green, during a 'live' broadcast from the Falklands, is a case in point.

Of course, while media reports may assist an enemy, they may also deceive it, wittingly or not. As I understand it, Australian policy guidelines prevent the Defence Force using accredited correspondents for purposes of deliberate misinformation. Whether other countries have similar provisions, I do not know. No doubt this aspect of war reporting will form part of your discussions. I merely note that during his media briefing at the conclusion of fighting in the Gulf, General Schwarzkopf 'teased the press', according to the *Sydney Morning Herald*, for the leaked reports that fooled Iraq into expecting an amphibious landing on the Kuwait coast.

Incidentally, I should say that the General's television briefings were masterly. Even Peter Smark, a dedicated fighter in the cause of journalistic truth, conceded as much with his end-of-match scoreboard: Schwarzkopf 100, Media 2.[10]

The security implications of the defence view of the public interest are one thing. But there is another aspect to it that is far more contentious – one where the boundaries between the requirement for secrecy and the right to know are less clearly defined. I refer to the need to maintain domestic support and morale during times of tension and conflict. Indeed, Brigadier Simpkin in *Race to the Swift* has pointed out that while historically the aim of censorship has been to keep information from the enemy, 'in the face of modern surveillance by satellite and other means, the aim becomes the sustainment of morale on one's own side'. This is not something that should be lightly overlooked. The RAAF *Air Power Manual*, to which I referred earlier, comments: 'once a nation's will to resist is broken, it's enemies are in a position to impose terms. A high national morale is, therefore, the most valuable asset a nation can possess: it provides the foundation of its power to deter aggression and, if necessary, to accept the consequences of war.'[11]

For our generation, Vietnam remains the most notable example where national support for a war aim eroded over time, for the sorts of reasons I mentioned earlier. It is true that public morale is usually pretty high when conflict breaks out, provided that the reasons for it are publicly justifiable and sustained in the media. This of course opens a whole new front for debate. To what extent – if at all – does the media in a pluralist society have a 'patriotic duty' to support the nation's war effort? What weight should it give to critics and opponents of the war, let alone to perspectives from the other side?

With a few exceptions, I think the Gulf War coverage was mercifully free of the worst jingoistic excesses, although there was certainly some sniper fire at so-called 'unpatriotic' Western journalists reporting from Baghdad and complaints of bias against certain media commentators and outlets. This is a bit of a minefield for me to enter. But on the whole I tend to believe that people are well able to distinguish when opinions are too loaded one way or the other, and can make the appropriate intellectual adjustments. I say that because during the late war there were also some journalists who gave the impression that they were wearing Sam Brownes and battle fatigues, and who sounded as if they were giving the drums of jingo an early muffled beat.

So the performance of the media was something of a mixed show – and therefore, I expect, rather reflecting the nature of our society and its views on an issue like this. Indeed, one should never discount the legitimacy and real concerns of the peace movement which, as a general rule, is likely to attract increasing popular support the longer a war continues. In fairness, I should say that my overall impression of the Western media during the Gulf War was that it was much less at the polar points of view, and much more at the serious work face, giving us facts and honest analysis. And that sort of performance gives me confidence.

(The Baghdad press corps of Iraq, of course, was under the democratic direction of the Ba'athist Socialist Party).

It is certainly true that recent conflicts involving the Western nations – the Falklands, Grenada or the Gulf – were over so quickly and casualties, at least on the Allied side, so comparatively light, that public support was not seriously affected. Nevertheless, it would seem that both contemporary thinking and technology enabled the coalition forces in the Gulf to avoid many of the factors which, it is commonly held, led to the loss of morale and public support in Vietnam. There were no meaningless 'body counts'. An official estimate of the number of Iraqi dead has still not been given. There was little false optimism. Rather, official briefings stressed caution and understatement.

There was no saturation bombing of civilian areas. On the contrary, so far as one can judge, modern weapons systems were largely successful in confining their attacks to strategic targets. This is not to say that civilians were not killed. I have already mentioned the deaths in the Baghdad air raid shelter. But it is relevant to note that the coalition forces felt it necessary to respond immediately with evidence that the building also had military significance. It would be interesting to know if the tragic television pictures of the incident had any perceptible affect on public opinion within the Allied nations. If so, I suspect it would only have been marginal. Indeed, one survey suggested that a sizable number of Americans favoured bombing the hotel where journalists stayed in Baghdad – it was believed to contain a communications centre – after warning leaflets had been dropped first!

Having said that, however, I imagine there will be much debate during the conference as to whether the military's perception of the public interest is so broadly defined, that legitimate matters of discussion are sometimes kept from the public arena – not on grounds of security or public morale, but rather to avoid criticism or for reasons of internal military politics.

Again, I draw a few examples reported from the Gulf War. Malcolm Browne wrote of how a description of 'giddy' pilots was changed to 'proud' pilots by the censors, and of how a report of a briefing about the Stealth fighter-bomber was delayed for 24 hours while the 'bomber' bit was deleted.[12] There were complaints that the media, and particularly television, was used for 'propaganda' purposes by both sides. Robert Fisk wrote of how, in the Gulf, the relationship between reporter and soldier was 'becoming almost fatally blurred', and of how a desire to fit in with the pool arrangements, to work the system, was leading to 'a frequent absence of critical faculties'.[13] Some independent journalists apparently were threatened with loss of accreditation or even deportation. There were reports of film being seized. And in the United States itself, there were several legal challenges mounted against the Pentagon's media rules.

My purpose here is not to argue these issues, but rather to point to the sorts of areas where the 'friction' between your differing perceptions of roles and responsibilities in time of war come most acutely into collision – and consequently provide the subject matter for this conference. The only thing I would say is that one ought not to be too afraid of a critical media. Robert Fisk's reports of the Iraqi atrocities discovered after the liberation of Kuwait were that much more credible precisely because he *had* maintained his critical distance during the war. In any event, the truth will out eventually as I said earlier. Where it is hidden, the risk is always that the damage to public morale will be even greater when it is revealed. Besides, my experience of public life suggests that people are far more resilient – far stronger – than many believe. Citizens in a free society will face the truth of things, however unpleasant, provided those who lead them deserve their trust and confidence.

A recent US survey showed that eight out of ten respondents had confidence in military briefings during the Gulf War, and believed that the authorities had given out as much information as they could under the circumstances. Conversely, fewer than one in four had confidence in the media.[14] Whether these proportions would have remained the same had the war become a protracted one, is anybody's guess; though I trust that Peter Smark was indulging in a little hyperbole when he complained that the public 'probably wouldn't mind very much if a ministry of truth took all information sources by the throat'. I strongly believe that a vigorous, independent and critical press is essential for the public to maintain its confidence in the institutions of democratic society – just as a safe and secure democracy is necessary if a free press is to flourish.

Thus it is that I repeat the comment I made at the beginning of this address: the 'friction' between the media and the defence forces will always be there, and it is an eminently healthy thing that it should be so.

Let me conclude what has been a rather long speech with a quotation from Edwin Godkin, one of the first war correspondents in the Crimea. The appearance of journalists on the battlefield, Godkin wrote, 'led to a real awakening of the official mind. It brought home to the War Office the fact that the public had something to say about the conduct of wars and that they are not the concern exclusively of sovereigns and statesmen'.[15] A century on, and a revolution in communications later, that sentiment is still valid. I commend it to you.

NOTES

1. RAAF *Air Power Manual*, 1990, pp.6–7.
2. Richard Simpkin, *Race to the Swift, Thoughts on 21st Century Warfare* (Oxford: Brassey's Defence Publications, 1985), p.173.
3. *Sunday Age*, 17 February 1991.
4. *Sydney Morning Herald* (*SMH* hereafter), 27 February 1991.
5. *SMH*, 13 March 1991.
6. *The Age*, 5 February 1991.

7. Reprinted in Townsend Hoopes, *The Devil and John Foster Dulles* (Boston: Little, Brown & Co., 1973).
8. *The Age*, 9 February 1991.
9. *SMH*, 13 March 1991.
10. *The Age*, 2 March 1991.
11. *Air Power Manual*, p.15.
12. *SMH*, 13 March 1991.
13. *The Age*, 9 February 1991.
14. *The Age*, 2 March 1991.
15. Phillip Knightley, *The First Casualty* (Harvest, 1975), p.17.

Keynote Address

GENERAL PETER GRATION

I have heard it suggested that the history of the world is the history of human conflict – this being the case there must have been a journalist of sorts reporting each conflict. The military and media have long suffered mixed relations. However it is that very relationship between the two groups which holds the key to each achieving their aims during times of tension and conflict. As a military man, I could consider that my predecessors have created a rod for their own backs – as it was the military that gave us the first daily newspapers and therefore journalists.

As I recall, it was in 11BC when Caesar Augustus, displeased with the public utterances of an irregular news sheet 'published' by the Senate of the day, called upon a unit of the all-powerful Roman Army to terminate the circulation and substitute a version of their own on a daily basis. This was without a shadow of doubt the world's first 'daily'. It was called the *Acta Diurna* or news of the day ... its writers therefore being called diurnalists, which was later corrupted to journalists. Although there are some days when it might not seem such a bad idea to send troops in to replace some of our dailies with an army newspaper – I prefer to think that I have spent my career ensuring a democratic society which is proud of its free press principle.

Those very early days of military/media ownership – which I might add is still extant in many countries – soon gave way to the free press which did not present a problem to the military until the Crimean War. The man referred to as the 'father' of the modern war correspondent, Sir William Howard Russell – the first civilian to report from the front lines – made a name for himself by reporting on the inefficiency and mismanagement by the lords conducting the war. His reports led to outrage at home, with the Secretary of War hoping the Army would hang him and Prince Albert denouncing him as a mere scribbler.

In the Sudan, at the Battle of Omdurman (1898), Major-General Sir Horatio Kitchener referred to the correspondents as drunken swabs, threw them into prison and threatened to shoot the first one who wrote

15

anything about his campaign. These are among the first records of open censorship of the press by the military ... although following these events, the British government did develop a more subtle approach to censorship. In all fairness to Russell, it was later determined that he was reporting the truth, and even his severest early critics acknowledged that the ministers themselves would not have been made aware of the Army's deplorable state had it not been for the power of the press.

By the start of the First World War, the British had learnt that the press was indeed a powerful tool and had used it to boost popular support for the war effort through mass communication of what could be called propaganda. Press at the front line were fed exaggerated untruths and were barred from reporting on the actual horrors of war. It has even been suggested that correspondents were offered knighthoods in return for not reporting on the mass slaughter of trench warfare. During the Second World War the media again were positive in their approach to reporting, ensuring that they did nothing to swing popular support from the efforts at the battlefront.

But the press during this era were a different breed to the modern media. They were parochial and, therefore, fiercely patriotic as opposed to the approach taken by some of their modern day counterparts. Not for them the approach by Radio New Zealand during the Gulf War who declined to call Iraq 'the Enemy' or the Anti-Iraq force 'the Allies', nor that of Radio Australia who thought it important not to be seen to give 'overt support for the government's political-military endeavour' by broadcasting family messages to our sailors in the Gulf.

At this point it will be useful to examine in more detail some elements of the military/media relationship today, to derive some conclusions on how it can best be managed, and to refer briefly to Australian Defence Force policy on public information in time of tension or conflict. We should acknowledge from the outset that there is the potential for a fundamental clash of interests between the military and the media. We are pursuing basically different agenda. This is not to deny the need to establish trust, good working relationships, respect and so on, as I shall argue later, but to recognise the reality that the potential for disagreement, disputation and hostility is always there and likely to emerge at any time.

For the military's part, our aim is essentially to win the war and to do so with a minimum of friendly casualties. We are concerned with what we see as the serious and weighty matters of national objectives and national prestige. We are above all concerned with the lives and well being of our soldiers, sailors and airmen. We regard the successful prosecution of the war as an absolute priority, and take a dim view of distractions from the media, or worse, what may be seen as attempts by the media to undermine our efforts.

For the media there are probably various agenda centred around exercising the public's desire and right to know what is going on. (I will come back to this 'right to know' in a moment.) This is usually manifest as the media seeing themselves as a public watchdog or 'whistle-blower' on military excesses or incompetence. Peter Robinson, Editor-in-Chief of the Australian *Financial Review*, sees the media giving '... A balanced view of the foul-ups, miscalculations and inadequacies of command and supply and an insight into the strain and agony affecting the ordinary soldier'. If there is political control of the media, he believes that 'we are in essence, being asked to believe that nothing has gone wrong, that a perfect military operation has proceeded without pain to the personnel involved, that there are no tensions between ... allies ...' and so on. Some might see this as an obsession with the negative aspects, but it is probably a legitimate role for the media in the hands of professionals, although never popular with its victims.

So the media and the military are following basically different and often contradictory agenda. But nevertheless there is a good deal of common ground on which we can build. Public support is essential to the nation's and the military's prosecution of the war and this will be strongly influenced by the media's reporting of the conflict. Contradictory agenda or not, the military and the media need each other.

Let me list for you four points of common ground which I think can be accepted without further discussion:

(1) Freedom of the Press as a principle is accepted without reservation – the problem is how the principle should be applied in war.
(2) There is inevitably going to be extensive media coverage of any modern conflict. The public will demand it; it is an essential part of maintaining support for our efforts in the war, and we the military might as well get used to the idea and work out how best the process can be managed for the national good.
(3) New communications technology has opened up new dimensions in covering a conflict, in terms of immediacy, quality of images and global coverage to a massed audience.

(4) The media will be a most powerful force in forming public opinion, one way or another, for or against the war. The quality of the performance of the media is therefore a matter of national importance.

Operations

Now I would like to turn to some aspects of the military/media relationship which warrant special mention, starting with the military's primary concern – operational security. It is essential that we do not reveal prematurely information which may prejudice the success of future operations and therefore endanger the lives of our own troops. I do not believe any sane person will dispute this principle, although there will always be argument about what constitutes operationally important information, and claims that the military are abusing the principle in order to withhold information of little or no operational significance.

For the military's part, the principle is absolute. We reject utterly the risk of endangering even one friendly life to make a good story, and have built into our policies various safeguards to prevent this happening, while still giving access to the media and avoiding full-blown censorship. In Australian media policy, this is the reason, indeed the only reason, why we insist on vetting accredited correspondent's material before transmission. For one thing, it is not always clear to the correspondent what is and what is not material of value to the enemy. For another, the matter is of such fundamental importance that we are not prepared to leave it on trust. There are too many historical examples of the breaching of security. I recall the British experience in the Falklands where, despite everyone's accepting the principle of not revealing operationally-important information, an embarked BBC representative reported the intention of the Parachute Regiment to assault Goose Green on a live transmission the evening before the attack, with arguably heavier casualties for the paras in the action. I recall also the British admiral during the same campaign who growled 'tell 'em nothing, and when it's all over, tell 'em who won'.

The Right to Know

The words 'the public's right to know' are at the heart of the media's case for untramelled access and uninhibited reporting of conflict.

Interestingly American experience after the 1983 Grenada operation suggested that the public's desire to know, as distinct from their right to know, needs some close scrutiny. The evidence seems to suggest that where the success of operations of war, and hence the saving of friendly lives, is at stake then the public does not demand at all to have instant and total access. *Time* magazine published a cover story at the time of Grenada titled 'Journalism under Fire' in which the opening paragraph gave what was regarded as the public's perception of journalists. It said 'They are rude and accusatory, cynical and almost unpatriotic. They twist the facts to suit their not-so-hidden liberal agenda ... and they are arrogant and self-righteous'. And remember this is the media criticising its own.

I think the point of this is that 'The Right to Know' is not an absolute in itself which gives the media *carte blanche* to do as it wishes. The public themselves will accept sensible limits, and this should give us a pointer to our general approach to managing the military/media relationship, and to controls on media activity in the war zone. I do not personally accept the argument put by some that *any* restriction will be counterproductive in the long run and will bring an ultimate cost in terms of creating an unrealistic or fatally flawed public view of what is going on. It simply does not follow.

In the past 20 years, the UK and US have tried various approaches to restricting media activity in the war zone without imposing full censorship. They have tried in varying degrees restricting who is allowed into the war zone, controlling the movements and access to events of those who do make it to the war zone, and vetting their output before transmission. Most would agree that the free-wheeling approach of Vietnam was not the way to go – with hundreds of correspondents of greatly varying quality free to enter the theatre, go where they wished and report whatever they saw fit. Arguably this was a major factor in the erosion and eventual withdrawal of home support. There was probably an over-reaction in Grenada in 1983 with the media denied all access for the first 48 hours, and perhaps in the Falklands where the extreme isolation and difficult access made it easy to limit severely the numbers of correspondents with the force.

We need more analysis of the Gulf War media coverage but it seems to have been successful on two important counts. The war was won in stunningly successful style, and the American public seems to have been highly satisfied with the coverage it received. In a poll, 80 per cent of Americans said they approved of all military restrictions on the reporting of the war and 60 per cent thought there should have been more. As I understand it, there was limited issue of visas to journalists to enter Saudi Arabia. Once in the theatre, journalists had to rely on military briefings, as the only media representatives allowed to join troops were those placed in pools. However the military briefings were professional, and accurate to the point of being overly conservative. The pools were escorted by 'minders' with strict rules on leaving or moving in the allocated areas. There was voluntary acceptance of reporting guidelines for correspondents seeking accreditation to the Riyadh information centre and copy was vetted for breaching of operational security.

The Quality of Reporting

Both the military and the media would subscribe in principle to the importance of fair and accurate reporting. The military, mindful of the need to sustain home support, are concerned that the media report accurately and factually, avoid bias, do not trivialise the issues and respect confidences. Presumably the professionals in the media share these concerns for reasons of professional pride and integrity.

But performance often falls short of the ideal. Commercial competition amongst the media does not always help. US Major General Patrick Brady on telling a reporter that 'we are always happy to help get it right' recounts the response 'I don't care if I get it right; I only care if I get it first'. There is sometimes a feeling amongst the military that the media somehow regards it as the military's job continually to provide sensational material. I recall the headline on Day 6 of the Gulf War: 'Sixth Day – War Drags On'.

The media have their problems too. Peter Smark in the Melbourne *Age* on 15 January 1991 wrote that '. . . the capacity of some members of the officer caste to blind themselves to the obvious, to hide errors, to justify nonsense is unlimited'. And in his view 'The official capacity to lie knows no limits'. If his views of the military as both liars and fools are representative, we do indeed have a long way to go with media/ military relationships.

The military for their part would like to be dealing with professionals who understand the complexity of military operations, who can distinguish the major issues from the trivia, and who accept that the military have a desperately dangerous and difficult job to do. An example of what not to do was the reprehensible reporting by the ABC during the Gulf War, without any checking, that one of our ships had been involved in a collision at sea. The story was without foundation. But collisions at sea can be disastrous, and the story caused great alarm among the families of crew members.

Much could be said on these matters, but let me highlight a few points:

- Peter Smark notwithstanding, as a matter of policy we do tell the truth. For the operational security reasons I spoke of earlier some information may be withheld, but what is said should be true.
- As both parties need each other, there has to be a solid attempt at building a working relationship and developing some sort of mutual confidence, if not trust.
- There should be a tacit acknowledgement that no one is perfect. The military should accept that the media will get it wrong now and again, and the media should accept that in the immensely complex business of planning and executing operations of modern war, some things are bound to go wrong. Hopefully the inevitable minor mishaps will be seen for what they are and not blown out of proportion. Much of the media's harping on the Australian Defence Force's Fiji operation in 1987 was in this category of harping on trivia. This of course is not a plea for the military to be let off the hook for major foul-ups – it is a plea for proportionality.
- There should be some sort of quality control over the correspondents reporting the conflict, desirably exercised by the profession itself. It is not good enough that any cub reporter can roam unrestricted around a theatre of operations understanding little of what he sees, but nevertheless turning out copy that presumably will be read or viewed by someone. This is the idea behind having accredited correspondents nominated by the profession. In similar vein, the media for their part are entitled to deal with military officers who understand the rules and who appreciate the pressures, deadlines and operating requirements within which the media must work. Some process of education on both sides would help.

Solutions

Well so much for the problems. What are we do to about them? I think underlying it all must be the recognition that there will always be the potential for a fundamental clash of interests between the military and the media based on our different aims and agenda. It is therefore not so much a matter of eliminating problems, as managing the process to the greater benefit of both sides.

In the Australian Defence Force we have had a policy in place for some years that seems to me to come to grips pretty well with the issues traversed this morning. We do not claim that it is perfect and we will change it if need be in the light of our own and other's experience. This conference may well suggest changes. The central idea is to seek to build a solid relationship between the military and the media, established in peace but carrying over into war. The relationship relies on developing an understanding each other's special needs, and a confidence on the one hand that the media are hearing the truth, and on the other that it will be reported accurately, proportionately and without bias.

We accept the need for education on both sides. We now go to some lengths to educate servicemen and women in the techniques of dealing with the media and on ways and means of meeting media requirements within operational constraints. Similarly we hope that the media will appreciate the need to get a better understanding of the military and the complexities of military operations. The best time to do this is in peace – before operations start. A media not familiar with the military in peace must go through a steep learning curve to be able to report effectively in combat.

We accept that media coverage of conflict is not only inevitable but important, and the public information (PI) plan is an important part of all operational planning.

We tell the truth although we might choose to withhold some information for operational security reasons. I have not spoken this morning about disinformation – the deliberate planting of false or misleading information within officially sourced statements. This is a complex area, but suffice to say that our public information policy makes it clear that disinformation is an Intelligence and not a PR/PI function and is not to be used against accredited correspondents.

We have chosen to tackle the management of the flow of information through a system of a limited number of accredited correspondents, selected by media representatives (the Defence Media Advisory Group) who once they arrive in the theatre of operations are free to move about freely and without minders. They are given generous technical assistance with their preparation and transmission of copy through a media support unit. In return we require that they submit copy for vetting on the spot of any material which might jeopardise operations. This is not censorship – it is concerned only with operational security, and material that is critical, inaccurate or whatever but not affecting operations will be allowed to pass. By contrast, unaccredited correspondents will be given little assistance. Brigadier D'Hage, the Director General of Public Information, will be giving a more extensive account later in the conference of the Australian experience.

There are challenges in all this for both the military and the media. We are facing up to ours. I welcome this conference, the first of its kind, and have no doubt that it will make an important contribution to this timely and most important issue. I look forward to reviewing the results.

Defining Limited Conflict:
A Case of Mistaken Identity

DR STEWART WOODMAN

The Nuclear Dilemma

On 6 August 1945 the first atomic bomb was dropped on the Japanese city of Hiroshima. In that and the subsequent raid on Nagasaki three days later more than 100,000 people died, a similar number were injured and much of the two cities was destroyed. Few would not argue that those events dramatically changed the concept of warfare. There had been other shifts into new and exotic areas of capability in the past, such as the use of chemical weapons in the trenches of the First World War. The latter could produce relatively indiscriminate damage, including to civilian populations, but none had had the capacity to override so completely the effectiveness of other defensive systems and to threaten such enormous destruction. Furthermore, the possession of nuclear weapons by only a few nations and the difficulties, costs and long leadtimes involved in attempting to acquire it underpinned a new global balance.

In the wake of these developments, it is not surprising that the focus of the international strategic debate was, for the superpowers, in ensuring that they did not become comparatively disadvantaged in the development and maintenance of their nuclear arsenals. For middle powers, it was in seeking guarantees that those nuclear capabilities would not be resorted to in war. This focus was reinforced by the fact that the major concentrations of conventional military forces after the Second World War fell under the strategic nuclear umbrella of either the United States or the Soviet Union. An extensive range of control measures, including the Nuclear Non-Proliferation Treaty, was introduced subsequently at both the global and regional levels for the purpose of limiting the spread and possible use of nuclear weapons.

The superpowers themselves have attempted fitfully to introduce strategic arms limitation measures. The United Nations has pursued a range of arms control initiatives which have gone some way to limiting the further spread of nuclear and other exotic technologies but have had little impact on the strategic priorities of, and level of competition between, the superpowers. The effect of regional initiatives such as the South Pacific Nuclear Free Zone, ZOPFAN and the Indian Ocean Zone of Peace, has also been limited. This has been not only because of superpower strategic reach and global deployment patterns but because many regional countries saw themselves as having an investment in that competition either for preserving global stability or in terms of their own direct security interests and needs.

Indeed, it can be argued that it has only been the failure of the major powers to be able to afford to compete that has brought them to modify their stances. The Intermediate Nuclear Forces (INF) Agreement reached in December 1987 and the subsequent progress towards arms control, including the difficult issue of verification[1], have for the first time in 40 years allowed the strategic debate to escape its preoccupation with the nuclear holocaust.

What has been recognised much more hesitantly is the impact that the possession and use of nuclear weapons has had on the role and use of warfare as an instrument of state. Until Hiroshima, the shape of conflict had been primarily determined by the military imperative, that is, the reach and impact of available military capabilities. War in the nineteenth and early twentieth centuries had been primarily about territorial supremacy whether in defence of the state or in its expansion. The introduction of nuclear weapons meant that the ultimate cost of warfare – mass destruction, including potentially to one's own state – was no longer acceptable. In that dimension at least, war had outrun its utility as an instrument of state policy. As Michael Howard wrote in 1979, 'in a grotesque inversion of logic the means now dictate the ends'.[2]

Consequently, the emphasis in strategic planning was on establishing boundaries that would avoid larger scale conflict going over the nuclear threshold. It was only more gradually that strategic thinkers began to recognise that there was a range of alternative uses of military force (rather than just the upper limits) that could and, indeed, might need to be exploited. That is, that despite the existence of nuclear weapons, there was an overlay of more limited conflict in which the use of force was possible without risking unacceptable consequences.

Limited War

Perhaps not surprisingly, the recognition of the possibility of more limited conflicts in the immediate aftermath of the Second World War only arose with their actual occurrence. Furthermore, both the initial reaction to them and the strategic theology that grew up to explain them was greatly influenced by the global preoccupations of the major powers. Western strategic analysts struggled with the problem first on two planes. There was the question of the conditions under which it might be possible to fight a conventional military war in Europe without the resort, or at least the first resort, to nuclear weapons.[3] This was difficult given the Soviet Union's predominance in the size of its conventional military forces deployed to the European theatre. Second, the issue arose of whether the nuclear theatre could be split into strategic and tactical phases, with the use of tactical nuclear weapons being acceptable to offset deficiencies in conventional capabilities.[4]

The debate was, however, given a new focus by the Korean War. The United States reaction to the North Korean invasion of the South was marked by considerable uncertainty. On the one hand, it was concerned that the attack was part of a plan for Communist expansion and possibly a prelude to a general war. There was thus a need both to discourage further Soviet aggression and to demonstrate US preparedness to its European allies to commit forces in such circumstances. On the other hand, the US was wary of an overcommitment which would weaken its capabilities in the primary European theatre, a concern reinforced by NATO pressure on the US to avoid expansion of the conflict and to bring it to a swift conclusion.[5]

Furthermore, while Soviet forces did not become directly involved and nuclear weapons were not used, major conventional engagements with Chinese forces occurred after the United Nations force had repulsed the North Koreans and crossed the 38th parallel. The military's hands were tied, however, by the refusal of permission either to bomb bases or supply lines in China or to blockade Chinese ports. Both they and the American public had difficulty with coming to grips with a conflict which, despite intense battles and significant casualties, did not lead to any form of decisive military victory.[6]

The lessons of Korea did not flow through immediately into official policy. Secretary of State John Foster Dulles continued to insist that 'There is no local defense which alone will contain the mighty manpower of the Communist world. Local defence must be reinforced by the threatened deterrent of massive retaliatory power'.[7]

Others including William Kaufmann and Bernard Brodie were more sceptical. They emphasised that the existence of weapons of unlimited capacity made it necessary to find some way to fight without using the full military power that was at hand. The focus of their concern was on 'local limited war' in Third World areas away from Europe and was given added point by the difficulties the French were experiencing in maintaining control in Indo-China. At the same time, British strategic planners had begun to focus on the prospect of a limited nuclear war in Europe and the relative advantages of conventional and tactical nuclear capabilities to their defence.[8]

By 1957 the works of Robert Osgood[9] and Henry Kissinger ensured that the concept of limited war was firmly on the public agenda. Kissinger argued that:

> The prerequisite for a policy of limited war is to reintroduce the political element into our concept of warfare and to discard the notion that policy ends where war begins or that war can have goals distinct from those of national policy.[10]

Consideration was given to how the limits of conflict might be set to avoid escalation, including restrictions on the types of targets, weapons systems, and the geographical extent of conflict. The importance of limited political objectives was stressed and the emphasis was more on attrition than a decisive defeat that could lead to escalation. There was, however, less agreement on whether the use of tactical nuclear weapons would be appropriate.[11]

'Limited war' never escaped the belief that each occurrence was but part of a protracted struggle between two nuclear-armed power blocs and its nature was defined more by the need to avoid general war than the intrinsic nature of limited war itself. When Soviet advances in missile technology swung American attention to the effectiveness and potential vulnerability of its strategic nuclear forces, limited war became absorbed as but one element of an escalation continuum along which the superpowers might seek to outbid each other.[12] Additional funds were not earmarked for specific limited war capabilities and indeed limited war was still seen militarily as implying large conventional forces. It was only in 1961, following Khrushchev's endorsement of 'wars of national liberation' that the US began to enhance significantly its potential to intervene directly against communist-backed insurgencies in Third World countries.[13]

It was, however, in Vietnam that the real complexities of limited war and the inadequacies of existing strategic theories were most graphically revealed. North Vietnam's determination to overrun the South left little scope to force a backdown short of total military defeat while the United States, despite its higher capability forces, was reluctant to pay the price of a military assault that would crush North Vietnam or risk the prospect of Chinese or Soviet intervention.[14] Politically, the US was caught between the use of military force to help stabilise South Vietnam, even though that very intervention could be portrayed as damaging to the political credibility of that government, while convincing American domestic opinion the threat was sufficient to justify large resources, a protracted commitment, and significant casualities.[15]

'Limited war' had thus moved away from being part of a global balancing between the superpowers to have specific regional connotations, with asymmetries that offset the dominant US capability, and which demanded a much clearer enunciation of US interests and objectives if a commitment was to be sustained. In consequence, the concept of limited war took on two distinct meanings. The first was in relation to the use of conventional and tactical nuclear weapons in the European context to be able to deter Soviet aggression at any level of conflict. Under the strategy of flexible response, NATO doctrine no longer envisaged automatic and early escalation to the use of nuclear weapons in the event of a Soviet attack.[16] The other range of possible conflict situations which did not involve direct US/Soviet military competition were grouped under the heading 'low-intensity conflict'.

Low-Intensity Conflict

The term 'low-intensity conflict' was developed in the 1970s to describe a diverse range of politico-military activities less intense than modern conventional warfare.[17] While most frequently associated with counter-insurgency and counter-terrorism, it has been extended to cover a whole range of situations from peacekeeping and displays of force up to conventional military operations with limited objectives and of short duration. What was most significant was the underlying belief that these types of conflict were substantially different in their nature to sustained conventional warfare and required alternative organisational concepts, institutional responses and policies to handle them effectively.

American planners were quick to recognise certain key elements which set low-intensity conflict apart from planning for more conventional military operations. These included the primacy of political objectives, the close relationship between political direction and the use of military force, that victory could not be achieved through massed firepower, that the enemy would often be elusive and direct engagements between larger formations would seldom occur, the unique character of each low-intensity conflict situation, and the critical importance of both domestic and international opinion.[18] They highlighted the inappropriateness of conventional forces to many low intensity conflicts and stressed the need for a well constructed politico-military strategy and for flexible forces able to handle a number of different conflict situations.

These concepts were not, however, put into practice immediately. American low-intensity conflict and special operations capabilities had been allowed to run down after Vietnam in terms both of equipment and training. This was clearly illustrated by the failed attempt to rescue the American hostages from Iran in 1980 and the criticisms levelled at the military following the invasion of Grenada in October 1983 after a pro-Soviet Marxist government had seized power on that Caribbean island.[19] President Reagan greatly expanded the funds available to support low-intensity capabilities ($440m in 1981 to $2.5bn in 1988), but as late as 1987 the US Congress itself felt compelled to push through legislation requiring that the Pentagon reorganise itself to respond more effectively to these more limited forms of conflict.[20]

The intellectual debate on more limited forms of conflict has thus been developed against a quite specific frame of reference. It has been dominated by the superpowers' strategic preoccupations, both directly and in the Third World. It has also been influenced by some of the more difficult decolonisation crises to face France and Great Britain since 1945. What has tended to be lost sight of is that those situations are only part of the range of limited conflicts that have arisen in recent decades and, given the changing role of the major powers, may be less likely to arise in the future.

The Other Dimension

As the world has shed the shackles of colonialism, the emerging nations have begun to assume greater responsibility for both economic development and the state security of the state. In doing so, they have also discovered the potential effectiveness of military force as an instrument for political bargaining between states, even where considerable disparity exists between their levels of capability.

The Cod Wars

In 1958 and again in 1972, the small North Atlantic community of Iceland, armed with only a few gunboats, challenged the might of the Royal Navy and the political will of Great Britain and other NATO powers. The issue was the protection of Iceland's fisheries resources and its plans to extend its control first to 12 nautical miles and later to almost 50 nautical miles (the edge of the continental shelf) from the coast. This excluded British and West German trawlers which had traditionally fished those areas. Despite the protection afforded by Royal Navy frigates to fishermen defying these new boundaries, Icelandic vessels undertook a protracted campaign of harassment through boarding vessels, cutting of lines, dangerous manoeuvring and the firing of warning shots. Iceland's use of force was accompanied by stubborn political bargaining, including the threat in September 1973 to break off diplomatic relations with Britain, and hearings before the International Court. The management regimes subsequently established in 1961 and 1973 did not bring about the total exclusion of foreign fishing vessels but did give Iceland far greater control over fishing activity in adjacent maritime areas.[21]

Indonesian-Malaysian Confrontation

Shortly afterwards in 1962, Malaya announced plans to include Singapore, and Sabah and Sarawak on neighbouring Borneo in a new federation of Malaysia. Its neighbour Indonesia, fresh from the revolutionary fervour of wresting West New Guinea from the Dutch, branded the proposal neo-colonialist and declared that it would oppose it through diplomatic isolation, the severance of trade, and possibly military action. Initially, Indonesian involvement focused on training and assisting rebel guerrillas to operate in Borneo. Gradually it extended to more major ground force raids to ferment disturbance and discontent in Sarawak. Ultimately incursions were even made across the Straits of Malacca onto the Malayan peninsula. The latter generally involved small groups of between 10 and 30 personnel intent on either sabotage or on organising indigenous uprisings.[22]

Indonesia's strategy was to combine direct but very limited military pressure with a vigorous propaganda campaign and protracted, if sometimes elusive, diplomacy. When Malaysia took the issue to the United Nations in September 1964 following the attempted Labis airdrop by three C130 aircraft, Indonesia surprisingly made no attempt to deny the action. It claimed instead that it should be seen in the context of imperial and colonial aggression by Britain and appealed to the non-aligned Afro-Asian members of the Security Council.[23] Throughout the campaign, however, Indonesia was concerned, despite its rhetoric, to keep hostilities below the threshold that would justify Britain using its superior air and naval strike capabilities against Indonesian bases.[24] Internal unrest within Indonesia and the overthrow of President Sukarno finally brought Confrontation to an end late in 1966.

Other SE Asian Rivalries

In recent years, there have been other examples of the use of military force between regional states for specific or limited purposes. There has been protracted rivalry for control over the tiny island groups of the South China Sea, first between China and Vietnam over the Paracel Islands and more recently between those nations and other South-East Asian countries over possession of the numerous reefs and islets in the Spratly group. Although tiny, some almost disappearing under the water at high tide, these islands are located across strategically important shipping routes and provide access to considerable marine and seabed resources. While generally beyond the range of regional aircraft, several nations have deployed small garrison forces to protect their possessions while naval vessels have exchanged fire on a number of occasions.[25]

On the mainland, China conducted a large scale raid and subsequently more limited harassments across its border with Vietnam during 1979. The hostilities appear to have been primarily to warn Vietnam not to become too ambitious or attempt to undermine Chinese influence in Indo-China in the wake of Vietnam's occupation of Cambodia. China at the time was deeply concerned by the apparently close strategic relationship between Vietnam and the Soviet Union.[26]

The Falklands/Malvinas War

On the other side of the world, Britain and Argentina clashed militarily in 1982 for control of the Falkland Islands. Although Argentina's claim to sovereignty originated in the 1820s, the islands had remained under British rule until the 1970s when, following debate on the issue in the United Nations, Argentina began to pursue its claim more vigorously. Negotiations, however, proved difficult and protracted and, following a relatively minor immigration incident on the small island of South Georgia in March 1982, Argentine forces moved quickly to occupy the islands. Vigorous attempts were made, particularly by the United States, to negotiate a settlement but domestic pressures within Argentina and the direct challenge to Britain's credibility as an international power gave the parties little room to manoeuvre.[27] While negotiations continued a British naval task force was assembled and dispatched to the South Atlantic.

The ensuing conflict was to witness a quite intense but brief engagement between Argentine air and ground forces and the British task force. The shape of those hostilities was, however, strongly influenced by the continuing political negotiations and the remote location, both geographically and politically, of the territory in dispute. Military actions were confined to the Falklands area and British steps to declare an exclusion zone and to retake initially the relatively inconsequential South Georgia were clearly designed to place pressure on Argentina to back down before a major confrontation. There was close political involvement in the conduct of operations, even down to the tactical level; the forces were put together quickly to undertake tasks for which they were not primarily designed; and there appears to have been considerable debate within the British Cabinet at least as to just what its national objectives were.[28]

Defining Limited Conflict

There are thus a whole range of conflicts which are, in one respect or another, limited. They extend from limited forms of conventional conflict through counter insurgencies and guerrilla warfare to small scale encounters such as the Cod Wars where few combat capabilities were exercised. Some attempts have been made to classify these according to the key features which make them 'limited'. British political scientist John Garnett has identified four key factors in that debate. These are limitations of geography, objective, military capabilities employed and the targets selected for attack.[29] However, while these are undoubtedly features of many limited forms of conflict, they are not consistently applicable, may relate to only one participant in a dispute, and frequently will represent relative rather than absolute judgments. Ultimately, the unique character of each limited conflict is acknowledged as is the importance of the perspective from which it is being analysed.

What is it then that sets limited conflict apart, other than it is not total war, general war or global war and it is broader than concepts such as guerrilla warfare and low-intensity conflict? Is there sufficient consistency in its characteristics to allow the concept to be discussed without becoming bogged down in definitional debates, boundary disputes or exceptions to the rule? Is limited conflict only a concept by default?

The answer to that question lies in two simple but interrelated propositions.[30] The first is that the concept of 'limited conflict' does not relate to the physical characteristics of a particular conflict. Rather, it describes the way in which a nation approaches the use of military force in pursuing its objectives. The point here is that at least some of the features frequently used to define limited forms of conflict (for example, size of forces, small geographic area) are simply consequences of the fact that a government has decided to use military force in a manner well short of all-out military confrontation. Whether or not those factors exist, and to what extent, will depend upon the individual circumstances of the conflict. Approaching limited conflict in this way also overcomes the problem of asymmetry, frequently noted in American literature[31], where two parties to a conflict are employing military force on two different bases.

The second proposition is that limited conflict relates to the use of military force between states for purposes other than challenging the territorial integrity of a country, except for more distant possessions. On face value, this proposition may appear to be too simple to be meaningful. It does not rule out the use of military force against the homeland of a nation for purposes short of territorial gain. Nor does it preclude conventional military engagements from occurring. It certainly does no justice to the copious volumes of literature that have been devoted to this issue. But perhaps we have been asking the wrong questions. The point is that when the territorial integrity of a state is under challenge, either in large part or small, many factors about the use of military force are set virtually automatically. There is no question that the objective is to defend the state, that the full range of available military resources will be deployed for this purpose if necessary, and that the government will have substantial freedom to draw upon wider national resources and to exercise a degree of control over national life to utilise these.

The Elements of Limited Conflict

However, as soon as that national objective changes away from the territorial imperative, the conduct of military operations enters a new dimension. A whole range of different planning considerations come into play and it is in fact these that are the essence of 'limited conflict'. They are as follows:

(1) The government will need to develop and articulate not only the national interests that are at stake but also the reasons for, and the costs and benefits of, using military force as distinct from other means such as diplomacy and economic pressure. A choice has to be made and, in that context, the resort to military force is a most serious step because it unleashes potentially a whole range of different planning considerations.

(2) Success will be dependent on the interplay between military force and the desired objectives. While specific tactical victories may be important to reinforcing a country's bargaining position in a dispute (e.g., the British concern in the Falklands War to take Goose Green before UN deliberations.[32]), a successful outcome will be measured against the preparedness of an adversary to accept either a specific policy or balance of interests between the two nations. Importantly, it is possible for the military dimension to outrun the desired political objectives unless control is exercised over the use of force. The danger of creating grounds for intervention by a third party was well illustrated by the delayed Chinese involvement in the Korean War.[33]

(3) Because of the critical nature of the political-military interplay, political leaders will have a much more direct interest in the ways in which and the means by which military force will be applied. There will be a much closer relationship

between the strategic and tactical levels of command with political leaders needing to be informed of and, as required, make decisions about quite detailed and specific military initiatives. The decision of the British War Cabinet to authorise the sinking of the Argentine cruiser *General Belgrano* is a case in point.[34] Clear command and control arrangements and the real time transfer of information between the military commander and the government will be essential.

(4) There will be constraints on how military force is applied. Certain targets and areas of operation considered important to effective military operations may be denied to the commander on wider policy grounds. Tight rules of engagement are likely to apply at the tactical level, potentially requiring much greater sensitivity at lower levels of military command.[35] There may also be pressure to match the characteristics of the force deployed as closely as possible to the political objectives. Some of the confusion concerning Australia's possible intentions during the first Fiji coup was undoubtedly engendered by preparations to deploy the Operational Deployment Force which has the potential to operate at brigade level.[36] The size and nature of the forces deployed, and their concept of operations, will be an important tool for managing the conflict, signalling both intentions and resolve and influencing the adversary's course of action and his bargaining position.

(5) The commencement, and particularly the continuation, of the use of force will depend on the maintenance of popular support. In the defence of the nation, the linkage between defence and civilian interests is generally complete. In limited conflict, the costs in terms of casualties, diversion of resources, and controls on civilian activity will only be acceptable while national support can be maintained for the objectives justifying the use of military force. The longer a conflict continues, the more difficult this will be to maintain.[37] Hence, there will be pressure to keep the use of military force short, geographically confined, and to deliver tangible evidence of success. Initially, that success could be provided by tactical military victories, but increasingly it will relate to realising the policy objectives which the govern-

ment itself has set. This consideration was well captured in the six points which US Secretary of Defense Caspar Weinberger put forward in 1984 for determining US ground force involvement overseas in limited conflict situations.[38]

(6) The task of maintaining popular support will not be easy for a government because limited conflicts are likely to be far more open to observation and comment. Many aspects of civilian life are likely to continue in parallel with military activity. There is likely to be greater public pressure for the government to be accountable for its actions and the very requirement to articulate objectives will permit much closer scrutiny of ends and means. The media through both its access to the 'battlefront' and its capacity to challenge publicly the government's motives will be a key element in this process.

(7) Militarily, the adequacy of national defence capabilities will depend not upon absolute force-on-force comparisons but on their appropriateness and flexibility to handle frequently quite limited conflict situations. There will be emphasis in particular on intelligence gathering and surveillance assets to provide the transparency at both the strategic and tactical levels important to underpinning the integration of political and military initiatives.[39] Operationally, it would be necessary to permit the effective engagement of an adversary who will often be exploiting indirect and possibly covert means of applying force. There will also be additional pressure in many situations for great precision in the delivery of firepower to maximise its impact while minimising the prospect of collateral damage.[40] Advanced technologies have their place in limited conflict but in relation to control rather than absolute combat power.

(8) Furthermore, while the use of military force may be carefully planned (as it almost certainly will be when territory is at stake), in limited conflict it will frequently be spontaneous, at least in the first instance. It will be a 'come as you are' party with little, or at best ambiguous, warning in relation to force build-ups or the specific change of political intent. That judgment, of course, has implications for the capabilities required within the force-in-being and the readiness at which key assets need to be maintained.

There may be other common features but these would appear to be the key elements that set limited conflict apart. How prominent each of those particular elements is will depend on the particular circumstance, including just how closely an issue is seen to be linked to national security. They are also likely to be much more obvious in a liberal democracy engaged in hostilities than in more authoritarian forms of national government.

The Definition in Practice

What, however, is the impact in practice of defining limited conflict in this way? Looking back over the conflicts that have occurred since 1945, the types of use of force that would be classified as limited include US actions in Korea, Vietnam, Grenada and Panama, the Indonesian and British actions during Confrontation, and Chinese aggression against both Vietnam in February 1979 and in the Spratly Islands. Excluded as a general rule would be the Arab-Israeli Wars, India's border conflicts with both China and Pakistan, and the Iran-Iraq War (1980–88). Somewhat ironically, Iraq's invasion of Kuwait would not fall within the definition of limited conflict but the US – led response to it would do so.[41]

It is also instructive to look at Australia's own defence planning. Australia is fortunate in that it does not face any identifiable military threat and there are no forces in the region large enough to attempt a lodgement on the Australian mainland. Defence planning does, however, recognise the more limited forms of military pressure that could arise, the essentially political objectives behind that use of force, and the different strategic vulnerabilities that would need to be taken into account where the threat stops short of even temporary occupation of part of the mainland. The potential for such threats to arise within short timeframes is acknowledged, together with the importance of intelligence and surveillance to a timely and controlled response and the likely constraints on Australia's use of its long-range strike assets. The linkage between the use of military force and national political objectives is an important planning factor as is the vulnerability of national decision-making to domestic political pressure should the use of military force not bring about a relatively speedy resolution of the issue.[42]

Where, however, do terrorism and counter-terrorist activities fit within this definition? While there is convincing evidence that countries such as Libya, Iran, Syria and Cuba have consistently supported international terrorist organisations, terrorism is not an accepted instrument of state. It is frequently indiscriminate and random in its impact, and in many circumstances is more akin to criminal violence and political protest than to the application of military force against another nation. Combating terrorism is also primarily the responsibility of civil law enforcement agencies, such as the police, immigration and customs, and the emphasis is on prevention rather than engagement.

At the same time, there is no doubt that the way in which terrorism has been exploited in the Middle East and in Northern Ireland by organisations such as the Palestine Liberation Organisation and the Irish Republican Army is closely akin to many aspects of unconventional warfare or insurgency. In seeking to challenge either the existence of a state or the political authority of a government, they are prepared to challenge national security forces directly and systematically.[43] Much hinges on whether one is prepared to acknowledge those organisations as the legitimate representative of a dispossessed state, an issue which raised considerable sensitivity during the early 1980s in relation to the rights of terrorists under the Protocols to the Geneva Convention.[44] Where, however, a nation believes that sufficient linkage can be established between acts of terrorism and a particular state, then any specific military response that it made would fall within the definition of a limited conflict. The punitive raid by US aircraft on Libya in 1986 is a case in point.

Finally, what is the significance of defining limited conflict in this way in relation to the role of the media? In broad terms, limited conflict is the area in which the media potentially becomes a free and independent player with the capacity to influence both the conduct of hostilities and, particularly through its impact on popular sentiment, the direction of government policy. When the territorial integrity of a state is under threat, both popular sentiment and the greater capacity of the government to control public life militate against a press which is critical of the war effort. Indeed, the media is likely to become either directly or indirectly a propagandist for the national cause.

In limited conflict the media could become, from a government and military perspective, a negative influence.[45] It has the capacity, and the media would say the responsibility, to analyse critically not only the government's objectives but also the military strategy being pursued and the details of operations at the tactical level while hostilities are continuing. The government may introduce some controls, either voluntary or enforceable, but the emphasis will generally be on engaging the media both to convince it of the correctness of the government's approach and to ensure that information that could prejudice effective operations (including the morale of the fighting forces) is not released prematurely.

While a media blackout might be maintained for a short critical period, the government will largely rely on the media to take its message to the people and possibly as an additional source of intelligence. Questions on the responsibility of the media, the effectiveness of self-regulation, and the possible need to brief editors in advance of certain events to prevent misinformation or dangerous leaks will clearly be important. In previous conflicts, the focus on press reporting alleviated some concerns about the early release of sensitive information. Today the speed of communications and the quality of graphic imagery, often at speeds faster than that available on military networks, give the media much greater leverage. In liberal democracies, at least, the power of the government to legislate to control media access and reporting will be far more difficult to sustain.

The Conflict Continuum

In conclusion, the term 'limited conflict' thus relates to the use of military force by a state to further or protect its national policy objectives in circumstances where the territorial integrity of the nation's 'homeland' is not directly under threat. It is also a concept which describes not the physical characteristics of a conflict but the process by which a nation decides upon, deploys and sustains the use of military force. The distinction based on territorial integrity may seem very simple but it is, in fact, the threshold at which the use of military force, and its relationship to the other instruments of national policy, enters a different dimension and a whole range of additional factors – not of great significance in more general conflict – are brought into play.

Where this fact has tended to be obscured, particularly in the literature on this subject, is that the major powers such as the United States have not, in the context of global strategic competition, drawn a clear distinction between the security of the nation and their broader, yet frequently still important, security interests. Some of the difficulties they have faced in those situations, including the need frequently to change policy directions, would suggest that they might have been better placed if they had done so. In the context of current pressures for a drawdown in the superpowers' forward deployed forces, that discipline is inevitably being introduced.

Current strategic theory portrays levels of conflict as a continuum. The only clear break that has been acknowledged has been that of a major nuclear exchange, at which point capability outruns political objectives. The remainder of the continuum is described in terms of the physical characteristics of the conflict. This paper has argued that the concept of limited conflict represents a second but no less important break in the continuum – that is, a point where the relationship between military force and political objectives changes fundamentally. It is, however, a break determined not by capability but by the relevance of the use of military force to the state.

NOTES

1. J. Dean, 'Europe's New Security Blanket', *Pacific Research*, Vol.4, No.1 (Feb. 1991), pp.7–10.
2. M. Howard (ed.), *Restraints on War*, (Oxford: Oxford University Press, 1979), p.8.
3. The conceptual difficulties which planners faced in coming to terms with hostilities below that threshold are well illustrated in K. Knorr and T. Read (eds.), *Limited Strategic War* (London: Pall Mall Press, 1962).
4. For a succinct study of the evolution of American thinking about limited war in the 1950s and 1960s, see R. E. Osgood, 'The Post-War Strategy of Limited War: Before, During and After Vietnam', in L. Martin (ed.), *Strategic Thought in the Nuclear Age* (London: Heinemann 1979), pp.93–130.
5. M. H. Halperin, *Limited War in the Nuclear Age* (New York: John Wiley & Sons, 1966), pp.39–45; R. Brown, 'Limited War' in C. McInnes and G. D. Sheffield (eds.), *Warfare in the Twentieth Century: Theory and Practice*, (London: Unwin Hyman, 1988), pp.166–68.
6. Gen. MacArthur's unwillingness to accept political constraints on the conduct of operations and his criticism of the US administration on this issue finally led President Truman to relieve him of his commands in Korea and Japan in April 1951. This action was subsequently the subject of a detailed Senate investigation, B. I. Kaufmann, *The Korean War* (Philadelphia: Temple University Press, 1986), pp.144–79.
7. M. H. Halperin, 'Limited War', Occasional Papers in International Affairs, No.3, May 1962, Harvard University, 1962, p.2.
8. Ibid., pp.3–4; I. Clark and N. T. Wheeler, *The British Origins of Nuclear Strategy 1945–1955* (Oxford: Clarendon Press, 1989), pp.147–49.
9. R. E. Osgood, *Limited War* (London: University of Chicago Press, 1957).
10. H. Kissinger, *Nuclear Weapons and Foreign Policy* (New York: Harper & Bros., 1957), p.141.
11. Brown 'Limited War', p.170. Kissinger began as an advocate of limited nuclear war

but was later to change his views, H. Kissinger, 'Limited War: Nuclear or Conventional? – A Reappraisal' in D. G. Brennan (ed.), *Arms Control, Disarmament and National Security* (New York: George Braziller, 1961), pp.138–52.
12. This continuum was most fully developed in Herman Kahn, *On Escalation: Metaphors and Scenarios* (London: Pall Mall Press, 1965).
13. S. C. Sarkesian, 'The American Response to Low Intensity Conflict: the Formative Period', in D. A. Charters and M. Tugwell (ed.), *Armies in Low-Intensity Conflict: A Comparative Analysis* (London: Brassey's Defence Publishers, 1989), pp.28–9; William Olson, 'The Concept of Small Wars,' *Small Wars and Insurgencies*, Vol.1, No.1 (April 1990), p.41. Seymour Deitchman, *Limited War and American Defence Policy*, (Cambridge, MA: MIT Press, 1969) is illustrative of the US struggle to come to terms with the idea of limited conflict in the 1960s.
14. A. Short, *The Origins of the Vietnam War*, (London: Longman, 1989), p.227ff; W. Williams, T. McCormick, L. Gardner and W. Lataber (ed.), *America in Vietnam: A Documentary History* (New York: Anchor Books, 1978, pp.218ff.
15. The freedom which the media had to comment on the conduct of operations in the Vietnam War has been seen by some commentators as a significant cause in the failure of US policy. The media's role is discussed in detail in D. Hallin, *The Uncensored War – The Media in Vietnam* (Berkeley, CA: University of California Press, 1989).
16. D. Schwartz, *NATO's Nuclear Dilemmas* (Washington, DC: Brookings Institution, 1983), pp.136–92.
17. L. B. Thompson (ed.), *Low Intensity Conflict* (Lexington, MA: Lexington Books, 1989), p.2.
18. S. C. Sarkesian and W. L. Smith (ed.), *US Policy and Low Intensity Conflict* (New Brunswick: 1981 Transaction Books, 1981), pp.1–66.
19. For a succinct assessment of the Grenada operation, see L. E. Russell, *Grenada 1983*, Men-at-Arms Series, (London: Osprey Publishing, 1985).
20. Thompson, *Low-Intensity Conflict*, pp.6–15.
21. A detailed description of the 'Cod Wars' may be found in *Keesing's Contemporary Archives*, Vol.11 (1957–58), pp.16478–80; Vol.18 (1971–72), pp.25234–6; Vol.19 (1973), pp.25869–77, 26028–32, 26237–9.
22. J.A.C. Mackie, *Konfrontasi: The Indonesia–Malaysia Dispute, 1963–1966* (Oxford: Oxford University Press, 1974), pp.111ff.
23. Ibid., pp.264–67.
24. J.A.C. Mackie, *Low Level Military Incursions: Lessons of the Indonesia-Malaysia Confrontation Episode, 1963–66*, SDSC Working Paper No.105, ANU, Canberra, 1986, pp.17–18.
25. M. Richardson and B. Cloughley, 'Storm Signals in the Spratly's,' *Pacific Defence Reporter*, Vol.17, No.11, (May 1988), pp.5–7.
26. J. Camilleri, *Chinese Foreign Policy* (Oxford: Martin Robertson, Oxford, 1980), pp.225–38.
27. For a analysis of the political manoeuvring preceding the Falklands War, see D. Kinney, 'Anglo-Argentine Diplomacy and the Falklands Crisis' in A. R. Coll and A. C. Arend (eds.), *The Falklands War*, (Boston: Allen and Unwin, 1985), pp.81–105.
28. 'Latin America: The Falklands War', *Strategic Survey 1982–1983*, (London: IISS, 1983), pp.116–23; R. L. Scheina, 'The Malvinas Campaign', *Proceedings US Naval Institute* (henceforth USNIP), Vol.109 (May 1983), pp.98–117.
29. J. Garnett, 'Limited Conventional War in the Nuclear Age', in Howard, *Restraints on War*, pp.79–102 and J. Baylis, K. Booth, J. Garnett and P. Williams, *Contemporary Strategy*, Vol.I, (New York: Holmes and Meier, 1987), pp.191–94.
30. This study adopts the approach that the purpose of definitional concepts such as

'limited conflict' is as a tool to assist our understanding of the characteristics of those conflicts and the actions of the various players involved in them. In some circumstances concepts of this type may need to do no more than describe the physical characteristics of particular situations or subjects to draw useful parallels or comparisions between them. In others, however, the similarities may lie in different areas such as planning principles or methodologies or the purpose behind the actions involved. These may still be reflected to some extent in the physical characteristics of those situations but those descriptive parallels will generally be either too superficial or heavily qualified to provide useful guidance.

31. This difficulty has been most frequently referred to in the context of the Vietnam War and America's failure to counter the commitment of the North Vietnamese despite far greater US potential strength. It highlights the importance of any nation preparing to engage in the use of limited military force to appreciate the adversary's motives and, as far as possible, the extent to which he is prepared to fight and can maintain popular support for, or acquiescence in, that course of action.

32. E. O'Ballance, 'First Thoughts: The Falklands Islands Campaign', *National Defense*, No.69 (Sept. 1982), pp.38–9.

33. For an assessment of why China entered the Korean War when it did, see A. S. Whiting, *China Crosses The Yalu* (New York: Macmillan, 1960).

34. D. Kinney in Coll and Arend, *The Falklands War*, pp.101–102.

35. D. A. Charters, 'From Palestine to Northern Ireland: British Adaption to Low-Intensity Operations' in Charters and Tugwell, *Armies in Low-Intensity Conflict*, p.171.

36. There also appear to have been some differences of views as to just what Australia's response should be, D. Scarr, *Fiji: Politics of Illusion – The Military Coups in Fiji*, (Kensington, NSW: New South Wales University Press, 1988), pp.78–79. Subsequently, Australia's Foreign Minister, Senator Gareth Evans, was careful to point out that 'we should bear in mind that in many situations it may be more appropriate to respond to a request for assistance with a civilian rather than military capability. The mere presence abroad of Australian military forces and equipment sends messages, which may be intended to be reassuring but might be seen in fact as threatening', 'Australia's Regional Security,' Ministerial Statement by Senator the Hon. Gareth Evans QC Minister for Foreign Affairs and Trade, Dec. 1989, p.21.

37. Gen. Frederick C. Weyand, writing in 1976 about the Vietnam War, noted that 'when the Army is committed the American people are committed, when the American people lose the commitment it is futile to keep the Army committed', quoted by Sarkesian in Charters and Tugwell, *Armies in Low Intensity Conflict.*, p.41.

38. At the US National Press Club on 28 November 1984, the Defense Secretary stated that the six tests that should be applied when weighing the possible use of US combat forces abroad were:
    - the issue must be 'vital to our national interests or that of our allies';
    - combat troops must be committed 'wholeheartedly, and with the clear intention of winning';
    - the need to have 'clearly defined political and military objectives' and to know precisely how the forces can accomplish them;
    - the relationship between objectives and the forces committed (size, composition, disposition) must be continually reassessed and adjusted if necessary;
    - there must be a reasonable assurance of the support of the American people and of Congress, which cannot be achieved 'unless we are candid in making clear the threats we face';
    - the commitment of combat forces should be as a last resort.

39. F. Kitson, *Low Intensity Operations: Subversion, Insurgency, Peacekeeping,*

(London: Faber, 1971), p.95.

40. Although only a small proportion of the total ordnance used during the Gulf War with Iraq, US use of laser and other precision guided weapons provided important political as well as military advantages, including managing on-going domestic support for the operations.

41. The United Nations did not accept the legitimacy of Iraq's claimed annexation nor, by the time of the UN deadline and attack, had Iraq introduced any civil administration or other permanent mechanisms for the supply and support of the local population that might reinforce its claims.

42. *The Defence of Australia 1987*, Policy Information Paper presented to Parliament by the Minister for Defence, Kim C. Beazley, March 1987, AGPS, Canberra, 1987, pp.23–33; *Review of Australia's Defence Capabilities*, Report to the Minister for Defence by Paul Dibb, March 1986, AGPS, Canberra, 1986, pp.42–73.

43. P. Wilkinson (ed.), *British Perspectives on Terrorism*, (London: Allen and Unwin, 1981); Y. Alexander and A. O'Day (ed.), *Terrorism in Ireland* (London: Croom Helm, 1984 and *Ireland's Terrorist Dilemma* (Dordrecht: Martinus Nijhoff, 1986); A. Gresh, *The PLO: The Struggle Within* (London: Zed Books, 1985); H. Schoenberg, *A Mandate for Terror* (New York: Shapolosky Publishers, 1984).

44. P. Wilkinson, 'The Laws of War and Terrorism' in D. Rapoport and Y. Alexander (ed.), *The Morality of Terrorism*, (New York: Pergamon Press, 1982), pp.308–24.

45. See Hallin, *The Uncensored War*; also comments on the Falklands campaign by former British Secretary of State for Defence, John Nott, 'The Falklands Campaign', *USNIP* Vol.109 (May 1983), p.136; and on Grenada Maj. Gen. W. Sidle (Rtd), 'The Public's Right To Know', *USNIP*, Vol.111 (July 1985), pp.37–43.

The Case for the Media

PROFESSOR CLEM LLOYD

> Two things people should not watch are the making of sausage
> and the making of war. All that front page blood and gore
> hurts the military. We are guilt by association.
>> US Air Force surgeon, Dr William Burner (1991)

> There can be few professions more ready to misunderstand
> each other than journalists and soldiers.
>> Major S. F. Crozier, Assistant Editor of *The Field*[1] (1982)

In the early 1890s the great Irish dramatist, Oscar Wilde, had a vision
of how future wars would be conducted. A single soldier from each
side, said Wilde, would stalk the other along the frontier, each armed
with a phial of liquid chemicals. Wilde was prophetic in his sombre
allusion to future chemical and biological warfare. His vision of a
modern conflict reducible to the symbolic level of Homeric combat
between Hector and Achilles, however, has not materialised.
Phenomenal advances in technology have not reduced the numbers of
combatants or the volume of armaments and military material on the
battlefield. Nor has the deterrent effect of total warfare reduced the
incidence of limited conflict, which has become virtually endemic in
the aftermath of World War II.

The pervasiveness of limited conflict has been accompanied by a
remarkable growth in the demands of news outlets and journalists for
coverage. Devising systems of media access and facilitation consistent
with national strategy and battlefield tactics has emerged as one of the
most intractable problems preoccupying the contemporary military.
The experience of over 45 years of limited conflict since World War II
ended has failed to shape co-operative arrangements consistent with
the objectives of both media and military. The decisive Allied victory
in the 1991 Gulf War has left the military very much in the ascendancy,
and the media face serious obstacles in restoring a balanced relationship and renewing conventional rights to report and interpret limited
conflict.

This paper is an attempt to analyse the media-military relationship up to and including the 1991 Gulf War, and to make some assessment of what might happen in future limited conflicts. It is not written from the perspective of the war correspondent or the foreign correspondent. The author claims no particular expertise in either area. The paper does, however, reflect a lengthy experience with public policy formulation and administration, including defence policy, and a life-long interest in military history and media practice. It begins with a brief examination of the history of media coverage of total wars and limited conflicts, culminating in the decisive impact of the Vietnam War. It considers the thesis that Vietnam transformed the fundamentals of the media-military relationship and profoundly influenced practice in subsequent limited conflicts. The Australian experience is singled out for more extended treatment, with the Vietnam and Iraqi conflicts as the principal reference points. The paper concludes with a somewhat pessimistic assessment of the media's involvement in future military conflicts.

Access, Movement and Co-operation

The needs of the journalist reporting military conflict may be defined under three basic heads: access to the battlefield; mobility on the battlefield; and reasonable access to official military information. The resolution, or non-resolution, of these requirements by negotiation between military and media determines the effectiveness, and the ultimate value, of media coverage. If all three requirements are denied, then obviously journalists cannot do their job. If only formal access to military information is provided, then the journalist's effectiveness depends on its quality, quantity and regularity. If access to official information and access to the battlefield is provided, but with restricted movement, the quality of news coverage is again heavily dependent on the honesty and co-operation of official sources. A journalist with both battlefield access and mobility can function effectively even in the absence of official information and co-operation. The ideal mix has been defined by the *Washington Post* Correspondent, Patrick J. Sloyan as the 'combination of common sense, common courtesy and open access that governed coverage of the American military through two world wars, the Korean conflict and Vietnam'.[2] The contemporary media would argue that this traditional compact between soldiers and journalists has been destroyed by military practice in the Falklands, Grenada, Panama and, most importantly, the 1991 Gulf War. Some guidance from history is necessary to throw light on how this has happened.

As with the origins of British constitutional and administrative practice, the contribution of the war correspondent can be traced back at least to the English Civil War of the 1640s. Its battles were reported for the rudimentary news journals, or 'diurnals', of the time, although we know little about how it was done. Reflecting the rapid fluctuations of that war, some talented journalists were tempted to report the war for both sides and, indeed, may have done so:

> I doe find that whosoever undertakes to write weekly news in this nature, undertakes to sail down a narrow channel, where all along the shore on each side are Rocks and Cliffs that threaten him; and though for the present one side seems not so full of sand or Dangers as the other, and therefore many of us ... do seem to lean to that side most, yet who knows that new tides may rise, and rolling sands may remove to the other shore.[3]

Factionalism on both the Parliamentary and Royalist sides made it difficult to present a totally impartial report. One journal supporting Oliver Cromwell delayed publication so that the contributions of the two main Parliamentary factions to the Battle of Naseby could be given equal coverage.

In harsh practice, access to the battlefield has always been guaranteed to luckless populations caught between warring forces. Many of the great fictional accounts of battles are seen from the viewpoint of civilians and not soldiers. Tolstoy in *War and Peace* describes the Battle of Borodino through the eyes of Pierre, an aristocrat who stumbles clumsily about the battlefield. Stendhal in *The Charterhouse of Parma* vividly portrays the fringes of the Waterloo battlefield through his hero, Fabrice, who barely comprehends what he sees. Zola in *The Debacle* uses a variety of civilians to provide a shifting focus on the manoeuvres of both French and German armies at the climactic Battle of Sedan (1870) in the Franco-Prussian War. This shifting of viewpoint from side to side, was a luxury largely denied the war correspondent, at least until the advent of Cable Network News. It was, however, possible for the war correspondent to share a vantage point with civilians to watch a battle or extended military manoeuvre. Where civilians were blended willy nilly into battle areas the correspondent did not need exceptional privileges of access and movement. Thus, journalists watched the Charge of the Light Brigade from the heights at Balaclava, as did army wives and camp followers of the British Army. The press correspondents who covered the First Battle of Bull Run (1861) in the American Civil War, had no greater privileges than the hundreds of citizens who flocked to watch the battle and were caught up in the shambles of precipitate defeat.

Great set-piece battles provided vantage points for civilians, including war correspondents. Rapid military movement masked the presence of journalists and gave them the access and mobility that they needed. The 'Golden Age' of the war correspondent is invariably defined as roughly the period between the Crimean War in the 1850s and the outbreak of World War I in 1914. Despite frequent discouragement and hostility, journalists roamed freely and drew upon multiple sources in the field. William Russell of *The Times* of London was able to establish standards for later war correspondents in the Crimea despite the adjurations of senior British officers: 'If I were you I should go away! I should indeed'.[4]

In the American Civil War, military hostility to war correspondents was tempered by presidential politics with Abraham Lincoln intervening to spare correspondents execution by General William T. Sherman and court martial by General Ulysses S. Grant. Lord Kitchener's oft-quoted imprecation to assembled journalists before the battle of Omdurman (1898), 'GET OUT OF MY WAY YOU DRUNKEN SWABS',[5] did not present them from providing a vivid picture of the River War. Access to the field and freedom to move with the troops vanquished official hostility and lack of co-operation.

The strict delineation of military and civilian space was largely caused by the static warfare on the Western Front during World War I. Civilians were withdrawn from the battle zones, leaving depopulated areas under military control. The replacement of mobile warfare by trench warfare and the absence of a masking civilian population simplified the control and manipulation of the press. Kitchener threatened to shoot journalists who entered battle zones without authority or escort. The mobile journalist able to venture at pleasure into war zones was supplanted by the château journalist who became virtually an appendage of the general staff. A so-called 'eyewitness' system was developed so that official representatives of Allied participants could provide an authorised coverage. Their reports were published under the by-line 'Eyewitness', although few observed actual combat and their occasional forays to the trenches were strictly supervised. The system produced one outstanding exception to manipulated coverage: Australia's official war correspondent, C. E. W. (Charles) Bean who won the confidence of the Australian Imperial Force at Gallipoli. In the latter stages of the war, fresh life was breathed into war reporting when American journalists arrived with their expeditionary force. They restored some of the independence and mobility of traditional military news gathering, while failing fully to exploit their opportunities. Despite these limited exceptions, World War I set extreme standards for restrictive consorship, military mendacity and manipulation of journalists and news coverage until the early 1980s.

The limited conflicts of the 1930s restored some of the traditional access and mobility while creating problems of logistics and objectivity. Journalists covering the Abyssinian War in 1936 found it easier to get war news from Mussolini's invading army than from Emperor Haile Selassie's hapless army defending its national boundaries. The Spanish Civil War coverage earned a largely undeserved lustre from the presence of distinguished writers such as Ernest Hemingway, George Orwell and André Malraux. Phillip Knightley has shown convincingly in *The First Casualty* that much of the reporting from Spain was heavily influenced by partisanship and manipulation.

In World War II access and mobility for journalists were much better although some military zones, particularly the Russian Front, were difficult to penetrate. In North Africa, where open terrain and sparse population encouraged separation of civilians and soldiers, journalists were given excellent access, mobility and formal co-operation. Much of the North African reporting was of good quality and, largely through the efforts of the correspondents, an aura of chivalry was created around the participants, a rarity in contemporary warfare. After the Normandy invasion, journalists moved freely behind, and sometimes in advance of, the Allied forces. Access of Australian journalists to forward war zones was vividly exemplified in the powerful camera images of Damien Parer. Ken G. Hall, the founder of Cinesound Newsreel and a colleague of Parer, acknowledged the importance of access to the front line in the work of the World War II cameramen:

> ... the cameramen were right there beside the men fighting in the trenches. When you see men fighting and dying ... then you know what war is all about. There was no one around to tell

Damien [Parer] what to do. At one stage the bureaucrats tried to order him home. But he said no, and went up the Kokoda trail [in the New Guinea Campaign]. He wasn't popular with the bureaucrats, but by golly he was popular with the men.[6]

It is impossible to generalise adequately about the smaller wars, limited conflicts, insurgencies and other military actions following World War II. Certainly, journalists were manipulated extensively in two of the most sustained conflicts – the Korean War and the protracted Algerian insurrection against the French. In Korea, this occurred although journalists acknowledged the access and mobility permitted. (Knightley demonstrated in *The First Casualty* the failure of the media, with some limited exceptions, to take up civil rights issues in both wars). Official policy in the Vietnam War discharged in an almost exemplary manner the three essentials of access, mobility and official co-operation. It also provoked a substantial re-thinking of the conventional canons governing relationships between the military and the media.

The Vietnam Experience

The Vietnam War generated a substantial literature on journalistic practice which it is impossible to summarise here. The received wisdom is that the US lost the war on the domestic television screens of America. The argument has been expressed most coherently by the British broadcaster, Sir Robin Day:

Television has a built-in bias towards depicting any conflict in terms of the visible brutality. You can say, of course, that that is what war is – brutality, conflict, starvation and combat – all I am saying is that there are other issues which cause these things to come about, and television does not always deal with them adequately ... One wonders if in future a democracy which has uninhibited television coverage in every home will ever be able to fight a war, however just ... The full brutality of the combat will be there in close up and colour and blood looks very red on the colour television screen ... If there are one people in the world who are never, but absolutely never going to understand the war in Vietnam it is the Americans who watched it on television. The war was meaningless to them; they don't know what happened at any single stage of that war and they never will and they are a lost generation as far as that is concerned and this is what worried me about television. The war was lost on the television screen of the United States.[7]

According to the British counter-insurgency authority, Sir Robert Thompson, the British would have lost the Boer War on television.[8]

This concentration on the impact of television is a gross over-simplification that has not gone unchallenged. The most important flaw in this widely-held truism is that it ignores the print media's contribution to the war's unpopularity even before TV reached its maximum impact. The distinguished columnist, Walter Lippmann, opposed the war virtually from the initial commitment of US troops, and President Lyndon Johnson acknowledged the effectiveness of his vehement opposition in the mid-1960s. Senator Eugene McCarthy, whose presidential candidacy was a rallying point for opposition to the war, described the turning point as the publication of a press photograph. This was a famous shot by Jimmy Olson of dead and bleeding marines on a tank leaving the Battle of Hue during the Tet Offensive in 1969.[9] The US military was steadfast in its conviction that blood and guts on television destroyed its aspirations in Vietnam.

The United States military in Vietnam amply discharged the three requisites of effective news gathering in war; it provided ready access to the battle zones; it encouraged a mobility unique in modern warfare and it gave access to official information. Furthermore, it generously extended the press freedoms of the American Constitution to all journalists covering the war. Yet the access and co-operation it gave journalists failed to achieve the public policy objective of stimulating a favourable coverage, and bolstering popular support for the war. The facilities for official information it provided were derided and satirised. Easy access and mobility prompted increasingly hostile coverage. Even so, the media strategy would probably have worked if the war had been short. Despite the mockery, many American journalists and news outlets made extensive use of official material, and did not pursue opportunities to work extensively in the field. They were content to stick close to official sources, even the briefings in Saigon despised as the 'Five O'Clock follies'. The longer the war lasted, however, the more pervasive became the scepticism of the journalists who worked in the field. The strength of the media presence in the field is demonstrated by the large numbers of journalists who died while discharging professional responsibilities to cover the war.

Subsequent analysis has detected many weaknesses in American Vietnam War coverage. Braestrup (1977)[10] and Hooper (1982) have argued convincingly that important elements of the coverage were marked by inexperience and sensationalism. Braestrup has shown that news coverage and interpretation of the Tet Offensive was defective. Yet the essential truth emerged: that the US and its allies had failed to secure South Vietnam, or to demonstrate convincingly that they would ever secure it.

Vietnam's Aftermath

Vietnam convinced the US military that it was essential in future limited conflicts to deny media access and mobility, and to limit and carefully control access to official information. Thus, a total news blackout was applied to the 1983 invasion of Grenada. An American diplomat, James H. Hughes, recalled listening to the complaints of US reporters who 'lolled' around the Bridgetown Airport during the three days of the invasion:

> They had not been allowed to accompany the US invasion force and the only news leaking out of Grenada was via heavily military censored sources. They were able to land in Grenada three days after the fighting was over, see the war damage and only then talk to those who witnessed the fighting first hand.[11]

Journalists who sought traditional access were turned back. Several who got to the island by rented motorboat were held on a US command ship for two days, although they were eventually permitted to file their copy. The only coverage accessible to the world media was supplied by Army public relations officers.

A similar censorship of news was applied with Operation 'Just Cause' the limited operation designed to remove Panama's General Manuel Noriega as head of state in December 1989. Following the media outcry over Grenada, a Pentagon press pool of ten journalists representing wire services, TV and radio networks, newspapers and photo agencies was created for deployment in future limited conflicts: 'Their reports would be circulated to all media. On paper they would be given unlimited access to generals as well as grunts, and provided [sic] top-priority transmission of films and dispatches through military communications circuits'.[12]

This pool was blooded during the Panama invasion in farcical circumstances. Pool journalists arrived in Panama hours after the fighting at the key points of Rio Hato and Patilla had ceased, and they were kept well away from continuing fighting at the Commandancia. The pool's principal sources were CNN broadcasts of Pentagon briefings from Washington, the first demonstration of the network's potency as a media, (and military), instrument. The military was able to paint Operation 'Just Cause' as largely free of casualties and virtually unblemished in its execution. It emerged subsequently that 23 American servicemen had been killed and 265 wounded in the three battles of day one. No eyewitness accounts, film or photos of these battles found their way into the US media and requests for official military footage were mostly declined because, as one official explained, 'combat photography is for combat use – internal use'. A subsequent investigation put most of the blame for the media fog on Defense Secretary Richard Cheney who simply deleted the Pentagon public information bureaucracy from planning the invasion.

The US bureaucracy was also strongly influenced by British practice in the Falklands War. The British largely responded to the orthodox interpretation of the media in Vietnam, although other complex factors were involved, particularly the British 'lobby' system and its reliance on unattributable briefings from official sources. When the briefings were withdrawn during the Falklands crisis, many defence journalists floundered. Other complications included the haste with which the Falklands Task Force, including the media contingent, was assembled, and the invasion's recalcitrant geography, with an elaborate maritime exercise culminating in a short decisive land campaign which was not covered adequately by journalists in the field. The journalists in the convoy found it extremely difficult to get stories back to offices and studio in the United Kingdom. Despite the strict controls there were complaints about security breaches, most importantly the disclosure by the BBC of plans for the advance on Goose Green. Again, the media's problems were analysed exhaustively after the war, and paper processes were devised to assure better news access in future limited conflicts. In both major powers these proposals were overwhelmed by the 1991 Gulf War.

The 1991 Gulf War

In the 1991 Gulf War the terrain, distribution of population and territorial boundaries facilitated a greater restriction of journalists' movement than in any ground war since World War 1. The 'smart technology' of the battlefield provided a potential capability to track the movements of journalists trying to work independently. A number of journalists evaded the various controls to work independently, although the volume of copy and film emanating from those who broke the system was insubstantial. A British journalist, Matthew Engel, encountered an Austrian magazine journalist in the middle of the desert. The Austrian asked for a lift back to Kuwait:

> ... I explained that we were up against a very tight deadline and there was no way we would have time to rediscover his car in this remote spot, and then drive the 400 odd kilometres back to Dhahran, which was the only place we could be sure of filing the pictures and copy. 'File copy?' He looked stunned. 'I thought you were soldiers'.

Conceding that he was looking rather 'butch' in an olive-green chemical suit and a helmet liberated from a TV crew, Engel described the strange meeting as his most surreal moment in a surreal war. According to Engel, any properly prepared journalist was dressed in genuine desert camouflage 'which bore a bizarre resemblance to a Laura Ashley print, and even then they still looked like hacks.'[13]

Arrangements made by the participants for their national journalists were swamped by the media management policies ordained by the United States. These derived from the American interpretation of Vietnam, supplemented by the field lessons drawn from Grenada, Panama and the Falklands. The traditional press freedoms enshrined by the US Constitution's First Amendment were given short shrift despite challenges in the US Federal Court backed by eminent journalists such as Walter Cronkite who looked back nostalgically to the moderate, reasonable censors of World War II:

> With an arrogance foreign to the democratic system, the US military in Saudi Arabia is trampling on the American people's right to know. It is doing a disservice not only to the home front but to history and to its own best interests ... The military has the responsibility of giving all the information it possibly can to the press, and the press has every right, to the point of insolence, to demand this.[14]

Cronkite's outrage was shared by Michael Gartner, the President of NBC News: 'Americans want to know, and if Americans aren't told, they'll raise hell about it. They want to know, and they have a right to know'.

The US Courts, however, affirmed military restrictions such as barring the media from the military base where military coffins had been brought back to America for 18 years. It emerged that Americans did not want to over-burdened by information in what became a rapid and relatively bloodless military victory. Buoyed by massive levels of public support for its policies, the American military got away with a policy epitomised by Engel: 'The Saudis placed no restrictions on anyone's freedom of movement. It was the Americans who issued guidelines which in the end forbade journalists to do anything, except sit back in the hotels in Riyadh or Dhahran and wait to be told which side was winning.'[15]

The dimensions of the Gulf War prevented total news management similar to Grenada and Panama. Consequently, the successful strategy relied on rigorous censorship, strictly controlled briefing sessions, provision of authorised film and pictorial material, and posting of media pools under strict military regulation and guidance. The mixture worked superbly in a brief military campaign, but it probably would have broken down in a more protracted military conflict. It would be wrong, however, to conclude that the Vietnam media strategy would not have worked in the Gulf. Greater access and mobility combined with a steady flow of official military would probably have been just as successful for the US military. It would certainly have yielded a better news coverage.

Journalists responded ambivalently to the US media strategy. Official briefings and pooled film and print stories provided a basic news cover, relieving the apprehensions of American journalists contemplating further news blackouts on Grenada lines. Better a routine, mundane news cover than none at all. In any military conflict, much of the media will be satisfied with a routine cover largely drawn from official sources. This happened even in Vietnam, as Martin Woollacott has observed:

> In Vietnam days, the despatches of *Agence France Presse* were renowned for beginning their daily round up with the phrase: 'American B-52s last night unleashed their deadly cargoes on . . .' and then would follow a list of Vietnamese places. It was rather like filling in a form.[16]

Similar patterns of routine clichés soon emerged in the Gulf: ' "Wave after wave" of American and British planes continue their "relentless pounding". It is just as meaningless.'

Journalists who were nominated to pools often found the experience irksome and largely unproductive for gathering hard news. Their peers concluded that pool material provided fresher and more vital news than the incessant briefings at the Saudi Arabian military bases. Many journalists feared that pooling would be abandoned at the slightest provocation and they zealously protected this limited avenue to the battle zones. The military created the impression that journalists working outside the established pools would jeopardise the news opportunities of their colleagues. Journalists reaching combat zones and exercising a right of independent reporting engaged in acrimonious exchanges with pool colleagues and their military chaperons. At the sharp action at Khafji, where the Iraqis put up a spirited resistance, journalists from the London *Independent* were abused by an American pool cameraman who accused them of threatening other journalists' right to work: 'You asshole: You'll prevent us from working. You're not allowed here. Get out, go back to [Saudi Arabia].'[17]

The interlopers were warned by a US public affairs officer that they could not talk to US marines and the marines could not talk to them. The widely experienced British correspondent and author, Robert Fisk, described it as a disturbing moment:

> For the American reporter . . . the privileges of the pool and the military rules attached to it were more important than the right of a journalist to do his job. The American and British military have thus been able to divide journalists on the ground that those who try to work outside the pool will destroy the opportunities of those working within it.[18]

French camera teams who filmed the engagement had their film confiscated. In another incident, a *Sunday Times* journalist located a British regiment in the desert but was ticked off by a British major escorting a press pool because his initiative would 'ruin it for the others'. A uniform coverage dictated by military sources was reinforced by appeals to journalistic fraternity and solidarity.

While pooling may have merit in providing a basic coverage, it is essentially inequitable. The pools are oriented in favour of wire services and the TV network news. It is a form of lotto system with many news organisations excluded completely. No rotational system can guarantee fair access for more than 2,000 journalists. Pooling also lends itself to manipulation by getting key journalists out of the way and ensuring they do not intrude into military operations:

> The few dozen who believed they were lucky and were selected to join military pools spent the weeks of the Air War in extreme discomfort writing tedious pieces about regimental mascots and cookhouse orderlies from Nottingham or Nebraska, then were unable to get their copy out quickly enough when the ground war began.[19]

A British journalist assigned to report British armoured brigades for all British evening newspapers spent weeks living in a tank and digging his own trenches, hearing nothing from media sources except a complaint from the *Kent Messenger* that he had not interviewed any soldiers from East Anglia.

Even with the short duration of the 1991 Gulf War, there were signs that the pool system was fraying. More positively, there was evidence of significant non-compliance with the rules about keeping out of the battlefield. According to Engel, those who co-operated with the system were 'completely stuffed' by the military: '... I never met any non-pool journalist who had signed the guidelines, still less took any notice of them.'

Enforcement of stringent rules was often lenient. Engel and several colleagues intruded into a battle sector and were arrested by a marine captain who threatened to take them back to Dhahran for deportation. The order was countermanded by a superior officer, an admirer of Engel's newspaper, the *Guardian*: 'The captain was left fulminating. He lost. We won. But he was quite right. He was fighting a war and I was prancing around his battlefield in an olive-green noddy suit'.

The television coverage was even more assiduously uniform, combining pool material with official military film. According to the French cinema and TV historian Marc Ferro, everyone saw virtually the same pictures:

> Instead of several national newsreels putting out their own material simultaneously, there is now something like a supranational picture-producing system.... Whoever provides the material [from the Iraqi War], whether it comes from the Americans or the Iraqis, it is shown on all channels, even if each one makes its own selection ... Today, even though most TV

channels have special correspondents either they see the same things, or else the slower reporters are pipped at the post by the quicker ones.[20]

Ferro recalled that during 1939–40, French newsreels did not include German war footage which could have been obtained from US sources. The TV networks had no such scruples in 1991.

This uniformity was mostly gratifying to the Allied command. The one wild card was Baghdad where, ironically, the Iraqi censors shaped a product for national ends that was generally consistent with Allied objectives. The principal exceptions were Peter Arnett's extended interview with Saddam Hussein, and TV coverage from Baghdad of an air raid shelter bombed with substantial casualties. This was the only occasion when the Allied media strategy faltered, the only time there was blood on the screen. As an artifact created for the Allied command, the seamless flow of television footage was otherwise unflawed. The first film coverage of war was shot by French Army units early in World War I. It was intended not for public consumption but for the high command who wanted to know how their weapons compared with those of the enemy. How much has really changed?

Are There Alternatives?

Are there alternatives to tightly controlled and largely uniform news coverage of conflict? The traditional answer is the skill, enterprise, and courage of dedicated journalists with access, at their own risk, to the battlefield, the freedom to work in the field and to move about it with relative freedom, subject to operational security. The parameters have been summarised by Sloyan: '... wide – and responsible – access to combatants, not in sanitized arranged encounters but as close to the time and scene of missions and battles as the troops in the field can facilitate without endangering the lives and security of the fighting forces.'[21]

The most sustained attempts in the 1991 Gulf War to assert traditional field conventions for journalists was made by French media organisations. After several French TV crews managed to evade their military minders and interview French soldiers in unauthorised areas, the French Defence Ministry imposed severe restrictions on access. This followed an earlier row when French journalists briefly boycotted their army and refused to report its activities. The Defence Minister,

Pierre Joxe, proposed the 'immersion' of journalists in the front line, allowing them to visit fighting units on 24 to 36-hour assignments. The proposal was accepted enthusiastically by French field commanders craving media attention after months of isolation in the desert. Joxe, however, backed away even though journalists eligible for 'immersion' were willing to accept military censorship of their reports. Precedent was drawn from regulations prepared in 1944, presumably for correspondents covering the Free French liberation forces.

Joxe also suggested a 'French School of War Coverage' which would permit an elite group of up to a dozen correspondents, chosen by consensus if possible, to cover fighting units on a permanent basis. Other journalists would have to be content with brief one or two-hour visits to the front. The media interpreted these moves as an attempt by the French Ministry of Defence to get its own approved defence specialists to the front. If consensus could not be attained, then access was to be restricted to sporadic visits to the 'rear of the front line'. Two journalists were chosen by Joxe as pilots for 'immersion', one representing *Le Parisien Liberé* and the other the *Agence France Presse*. (This journalist was also a reserve army captain).[22] The quick ending of the war quashed both 'immersion' and the 'French School of War Coverage', at least for the moment.

French journalists probably had a more dispiriting time in the Gulf than colleagues covering other national contingents. US censorship requirements affronted Gallic sensibilities and two French journalists were actually deported for breaches. Withdrawal of accreditation is a potent threat to the independent activity of the war correspondent but scope remains for continued reporting outside the system. Lack of accreditation may even stimulate independence and enterprise in news gathering. The threat of deportation is a deterrent to even the most persistently independent journalist. The war's swift conclusion prevented the testing of journalists' asserted rights of access and mobility, and the growth of non-compliance. It also prevented the media from exploiting their own 'smart' technology to penetrate the mysteries of the battlefield, such as night-vision cameras and portable satellite communications.

Another danger of rigorous news control by the military is the temptation it arouses to seek news from the enemy. This was largely avoided in the Vietnam War because of the access and mobility provided by a tolerant military command. In the Falklands War the United Kingdom recognised only British correspondents in the war zone, turning the media of other countries, particularly the United States, to Argentine sources. This produced some media coverage favourable to the Argentinians, even in the United Kingdom. The dangers were far more evident in the 1991 Gulf War, although stifled by crushing victory.

Australia and Limited Conflict

What lessons can we draw from the Australian experience in the 1991 Gulf War? Again, the logical starting point for assessment is the Vietnam War. The initial commitment of the Australian battalions to Vietnam was accomplished in an atmosphere of general media support. This was reflected in good relations between the initial battalions and the journalists who accompanied them. Journalists trained with Australian troops on the transport ships and they went with units on field operations without complaint that they were intrusive or threatened security. The result was favourable reporting by Australian journalists of Australian military operations. Correspondents wrote books praising the operational performance of Australian units; such were Ian Mackay's *Australians in Vietnam* and Gerald Stone's *War Without Honour*. After this good start, however, the relationship gradually soured, particularly after the Australian units were moved as a Task Force to Phuoc Thuy province.

The deteriorating relationship was not reflected in public recrimination or open animosity between the Australian command and journalists, although there were some clashes. It emerged rather in an unwillingness of some Australian journalists to cover the Australian military. This attitude permeates *Vietnam, A Reporter's War*, a fine account of reporting in Vietnam by the Australian journalist Hugh Lunn.[23] Considering the Australian military to be uncooperative, Lunn mostly worked in the field with American and South Vietnamese units. The legendary Australian cameraman, Neil Davis, also preferred to work with the Vietnamese and Cambodian armies. This reluctance partly reflects the reality that the big battalions generated the most news, but undoubtedly some Australian journalists felt it unnecessary to devote much time for the Task Force.

Re-assessment of news coverage from the war suggests that Australia's participation was not intensively covered. The major Battle of Long Tan was covered by journalists flown to the field once the battle was over. Long Tan was sparked by an unexpected attack on an Australian company and it would have been extremely fortuitous if Australian correspondents had been in the field or even at Task Force headquarters at the time. More significant were the protracted operations at Firebases Coral and Balmoral in 1969 when Australian units moved from the Task Force area to intercept enemy infiltration north of Saigon. Australian casualties in Operation 'Coral' were comparable to Long Tan and the risk of serious setback was just as real. Little of the operation's importance or the risks involved emerged in the Australian press. There is no reference in Lex McAulay's detailed history of Operation 'Coral' to the presence of Australian journalists in the field.

Pointing to gaps in the record is not to denigrate the dedicated efforts of the small group of Australian correspondents who tried to give an authentic and accurate account of how Australians fought the war. Pre-eminent was Pat Burgess whose personal courage and rapport with Australian troops was comparable to C. E. W. Bean. Burgess produced many vivid vignettes of the Diggers in Vietnam, phrased in prose that was invariably lucid, emotive and idiosyncratic. Even Burgess, however, was constrained by the limited space available in the tabloid *Sydney Sun*. The activities of the Australian Navy and the RAAF were given only cursory treatment. The early rapport between the military and journalists faded as senior Task Force officers became preoccupied with strict operational security and much less willing to take journalists into the field. The lack of encouragement given to journalists at Task Force headquarters during certain periods of the war was apparent even to casual visitors. Indeed, the indifference, even hostility, of one Task Force commander was evidenced in a disdain and lack of co-operation which extended even to press secretaries accompanying official visitors.

In the 20 years between the Australian withdrawal from Vietnam and its participation in the 1991 Gulf War, several experiments were made in establishing a workable relationship between the Australian military and journalists. These ventures were sometimes crude and impractical, but did show a mutual desire to establish better working relationships. A Defence Media Advisory Group (DMAG) was formed in 1986 to encourage consultation. The process was given some urgency by the possibility that Australian forces might be used in limited military operations in the South Pacific during the late 1980s. Ways of providing media access and mobility were tested in major military exercises, notably Operation 'Kangaroo' in 1989 which was attended by more than 150 journalists. The exercise worked well enough, although there was a complaint that the military had been slow to release the name of a soldier killed in an accident.[24]

Censorship was generally flexible and analytical articles critical of military performance and equipment were cleared for publication. The military had developed excellent facilities to assist journalists, but the spirit of co-operation prompted only limited national coverage. One analyst suggested that this was probably because there were not enough specialist military writers. The exercise report of Operation 'Kangaroo' in 1986, for example, suggested that most accredited correspondents preferred to stick close to the Media Support Unit and work on the briefing material provided. They did not exploit opportunities to venture extensively into operational areas to seek news. These findings were consistent, of course, with the Falklands experience which demonstrated the inability of many defence journalists to perform competently without regular briefings and access to official material. Martin Woollacott has described the reassurance which regular briefings give to journalists in unfamiliar, and potentially difficult, circumstances:

> The briefing room is another place which functions at a minimum of real information. The military authorities manage what they know, naturally, but it is also true know less than they care to admit. The schoolroom rituals reassure – the briefing officers in starched uniforms, the maps, the pointers. Things seem under control. But they are not.[25]

Apart from military exercises, the Australian military had no opportunity to test media procedures in the field before the 1991 Gulf War. In December 1990, while military forces were still assembling in the Gulf, Brigadier Steve Gower, said there would be no censorship:

> The press and the defence forces are always going to be uneasy bedfellows. But people want news – they demand news and we acknowledge that. We intend to make every effort to ensure that the media are there and are given the full story if the ADF [Australian Defence Force] is ever deployed. You have to be big enough and confident enough in your organisation and its work to be able to accept a certain amount of criticism. If the organisation is not as good as it should be the Australian people should know it. You can't go about hiding things.[26]

Despite some scepticism, the DMAG system was welcomed by

senior defence and foreign correspondents. David Jenkins described it as not perfect, but concluded that it was about the best journalists could expect: 'If nothing else, it seems to have built some trust in an area where suspicion traditionally runs deep'.[27]

Hopes for a balanced relationship were rudely dashed when the Australian commitment was limited to three ships and the tri-service commitment envisaged in several years of planning and consultation did not eventuate. ADF was not deployed. The central issue became the Australian media's access to the warships.

The brief but acrimonious controversy bruised both sides. Having got limited access to the ships, Australian journalists found that there was little hard news to report. The coverage turned to home-town news, with lists of service people on particular assignments and where they came from in Australia. This, of course, is not an unworthy news genre. The American journalist, Ernie Pyle, who specialised in such coverage during World War II, remains a revered war correspondent. The Falklands War showed conclusively that warships can be lethal places in contemporary warfare. The role of Australian warships in the Gulf was important and all aboard, including journalists, were exposed to risk. The expectations of the Australian media, however, were not geared to naval patrolling. News organisations and their journalists were irritated by what they construed as lack of formal co-operation and use of material on the national contribution suffered accordingly.

Limited Conflict and Journalists' Rights

There are no absolute rights for journalists. The US constitutional freedoms did not prevent what the American Society of Newspaper Editors concluded were unacceptable levels of censorship during the 1991 Gulf War. Nor did they get American journalists into the battle zones in sufficient numbers to provide independent coverage. Bolstered by spectacular success and overwhelming public support, the US military over-rode the attenuation of traditional rights. The media now face substantial difficulties in re-asserting and restoring long-accepted rights and privileges. Indeed, former rights and privileges may have vanished forever. The danger for the military is that the 1991 Gulf War may have reinforced the military in a fundamental misinterpretation of Vietnam. The media still has some good cards to play, particularly if they choose to exploit ruthlessly the technological innovations they now have.

Although the media have no absolute rights, there are qualified rights that precedent and convention might assert on their behalf. This is a crude listing: a right of reasonable access; a right of reasonable approach; a right to be accurately informed by official sources; a right to transmit accurate information to mass audience; a right to investigate; a right to communicate the results of investigations; a right to accept the hazards inherent in its activities; a right to withdraw from news gathering for professional reasons, such as filing copy, and for personal security. Of these perceived rights, all but the last appear to have been trammelled in various ways during the 1991 Gulf War. For the media, this was an appalling result.

Another disturbing aspect of the 1991 Gulf War was the open, even gloating, admission of the US High Command that it had deceived the media, and in turn the Iraqi military, by giving journalists false information. The media are in a difficult ethical situation here. The right of journalists to obtain information by subterfuge and deception if the public interest is great enough has been confirmed by no less an authority than the British Press Council. Journalists, therefore, can hardly complain if the public interest justifies the military deceiving it for the purpose of bamboozling an enemy. For journalists, there is a proviso that even if the public interest is considerable, dubious procedures should not be used if ethical alternatives exist. This restriction should also apply to the military. The resort to deceit by the military on this occasion was a conspicuous example of excess. A more detached and informed analysis by the media should also have disclosed the implausability of false strategic options such as a sea-based invasion of Kuwait by the Allies.

Military and Media

Some thoughtful analysts of media and military relations have detected similarities between the two castes. Alan Hooper, a former officer in the Royal Marines, listed 13 common factors: professionalism, initiative, responsibility, dedication, efficiency, delegation of authority, teamwork, self-discipline, decision making under the pressure of time, forward planning, logistics, flexibility and unsocial hours. In practical terms, both professions worked with raw data although the product differed, journalists converting it into news and the military into intelligence. Both depended on professionalism, self-sacrifice, and initiative. Both worked to deadlines. Both were little understood by the general public in what they did. That the journalist and the soldier were not kindred spirits was attributed by Hooper to the difficult circumstances under which they usually met.[28] The same point has been made more emphatically by General William C. Westmoreland: 'It may well be that between press and officials there is an inherent, built-in conflict of interest. There is something to be said for both sides, but when the nation is at war and men's lives are at stake there should be no ambiguity.'[29]

Journalists mostly have been even more dismissive of any lasting *rapprochement* between journalism and the profession of arms. The similarities noted by Hooper have a certain artificiality because they are largely based on how news is treated in the media office, not how it is gathered in the field. Much news is gathered by what are essentially bureaucratic means and the organisation of newspaper production and news broadcasting is predominantly bureaucratic. There remains, however, a spontaneity and flexibility about news gathering which defy analysis in terms of organisation theory. This individualism often increases strongly in proportion to the journalist's distance from the office, although not invariably; witness the reliance on bureaucratic processes of briefing and pooling which emerged in the Gulf. It is fair to note, though, that if many of these journalists had been assured of access, mobility and co-operation in the field they would have got their news by more direct means. The presence of journalists insistent on working independently is the most contentious issue, as Engel makes clear:

> ... the contest between the allied forces and the media was infinitely more competitive than the one between the allies and the Iraqis ... The professions of arms and journalism are essentially incompatible. The military depends on chains of command and people carrying out instructions precisely; journalism relies on lateral-thinking individualists. [In the Gulf] the military appeared to imagine that by handing out a certain number of pool places as though they were latrine duties, this would satisfy everyone. All the other papers would sit down quietly and wait to be escorted somewhere. Journalists had no intention of complying if they could avoid it ...[30]

Of the various solutions to the serious impasse between media and military proposed during the 1991 Gulf War, the French concept of 'immersion' has the most merit, provided it is not used merely to ratify military-approved journalists. The concept of 'national schools' of war coverage on the lines proposed by M. Joxe would do little to restore vanished independence. Journalists wanting to work independently in military conflicts should have considerable experience in international reporting, they should be physically and mentally fit, preferably they should have some expertise in defence matters, they should accept the professional risks involved, and they should acknowledge the dictates of operational security.

In the aftermath of the 1991 Gulf War, the media and the military remain poles apart, and a substantial exercise in reconciliation is clearly necessary. Doubtless, investigations will be conducted by the military, formal consultations will resume, new procedures will be agreed, and the relationship will be patched up. The media is entitled to be sceptical about whether the practices established in the Falklands, Grenada, Panama and the Gulf will change in future limited conflict. Perhaps the only chance for the media to re-establish some of its traditional prerogatives on the battlefield lies in a war of some duration.

Some Final Thoughts

Useful insights into the contemporary dilemmas facing journalists in military conflict can be drawn from the writings of C. E. W. Bean, Australia's greatest war correspondent. It was said of Bean that his dispatches were 'perfect'; he would watch a battle from a shell-hole with his notebook in hand, and describe the special features of each fight like an 'impressionist painter'.[31] Bean was intensely aware of operational requirements and he accepted the need for military oversight of journalists. He was not above altering dates and places to remove any value to the enemy from his copy. He was also unashamedly selective in what he presented as truthful reporting:

> It is quite possible that my letters and cables during some periods in the next few months may have to deal with safe subjects quite apart from news. There are certain periods in a war when the publication of news could become so risky that it is best suppressed altogether.[32]

Bean acted with the utmost propriety on the battlefield and he was

accorded remarkable privileges of access and movement. Apart from
the inestimable freedom associated with having no proprietor or editor
to answer to, he could report on whatever he liked and roam through
the lines virtually without challenge. He insisted that he was not the
man to feed the Australian people on 'soft pap', to offer them only
good and pleasant things no matter how grim the circumstances. In a
memorable justification of the front line journalist, he expressed
resentment at material emanating from 'headquarters journalists':

> Not one event in every five of those which [the Reuters cor-
> respondent] relates are true and most are wild, sensational
> inventions like the famous one about Germans enlisted in
> Australia shooting officers here from behind. This stuff has
> plenty of interest for the *Argus*. Mine has merely the interest that
> I risk my life hundreds of times over on the spot itself in order
> that they may know that every word is as true as it can be.[33]

Bean firmly rejected the view put to him by British officers that war
correspondents were a dying profession. He acknowledged the disap-
pearance of the romantic, free-wheeling war correspondent of the late
nineteenth century but insisted that the civilian population had to have
news of its troops. Even Napoleon had to tell the nation something,
and the alternatives of news supplied by military staff officers was
totally untenable. His summary of the official viewpoint which he
vehemently rejected is still highly relevant today:

> ... if the people is properly organised the authorities need not
> tell them anything at all ... in a properly organised nation the
> Government does not need war correspondents – It simply tells
> the people what will conduce towards winning the war. If truth is
> good for the war it tells them truth; if a lie is likely to win the war
> it tells them lies. ...

Bean rebutted this thesis, arguing that there were ways in plenty of
winning a war which conceivably did more harm than defeat:

> I quite agree you can't have the war correspondent running a
> modern war but I do think the people of any modern state worth
> living in will require some sort of information independent of
> their generals and general staffs as to what is happening: and they
> are not getting that in [World War I][34]

Again, the parallels with contemporary conflict need no emphasis.

During a lull on the Gallipoli battlefield in October 1915, Bean discussed the notion that the war correspondent was a dying breed with another distinguished practitioner, Ellis Ashmead-Bartlett. Bartlett's response should serve as a credo for all journalists contending with the frustrations of censorship, lack of access, and immobility: ' "He thinks we're dyin', does he?" said Bartlett ... "Well I'm glad we're dyin' game!" '[35]

NOTES

1. First quotation from Patrick J. Sloyan, *Guardian Weekly*, 10 Feb. 1991. Second from Alan Hooper, *The Military and the Media* (Aldershot: Gower, 1982).
2. Sloyan, *Guardian Weekly* (hereafter *GW*), 10 Feb. 1991.
3. Anthony Smith, *The Politics of Information* (London: Macmillan, 1938), p.135
4. Phillip Knightley, *The First Casulty, the War Correspondent as Hero, Propagandist and Mythmaker from the Crimea to Vietnam* (London: Deutsch, 1975), p.16.
5. Hooper, *Military and Media*, p.6.
6. Ken Begg, 'Canberra Diary', *Canberra Times*, 5 May 1991.
7. Hooper, *Military and Media*, p.116.
8. Ibid., p.121.
9. Sloyan, *GW*, 10 Feb. 1991.
10. Peter Braestrup, *Big Story: How the American Press and Television Reported and Interpreted the Crisis of Tet 1968 in Vietnam and Washington* (Boulder, CO: Westview Press, 1977), 2 vols.
11. *GW*, 3 March 1991, p.28.
12. Sloyan.
13. Matthew Engel, 'A Hack in the House of Sand', *GW*, 31 March 1991, p.22.
14. *Newsweek* quoted by Melbourne *Age*, 27 Feb. 1991.
15. Matthew Engel.
16. Martin Woollacott 'War in the Desert – from Biggles to Babylon', *GW*, 10 Feb. 1991, p.11.
17. Robert Fisk, 'Liberty to Report What Command Deigns to Reveal', *Canberra Times*, 8 Feb. 1991.
18. Melbourne *Age*, 9 Feb. 1991.
19. Engel, *GW*, 31 March 1991.
20. Marc Ferro, *Le Monde*, 3 March 1991, p.15.
21. Sloyan, *GW*, 10 Feb. 1991, p.18.
22. Ferro, *Le Monde*, 3 March 1991.
23. Hugh Lunn, *Vietnam: A Reporter's War* (Brisbane: University of Queensland Press, 1985)
24. David Jenkins, 'Wartime Relations', Australian Press Council News, Nov. 1989
25. Woollacott, 'War in the Desert'.
26. Jenkins, 'Wartime Relations'.
27. Ibid.
28. Hooper, *Military and Media*, p.64ff.
29. Ibid., p.6
30. Engel, *GW*, 31 March 1991.

31. Kevin Fewster (ed.), *Gallipoli Correspondent: The Frontline Diary of C.E.W. Bean* (Sydney: Allen & Unwin, 1983), p.16ff.
32. Bean, *Diary*, p.16.
33. Ibid., p.162.
34. Ibid., pp.163–64.
35. Ibid., (Oct. 1915).

Other Sources

Charlton, Michael and Moncrieff, Anthony, *Many Reasons Why* (London: 1978).
Department of Politics, Research School of Social Sciences, 'Press Cuttings Files, FA – Middle East, Gulf War Media, 1991.'
Glasgow University Media Group, *War and Peace News* (Glasgow, 1985).
Harris, Robert, *Gotcha: The Media, the Government and the Falklands Crisis* (London; Faber, 1983).
Maddock, K. and Wright B. (ed.), *War, Australia and Vietnam*, (Sydney, 1987).
Robinson, S., 'And TV Will Be There', *Weekend Australian*, 12–13 Jan. 1991.
Young, Peter, 'Reporting Conflict: The Relationship between the Armed Forces and the Media in Low Intensity and Limited Conflicts'. Unpublished sub-thesis, Master of Defence Studies, ADFA, 1987.

A Restatement of the Problem:
Theory and Practice

PETER R. YOUNG

Yesterday was basically a didactic day. A day designed to set the scene for the case studies that are to follow. As part of that learning process we were privileged to have the basic viewpoints of both the military and the media. We heard a masterful definition of limited conflict and an equally impressive insight into the technical versatility, reach and immediacy of the new high-technology global media. We were also made aware of the changing attitudes of the public towards the military and given an insight into what can be termed the sharp end of media/government cooperation in meeting the terrorist threat.[1] Having had the benefit of that background information, one would now like to attempt to set up a theoretical framework within which we can relate these lessons to our case studies over the next two days.

In brief, it is my contention that, with the advent of nuclear, biological and chemical warfare, the very nature of war has changed and that, with the possible exception of wars of religion, the pursuit of all future international ambitions will have to be fought as limited conflicts. I also believe that all, if not most, of the existing theory on the nature of the obligations of the citizen under the social contract in this new environment is largely outdated. As Grenada and the Gulf showed, the rule will be that the military will be able to retain control over the media only so long as they win, and win quickly. Beyond that, the expectations of a global audience, who now expect to have both sides of every issue presented to them as a right by the reach and immediacy of the new global media, will demand too high a political penalty if they are not met.

In order to develop this theme, there follow two assertions and four questions.

My first assertion, is that *the nature of war has changed*. While individual nations might possibly continue to opt for direct confrontation in pursuit of what they perceive to be overriding popular, religious or national interests, in general the penalties of nuclear, biological and chemical warfare are now so great that when force is required most international ambitions of the future will have to be achieved by limited conflict. That is by conflicts which will be circumscribed by geographical and weaponry limitations and by a system of safeguards in the shape of negotiating machinery designed to avoid any escalation to nuclear warfare. More important, such conflicts will be fought *without* recourse to the full mobilisation of the nations involved.

The second assertion is that *the existing body of theory and rights and obligations under the social contract in time of war has not kept pace with the changed nature of war and the priority that must now be afforded limited conflict.* As a result, one can argue that the expectations held by Western liberal democratic governments – and to an increasing extent, by totalitarian regimes, and their military forces is outdated. This is because the theory on which they base their expectations of public support is still rooted in mid-twentieth century concepts of nationalistic or 'patriotic' wars, or wars of survival, which are no longer relevant. They fail to accept the fact that the indirect or limited conflicts of the future will not affect the survival or even the welfare of the great majority in the belligerent nation. The current policies within the armed forces of Western liberal democracies – except in so far as they are manifested in the tightly controlled manner such as we saw in the Gulf in a short 'winning war' scenario – will not carry the levels of overwhelming popular support needed for governments to be able to impose the sort of media, or other restrictions that were acceptable in previous wars of survival.

These two assertions, it is contended, lead to four basic questions:

These are, first, whether the citizen holds an obligation to cede his rights to freedom of speech and information – or even support for the government of the day – in pursuit of limited conflicts which may not affect his own interests or even welfare and which may not pose any commonly perceived threat to national security, let alone any threat to national survival or personal liberty?

Second, whether Western liberal democratic governments have the right to impose censorship or other limitations on the freedom of the media in time of limited conflict which, while not posing any commonly perceived threat to national security or survival, may be opposed by a significant section of the community? And, correspondingly, whether the media does not have a duty to cater to that significant section of the community which may oppose the conflict?

Third, whether such governments (or even totalitarian regimes) now have or will have the physical or electronic capability to impose and maintain such restrictions in the face of the rising expectations of a better educated and informed population used, as of a right to the presentation of balanced information on all issues and the technological growth of the new internationalised high-technological media?

Finally, the question must be asked whether, given the poor track record of the Western military forces (and again by totalitarian forces, given the differences of their systems) in their attitudes and truthfulness in their dealings with the media in time of peace, there is any obligation on the media to enter into the sort of co-operative systems such as the Defence Media Advisory Group or Pentagon Pool presently being offered as the price of preferred access to the theatre of operations in time of limited war? This is especially in the case of Australia and the Gulf when the political minders, some of them perhaps fresh from masterminding a party political campaign, move in to pre-empt the military and renege on the bargain that has been entered into in good faith by both the military and media.

In summary, the question is whether governments will be able, or indeed have the right, to expect the same sort of support afforded in the past and to impose restrictions similar to those imposed in previous 'patriotic wars' in conflicts that fall far short of survival and when such conflicts could result in sharply divided opposition or even active opposition by a significant portion of the home community.

Let me first address the statement that the nature of war has changed. This I believe requires little amplification to such an audience. Given the proliferation of NBC weapons, no nation can afford to run the risk of escalation especially when so many nations now either have a declared or clandestine nuclear capability and the means to deliver into the home country's heartland either by air, submarine or missile. As a result, all wars of the future must by necessity be 'limited' – as were Korea, Vietnam, the Falklands and the Gulf. This sort of limited conflict – short of religious wars, which belong to a special category – is, I believe, the way in which all international ambitions of the future will be conducted.

My second assertion that the existing body of theory one has not kept pace with this changed nature of war is not as easy to prove, and asks for your indulgence in developing the argument. This leads down the well worn path of the doctrine of social contract. I hesitate to use such a timeworn undergraduate example in such distinguished company, but whatever your political convictions – be it ultra conservative or rabid anarchism each one of you as you drove here this morning stopped when the traffic light turned red. It was easy decision, based as it was on your perception of a common sense direction aimed at the individual and common good. In doing so, you validated the social contract, under which mankind has lived ever since the benefits of co-operation under a some form of leadership first became apparent in primitive hunting times. By stopping, you at once legitimised authority and re-enforced the mandate given to those who govern.

But that same mandate and abrogation of individual rights so freely given under the social contract – with common defence as a prime if not paramount consideration –, is a two sided 'bargain' between the ruler and ruled. The consent implied in that, bargain can be withdrawn, often by revolution, if that same authority impinges too far on civil liberties or threatens the life or property of the individual. To lose that consent in a democracy – or even in other more repressive forms of government is to risk the loss of legitimacy or mandate. As Manegold of Lauterbach – the thinker widely credited with first formalising the social contract – warned 'if in any wise the King transgresses the contract by virtue of which he is chosen, he absolves the people from the obligation of submission.'[2]

But throughout recorded history, whatever levels of democracy have pertained, and whatever the penalty for transgressing the bound of popular support for the mandate, the rights of the individual have been freely handed back to the state or central authority in time of war, or when the majority have perceived a threat to their liberty or survival and accepted as the 'right' thing to do by even the most libertarian of social contract thinkers. This voluntary abrogation of individual rights and the acceptance of restrictions in support of a common defence by the state has been a major feature of the social contract. The levels of loss of rights and the means and style of restriction may have changed, but, in general, the rule has been that *the greater the perceived common threat, the greater the tolerance for government imposed restrictions on rights*, including that cornerstone of democracy, freedom of speech. This abrogation of individual rights in the cause of common defence, was re-enforced in more secure or advanced democracies by the understanding that this voluntary loss was only to be of a temporary nature and that they would be returned once the emergency had passed.

Few would argue with this concept when the immediate penalty of defeat was enslavement or death. This view would have been understandable and acceptable right up until the Renaissance and well into the seventeenth century, with Locke believing that the most urgent concern of the body politic as a whole was external security.[3] Bentham was suspicious of defence and certainly of foreign conquest but accepted that territorial integrity had to be defended and that in time of war 'the State towered over the citizen', and that it was right for citizens to sacrifice their property and rights and even their lives for its survival as individuals developed a social interest stronger than their own.[4] Hobbes stated that while war was to be avoided, it was the obligation of all citizens to authorise all of the sovereign's actions in defence against a common enemy.[5] Rousseau believed that war was the prerogative of the ruler and the state and the citizen had an obligation to meet this prerogative, saying that when a man laid down his life in defence of the state all he was doing was 'handing back the very boon he had received at its hands'.[6]

Despite the growth and acceptance of libertarianism that followed, and the exchange of the tribal imperatives, for those of the demands of nationalism and patriotism called for by the twentieth century nation state and the massive social changes that we have experienced over the last century all the way to modern day politics, no one has seriously challenged this near universal agreement that the overriding duty of the citizen was to put aside his rights and place his property and life at the service of the state in time of threat.

On the wider scene, the Universal Declaration of Human Rights adopted by the UN in 1948[7], spelled out a broad range of human rights including freedom of the press but promptly limited them as ... 'subject to the requirement of the general welfare', leaving it to the sovereign nation to make its own interpretation – an interpretation which is an open license to censorship. Eighteen years later, the International Covenant on Economic and Social and Cultural Rights adopted by the UN[8] was more specific, guaranteeing a range of rights, but again, except 'in the interests of national security'. These limitations were re-enforced in the International Covenant on Civil and Political Rights adopted by the UN[9] in the same year which disallowed these rights 'in time of public emergency which threatens the life of the nation'. Article 8 of the same document restricted freedom of movement on the basis of 'national security'.

In 1949, the Statute of the Council of Europe, which set up the Council of Europe, made up of some of the strongest democracies in the world, and at a time when they had just suffered in the cause of democracy, spelled out a similar series of guaranteed rights, freedoms and obligations. Among them, was 'the right to receive and impart ideas and information regardless, without interference by public authority (and) regardless of frontiers'. But whilst guaranteeing these rights, it stated that the exercises of these freedoms carried duties and obligations which may be subject to formalities, conditions, restrictions or penalties as are prescribed by law and are necessary in a democratic society 'in the interest of national security, territorial integrity or public safety'.[10]

Again, we see the same caveat in the 1969 American Convention on Human Rights (Article 13). And when it comes to freedom of information, in the draft UN Convention on the gathering and transmission of news, which claims as its ambit, the right of the people to be informed, we have in Article 4, the open acceptance of the rights of nations to impose censorship, and under Article 11 actually allows any contracting state to derogate from its obligations in time of war.[11]

Closer to home in Australia, we have the eminent historian T.B. Millar as late as 1979 defending the Governments right to secrecy – an opinion echoed by both the *Sydney Morning Herald* and the Melbourne *Age* in their comments on the 1981 court action against the publication by the Fairfax organisation of classified information even in time of peace.[12] We also have the now infamous persecution of Mr Brian Toohey and Mr Pinwill over the publication of their book on the Australian Secret Intelligence Service (ASIS), *Oyster*[13], and, if further evidence is needed, I draw your attention to the Defence Department submission to the December 1988 Gibb Review of the secrecy provisions of the Crimes Act, which, despite its professed liberalism under the Defence Media Advisory Group (DMAG), would effectively restrict any mention of any military information whatsoever in a list of exclusions which runs to three pages.[14]

Only the contemporary thinker John Rawls comes close to addressing the wider implications of conflicts which might carry divided loyalties or what he terms 'unjust wars'. Rawls basic argument rests on a form of social contract in which a citizen owes no political obligations, only 'natural duties based on the principles of justice and fairness'. A soldier, he argues, might refuse to engage in certain acts or even campaigns if he reasonably and conscientiously believed they violated the principles of international justice. As Rawls puts it, it is the citizen's 'natural duty' NOT to be made an agent of grave injustice and evil to another *outweighs his duty to obey his Government*.[15] As

Parekh interprets it, Rawls believes that the aims of modern states in waging war are 'now likely to be so unjust that one might rightly abjure military service altogether in the foreseeable future.'[16] This is an acute observation, since most of Rawl's work was aimed at the rights of conscientious objectors, but it has equal validity to the support of limited conflict and in fact emerges as the major innovation in modern social contract thinking in time of war, especially when, as we have seen, every other commentator or authority down the ages to the present day stops short of applying or guaranteeing *any* principles of justice, fairness or liberty when it comes to the security of the state.

As Parekh so aptly sums it up when he measures Rawls' work against this wider scene, 'the political philosophical discussion on property, citizenship and the relations between Government and the economy, social classes and even war, continue to be dominated by the categories and assumptions inherited by our forbears'.[17]

The 1991 Gulf War proved my thesis of winning quickly. But if it had dragged on it might have been the catalyst for the sort of popular penalty that I believe lies in wait for the military forces of Western liberal democracies who remain secure in their belief in outdated theories that lead them to expect the same sort of continuing popular support they enjoyed in previous patriotic wars.

There is also of course a great body of argument in the differing theories of Elitism versus Democratic Participation. Time precludes me from speaking to that issue. Suffice it to say that elitism is alive and well and long ago won the battle for the hearts and minds of the military, the politicians and the minders on the basis that once the mandate has been given, then they should be allowed to get on with the business of governing – including the management and manipulation of information, especially in time of war.

But, having argued my two assertions that the nature of war has changed and that social contract has not kept up with that change, albeit so briefly, let me now address my four basic questions, which can be applied as a test to the case studies that will follow.

The first is whether the citizen holds the obligation to cede his right of freedom of speech and information in the event of limited conflicts which might not even affect his own interests or welfare and which may not pose any commonly perceived threat to national security let alone any threat to national survival or personal liberty?

My short answer is NO. I would not go as far as Rawls, but would maintain that neither the military or government have the right to expect the same sort of unquestioning obedience and voluntary abrogation of rights, or any control over the media on the basis of military security in conflicts short of survival. The military among you may take exception to this – as I might have done a few years back – but let me take you back to the rationale for your existence – the safe-guarding of democracy. And, without the imperative of survival inherent in national wars of survival or direct national interest, how can these outdated concepts of duty to the state and support for the military, in the sort of limited conflict one believes will be the norm in the future, be sustained. This is especially the case in the light of the statistics given to us by Professor McAllister and Dr Makkai yesterday, which show a general decline in support of the military with 'public opinion now less favourably disposed towards defence than at any time since the end of the Second World War'.[18]

Let us take for instance the example of any Australian involvement in Papua New Guinea (PNG), which would present a classic instance of a limited conflict. Despite some very real concern that might be expressed privately by the military over their lack of resources in the face of such a massive undertaking, we could confidently expect any intervention to be accompanied by the sort of managed news and political jingoism that we saw during the Australian commitment to the Gulf. But would it be feasible for the Australian Defence Force (ADF) to expect the sort of continuing support it enjoyed in the same area during World War II when PNG was crucial to our survival as opposed to a current campaign when the benefits would be much less apparent. Would it be feasible for the ADF to count on the same levels of support inherent in theories predicated on national survival when the campaign might not even impinge on the welfare of the vast majority of Australians. Could it count on the levels of support it believes to be its due if, as is very likely, the intervention quickly demanded the introduction of national service for a protracted and debilitating campaign with very little to show for it. The answer would not only be no, but also that the majority of modern Australians would not see themselves beholden in any way to support such a campaign. In fact, the reverse would quickly apply, in the shape of an active demand for a withdrawal.

There is a warning here for those who believe that jingoism will see them through. Certainly this is important and in the Falklands, the Gulf and Grenada, there was an initial overwhelming support for the campaigns and for military restrictions on the media. It was only later, however, when more rational judgements were made and when the issues were debated in parliament and Congress did the more cautious view emerge and the statistics change to a more thoughtful concern.[19]

The second question is whether the Western liberal democracies have the *right* to impose censorship or other limitations on the freedom of the media in time of limited conflict which, while not posing any commonly perceived threat to national security or survival, may be opposed by a significant section of the community. Again my answer is NO. This is a difficult statement to support, especially since there is almost no existing theory on the subject but, in general terms, the question remains by what *right* a Western liberal democratic government can even attempt to limit the citizen's rights to the levels of freedom of information enjoyed in time of peace when that 'peace' is not threatened. In much the same way that the citizen holds no obligation when neither his own safety or even welfare, or the security or even long-term welfare of the nation is at risk, I contend that, conversely, the government has no right to impose any form of restriction. Certainly not in time of limited conflict when, by the very nature of the term, a large part of the population might be opposed to the conflict on the basis of the information they had received in the lead up to the event.

Within a democracy, opinion *must* be served, and while the press has its limitations and is restricted by its audience, if that audience is there then there is a need for it to be served. No Western liberal democratic government has any right – beyond those spelled out in what I consider to be outdated convention or emergency legislation based on the security of the nation to inflict any form of limitation on the right to know during limited. Any limitations, such as we saw from the political minders in Canberra during the Australian commitment and the limitations put into place by both the British and American governments at the time of the 1990 Gulf deployment, are first of all illegal, and second, in terms of duration, not sustainable.

Third, we come to the question of whether Western liberal democratic governments (and totalitarian regimes) now have or will have the physical or electronic capability to impose and maintain restrictions on the media in the light of the rising expectations of a better educated and informed population used as of right to the presentation of balanced information on all issues by the new internationalised global media?

Again I contend that the answer is NO. Yesterday we heard perhaps one of the best expositions on the reach and immediacy of the new hi-tech media by Professor Melody. In essence, the message is that the microchip revolution has all but destroyed the power of the military to censor – except in what can be termed expeditionary forces to remote and inaccessible places – and it is instructive to remember that both the Falklands and the Gulf fall into this category. Anywhere else and the power and reach of the internationalised media would eventually outstrip even the most draconian measures imposed by the military – apart from the ultimate and politically dangerous final sanction of electronic jamming. Certainly the current appeals for operational security would quickly lose their sanction, in that, while I myself, Prakash Mirchandani, John Stackhouse or Frank Cranston might be constrained by patriotism, the two Japanese cameramen on the next hill or the two Italians over the other side of the river, or even the Australian freelance crews operating outside of the DMAG or on contract to a world news system such as CNN or ITN would have no such compunction. And, once it is up on the satellite, there is no way of denying it, and the cries from the scooped news editors back in the home nation would be horrible to hear.

In addition, the modern newsgathering organisations now have access to the same, if not better technology, than that available to the military. It is now possible for the major news organisations to field complete ground stations in static situations and to provide their reporters with suitcase size battery and solar-powered satellite sending systems or satellite based telephones. When reporting from Baghdad for CNN, Peter Arnett's main means of communication was the INMARSAT phone, a suitcased link with the world that he would drag out each evening, aim at the heavens whilst dialling the International desk at CNN in Atlanta.[20] Later, in the same article he refers to his back-up team arriving with a portable satellite video transmitter and tons of gear. This sort of communications – plus, of course, the old-fashioned systems of cable, letter and word of mouth, can only be stopped by either electronic jamming or the point of a bayonet – both of which have an instant appeal to the less thinking military mind but both of which eventually will have to be answered for in a free democracy.

Other means of information to be considered, and stopped, with all the eventual resultant political penalties, are the massive flow of travellers and information, from airline travellers moving around the world and the old-fashioned rumour mill. Thousands will still travel international during limited conflicts, as they did during the Gulf crisis.

Such international travel simply cannot be denied. Its travellers bring in papers, articles and even videos of events as well as their own knowledge of events. It was largely word of mouth and the actual sight and spoken experiences of wounded or drug addicted soldiers returning home that finally brought home to the USSR the message of a near disaster in Afghanistan.

We also have the fact that the new world audiences are now conditioned to expect to have every side of every argument presented to them as a right, not a privilege, but a right, And it would be politically disastrous even to attempt to deny that right over any length of time. To attempt to stem the massive tide of alternative means of communications such as travel and to close down the new high-technology means of communication now available to the media from a theatre of operations by such means as jamming or force, would, it is contended, be politically disastrous.

In summary, it is argued that beyond the most limiting of 'expeditionary' factors, it is already nearly impossible for the flow of information to be constrained and that this trend will continue at an accelerated rate in the future to such an extent that the military may find themselves little more than dismayed bystanders as a constant stream of alternative information was fed to a worldwide audience that now sees its rights to that information as a right in itself.

Finally, we come to the hardest, and certainly to such an audience as this, composed as it is of so many military, the fourth and hardest question of all. And this is, can we trust the military to do the right thing in time of war given their track record in peacetime? And here I must restrict myself to Australia where one can speak from experience. But to avoid charges of personal animosity, every example quote comes from a parliamentary report.

Regrettably, again the answer, despite the great hopes raised by the arrival of Brigadier D'Hage as the new Director General of Public Information, is a firm NO. The record of deception on the part of the Australian Defence Public Relations organisation, allied to what some might interpret as a vindictiveness against journalists who have been critical of government defence policy is not to be envied. In fact, many see them as little more than the outriders of the Minister's office.

At one stage, according to one defence public relations officer, the *Pacific Defence Reporter* was on a Defence PR 'blacklist' because the journal chose to exercise its independence. In an article in the *Reporter* itself, prior to his resignation, he stated that 'when criticised, Defence

PR reacts with indignation. It is almost as if they feel that nobody should criticise. One of the tactics employed by Defence PR is to discredit the critic, believing that running down the credentials of the critic will disprove the criticism'. He also made the charge that Defence PR refused or 'neglected' to provide information to the journal.[24]

The *Pacific Defence Reporter* today ranks as one of the leading journals of its kind in the region. It has played a very important role in fostering debate on defence and in calling for a stronger defence as well as being instrumental in many of the reforms in ADF conditions of service. When I started *PDR* in 1974 however, instead of being welcomed, a signal was sent around all military bases by the then DPI stating that officers should be encouraged *not* to subscribe to this journal, and Defence PR fostered another journalist with promises of access and finance to start a competing commercial defence journal.[25]

During 1983 and 1984 Defence PR portrayed a picture of a thriving, healthy and operationally-ready defence force. Yet in October 1984 the report on the Australian Defence Force, its Structure and Capabilities, known as the first Cross Report, described any potential enemies view of Australia's force in being as 'thinly spread and ill prepared'. In fact, the Committee was not satisfied that the ADF could meet even low-level threats, in 'a timely and effective manner'. The details of the report were equally damaging, yet right up until the eve of the issue of the report Defence PR strove to present an opposite image.[26]

For two years during 1987/88 the *Australian* ran a campaign attempting to waken the nation to the massive and damaging manpower losses in the ADF. This was countered at every level, using what can only be described as disgraceful methods to hide the facts. These facts were well known to the military leadership a year *before* the Minister herself described news reports of losses as 'inaccurate and mischievous'.[27] Only when the issue was examined by a parliamentary inquiry did the real truth emerge. The results of a near 60 per cent wastage during the lifetime till then of the Labour government led the Committee to state that, the effects of the wastage amount to 'a loss of operational capability', was undermining the organisational health of the ADF. The resultant lessening of the experience and competence levels of personnel was 'impacting on the capacity of the training and personnel management system to maintain the Force's integrity', with a concomitant fall in morale.[28] Right up until the eve of the Committee hearings when it was obvious what was about to emerge, Defence PR fostered the political line being put forward by the Minister.

It was a similar picture with pilot wastage, with elaborately stage-managed press conference being held to counter claims by defence writers that there was a serious shortage of pilots. In the same parliamentary report, the Committee not only confirmed the press reports but also stated that as the number of pilots graduating each year was only between 55 and 65, the fact that '42 pilots had given notification of their intention to resign in the first six weeks of FY 1988/9 can only be described as startling'.[29]

The performance of the defence industry was hallooed to the sky by Defence PR; it was one of the great successes of the Labour government. But when it was examined by the Joint Committee of Public Accounts in its 1986 Report No.243, Review of Defence Project Management, the majority of projects were revealed as either over time, over cost or subject to mismanagement. Up until then, the message from Defence PR was one of unrelieved success.[30]

When the news is anti-government, however, the same Defence PR organisation is much more muted. The Joint Parliamentary Committee on Foreign Affairs, Defence and Trade's report on the Management of Australia's Defence in November 1987, which generally called for more power to be given to the military at the expense of the defence bureaucrats was virtually ignored by Defence PR after it had been pre-empted and decried by the Minister. This was despite the fact that the report favoured the military, with one member of the Committee stating that, unless reforms were instituted, 'Australia could be headed for a (command) disaster that could rival that of the Crimea'.[31]

Another example was the Mine Counter Measure project, put forward by Defence PR as one of the biggest defence industrial success stories ever. It was only when the project was examined by parliament that it was revealed to be a costly lemon in the report on Priorities for Australian Mine Counter Measure Needs by the Joint Parliamentary Committee on Foreign Affairs, Defence and Trade in May 1990.[32]

An even worse case was the Army Reserve, which was highlighted by Defence PR as the major success of Exercise Kangaroo '89, only to be revealed as little more than a hollow sham by the Auditor General's Report No.3 of 1991 which identified major shortcomings in almost every area of the Reserve.[33]

There are many other examples, which the allocation of time to this particular question forbids. They include, the PC9 trainer debacle, problems over the Army communications systems, lack of airborne radar and airspace surveillance, delays over the Seahawk helicopter programme, conditions of service and the lack of the necessary hi-tech weaponry for the Navy – rectified only when they were dispatched to the Gulf. All these were boasted successes by Defence PR until proven otherwise, either by fact or in parliament.

There are, however, three others that cannot be dismissed so lightly. These are the Dibb Review and the resultant Defence White Paper and the report on the real state of the Reserves and the 'credible threats' behind the major exercise Kangaroo '89. The Dibb Review and the Government's White Paper released the following year in March 1987, were given the same optimistic treatment by Defence PR. The optimistic line that the White Paper was on track was held until its deathknell as it went the way of its 1976 predecessor. This was despite the fact that the funding was some 7 per cent below that deemed necessary by Mr Dibb and Mr Beazley and the timeframe had grown from 5 to 10 then 20 years for it to be achieved.[34]

In similar fashion, we have been given the Defence PR treatment on 'credible threats' designed more to meet what we have in the armoury than real threats. We then had the logistical fairy tale of Kangaroo '89, with the pre-positioning of stores and communications for an exercise which was billed as a 'come as you are' event designed to prove ADF mobility and sustainability in any defence of the North and North West.

There are many other instances, which collectively have left the few defence specialists in the Australian media with a jaundiced view of Defence PR. Again, like the examples given above, this view is well documented. Just over two years ago, the Department of Defence itself commissioned a review of its Defence PR by the prestigious firm of Hill and Knowlton. The tightly written 11-volume report was what can only be described as a damning indictment of a politicised, inefficient and largely irrelevant organisation with the central organisation described as 'too narrowly projected through prepared press releases, too pre-occupied with perceived Ministerial demands; and too subjugated to an awesome management heirarchy'.[35]

The report was only obtained by me under Freedom of Information, though it was claimed the next day that it was freely available. Beyond that, it was destined to be forgotten.

A year later, a second report was commissioned. A slim volume, written in the sort of text that you get at the very top of the eye test chart, with something like only 120 words to the page. The basic message, was that 'major success is being achieved by Defence Public Relations'.[36] Yet a careful tally of the manpower movements within Defence PR shows no appreciable change in the workforce that less than 18 months earlier had been castigated as not meeting Defence Management expectations and 'unlikely to match future needs without substantial change'.

I must apologise for having been so detailed over the Australian Defence Public Relations, experience however has taught me that if it is not documented in detail then it is easily discarded by an obviously defensive organisation. On the other hand, experience also shows that when faced with such documentation, the normal response is to ignore the facts and play the man. It is against this Australian experience plus the findings of the Siddle Report in the United States and the Parliamentary inquiry in the Britain after the Falklands[37] that one argues that the military and their public relations organisations, especially the politicised form that seems to be evolving, should be treated with caution.

This paper is little more than an extract from a closely reasoned doctorate that has taken almost four years to compile. The proof of every assertion, belief or example is available on request. My beliefs are also based on more than 20 years as a defence journalist – in print, radio and television. My general conclusion is that there has been little or no advance in theory in the face of what we must all agree is the changed nature of war. One would also argue that there has been almost no movement in current theory beyond that based on the outmoded concept of 'wars of survival'. Little or no work has been done in examining this theoretical problem from the position of the rapidly changing reach and immediacy of the new global high-technology media, the expectations of a better informed public or the increasingly secretive ambitions of increasingly elitist governments and their increasingly pragmatic military commanders.

In view of this lack of debate, I believe that neither Western liberal democracies or their military commanders are aware that their right to impose censorship or the citizen's perceived duty to cede his or her own rights are likely to be sustainable except over a very limited period – with that period qualified further by the need for a quick victory. The seeming success of the military at containing the media during both the Gulf and the Falklands Wars was due mainly to the fact that both were fought in extremes of terrain or climate that can categorise them as 'expeditionary' campaigns, and that neither would have achieved the same outcome in the face of any more extended conflict. The lessons learned are false, and we should be careful to avoid drawing too many conclusions from the Gulf, especially at this early stage when the real picture has yet to be shown and the full cost and consequences have yet to emerge.

The combination of the reach and immediacy and the, at least visual, credibility of the media, plus the expectations of the best educated audience in the world and the by now accepted 'right' to information, will be too much for any liberal democratic military to handle in any more 'conventional' conflict, that is any conflict where the media can operate on its own. It is against this background that I offer the verdict that from a military point of view, any future limited wars will have to launched with the minimum of media coverage, last for no more than six weeks, and be victorious. Beyond that time frame, or close to it, the political demand for that audience to be informed through the media will be be simply too strong to be denied. From the media point of view, my opinion is that they will soon become too strong to be denied – as was shown by CNN's success during the Gulf War. The danger will be in placing their trust in the military and in being drawn into the conflict as 'actors'.

All of this is of course highly contentious and at the moment only theoretical. And it will take a long time for the theory to be fully developed. Let me ask, however, that you apply these tests to the case studies we shall hear over the next few days. It might be instructive.

NOTES

1. Conference papers given on Day One of the 1st International Conference on Defence and the Media in Time of Limited Conflict by Gen. Peter Gration, Mr Allan Behm and Profs Lloyd and McAllister.
2. E. Barker, *The Social Contract* (New York: Dover Publications, 1950).
3. John Locke, *First Treatise* (1689), Section 92 & *Second Treatise* (1689), Sections 3, 11, 57, 134 & 139, Ch. 14, Para 160/61. See also P. Laslett (ed.), *Locke's Two Treatises of Government* (Oxford: Clarendon Press, 1960).
4. J. Bentham, *Constitutional Code*, (1827), p.127. See also J. Lively and A. Reeve (ed.), *Modern Political Theory from Hobbes to Marx*, (New York: Routledge, 1989) and Plamenatz, J., *Man and Society*, Vol. 2 (New York: McGraw Hill, 1963).
5. H. Warrender, *The Political Philosophy of Hobbes* (Oxford: Clarendon Press, 1957). See also Thomas Hobbes, *Leviathan* [1651] (New York: Dover Publications, 1950).

6. J. Rousseau, *The Social Contract or Principles of Political Right*, (1762), Chs. 5 and 6 (many editions). See also E. Vaught, *The Political Writings of Jean Jacques Rousseau* (Cambridge: Cambridge University Press, 1915).
7. United Nations Universal Declaration of Human Rights, 1948.
8. UN International Covenant on Economic, Social and Cultural Rights, 1986.
9. UN International Covenant on Civil and Political Rights, 1986. See Articles 4, 8 & 19.
10. Statute of the Council of Europe, 1948 and Convention on Human Rights, 1954.
11. American Convention on Human Rights, 1969 (see Article 13). Draft United Nations Convention on the Gathering and Transmission of News, 1969, see Article 11.
12. T. B. Millar, 'A Special Case for Secrecy', *Quadrant* (June 1981), pp.3–5. See *Australian Law Review Journal* No.55 (1981), pp.45–53, Commonwealth of Australia v. John Fairfax and Sons Ltd and others, Commonwealth of Australia v. Walsh and Another, and Commonwealth of Australia v. IPEC Holdings Ltd and Another. Heard before Mr Justice Mason, Canberra, Nov. / Dec. 1981.
13. B. Toohey, and W. Pinwill, *Oyster* (Sydney: Heinemann, 1989).
14. The Gibb Review, Discussion Paper No.20, Review of Commonwealth Criminal Law, Disclosure of Official Information, Oct. 1988.
15. J. Rawls, *A Theory of Justice*, (Oxford: Clarendon Press, 1972).
16. B. Parekh, *Contemporary Political Thinkers*, (Oxford: Martin Robertson, 1982).
17. Ibid., pp.199–200.
18. I. McAllister, and T. Makkai, 'Changing Australian Opinion on Defence – Trends, Patterns and Explanations', 1st International Conference on Defence and the Media in Time of Limited Conflict, 3–5 April 1991, see p.195 of this volume.
19. K. S. Morgan (ed), *The Falklands Campaign: A Digest of Debates in the House of Common, 2 April to 15 June 1982* (London: HMSO, July 1982).
20. W. Melody, 'The Reach and Immediacy of the New High Technology Media', Paper delivered at the 1st International Conference on Defence and the Media in Time of Limited COnflict, 3–5 April 1991.
21. Peter Arnett, 'The Baghdad Story', *Washington Post*, 17 March 1991.
22. Defence PR Signal – Personal Archives.
23. *Stratagem*. Personal notes on Interview with the Editor of *Stratagem*, July 1981.
24. J. MacNamara, 'Tin Gods and Chocolate Soldiers', *Pacific Defence Reporter* (Nov. 1977).
25. *Stratagem* op.cit.
26. Joint Committee on Foreign Affairs and Defence, *The Australian Defence Force: Its Structure and Capabilities (The First Cross Report)* (Oct. 1984).
27. *COSC Paper on Manpower*, Chiefs of Staff Committee (Classified Information available on request).
28. Parliamentary Joint Committee on Foreign Affairs, Defence and Trade, *Personnel Wastage in the Australian Defence Force – Report and Recommendations* (Nov. 1988)
29. *Personnel Wastage in the Australian Defence Force*, op.cit., p.67, 2.72.
30. *Review of Defence Project Management*, Vol.2, Auditor General's Report No.243, 1986.
31. Parliamentary Joint Committee on Foreign Affairs, Defence and Trade, *The Management of Australia's Defence* (Nov. 1987). See also Peter Young, 'Beazley to reject Defence Warning', *The Australian*, 1 Dec. 1987 and RSL Media Release, 9 Dec. 1987.
32. Parliamentary Joint Committee on Foreign Affairs, Defence and Trade, *The Priorities for Australia's Mine Counter Measure Needs* (Nov. 1989).
33. *The Army Reserve*, Auditor General's Report No.3, 1991, 24 May 1990.

34. *The Defence of Australia 1987*, Presented to Parliament by the Minister for Defence the Hon. Kim C. Beazley MP, March 1987, AGPS Canberra 1987. See also the Dibb Review, AGPS, 1987.
35. Hill and Knowlton, *No Heroes in Peace Time: Defence Public Relations Strategy Review* Vols.1–11 (Sydney, 28 June 1988).
36. Frank Small and Associates, *Defence Public Relations Strategy – Ongoing Community Monitor* (Sydney, Dec. 1989).
37. US Congress, House, *The Siddle Report: Report to the Joint Chiefs of Staff USA 1983*, Civil Liberties and the National Security State Hearings before the Judiciary House of Representatives November 23, 1983 and January 24, April 5 and September 26, 1984. See also *The Falklands Campaign: A Digest of Debates in the House of Commons 2 April to 15 June 1982*, op.cit.

PART II
CASE STUDIES

Vietnam:
A Critical Analysis

PROFESSOR CARLYLE A. THAYER

The role of the media (press and television) during the Vietnam War is a highly controversial subject. Assessments about its impact on American society vary enormously and have aroused about as much controversy as the war itself. Of significance to this conference is the fact that the controversy over the role of the media in a time of limited conflict has not just been confined to partisan political circles or the halls of academe but to the pages of military journals as references in the attached bibliography indicate. Quite obviously, the American military has drawn some lessons from Vietnam and has applied them to later conflicts, such as Grenada and Panama. The 'lessons of Vietnam', in so far as they relate to the relationship between the media, government and the military in a time of armed conflict, have also been the subject of study in Great Britain.[1] This presentation will offer an assessment of the impact of the media on the Vietnam War during the years 1962 to 1973 based primarily on the secondary literature.

At the outset it is important to understand the sources used and their limitations. It may be a surprise to learn that the US Army, through its Center of Military History, has commissioned a two-volume study of 'the military and the media' in Vietnam. The first volume, written by William Hammond, covers the period 1962–68 including the impact of media reporting of the Tet offensive. The second volume has not yet been published.

Hammond presents an historical study which adopts a qualitative methodology based on the official record and public sources including the news media. However, as the author notes:

> serious gaps in the chronicle of the war remain. . . . The records of the various agencies that dealt with the US government's public relations during the Vietnam War are a case in point. The archives of the MACV [Military Affairs Command Vietnam] Office of Information and of the Joint US Public Affairs Office

[JUSPAO] have all but disappeared, apparently the victims of the rush to evacuate Saigon. Also missing are the files of the Southeast Asia Desk of the Office of the Assistant Secretary of Defense for Public Affairs and the records of the Bureau of Public Affairs at the State Department.[2]

Hammond attempted to overcome the problem of missing data by reconstructing portions of the missing files by locating copies of the original documents in the archives of other government agencies or in personal collections, such as the Westmoreland Papers. Hammond also conducted extensive interviews with the key actors.

The second major source used in this paper is Daniel Hallin's *The 'Uncensored War'*,[3] an academic study which reviews press coverage from 1960 up to mid-1965 and then relies on television coverage thereafter. Hallin relies exclusively on the daily reportage by the *New York Times* as a representative of media reporting.[4] The *Times* was one of the few American papers to have a correspondent permanently stationed in Vietnam at that time. Hallin's analysis of television reporting rests on a random sample of evening news broadcasts by the three largest networks, ABC, CBS and NBC over the period 20 August 1965 to 27 January 1973. These samples ($N = 779$) were subject to quantitative content analysis.

As with the official US government archives, there are serious gaps in the television archives as well. Prior to 1968, the major American networks did not systematically retain copies of their television footage. In August 1968 the Vanderbilt Television News Archive was established and this problem overcome. Prior to 1968 the best archival source for television coverage was assembled by the US Army Photographic Agency (presently housed in the National Archives, it is known as the Defense Department Kinescopes). Gaps may be found here too, as the US Army only retained news considered relevant to the Defense Department. Hallin notes that the 'standards of relevance were vague and inconsistent', and that emphasis was given to stories dealing with military operations at the expense of stories relating to the nonmilitary aspects of the conflict.[5]

This paper also relies on other academic works, such as Peter Braestrup's exhaustive analysis of media reporting during the 1968 Tet offensive,[6] and other works (see bibliography, pp.113–15).

The Press as 'Adversarial Opposition'

It is a commonplace view that as the Vietnam War progressed, the American news media (defined here to include the press and television) became increasingly critical of most if not all aspects of the war. The press then moved from 'a relatively passive and conservative institution into an institution of opposition to political authority' and thus directly influenced American public opinion.[7] At its most extreme, criticism of the American press accuses it, along with the anti-war movement, civilian strategists, Democratic presidents, Congress, leftists, and liberals, of 'snatching defeat from the jaws of victory' – in short, the press assisted in stabbing the American military in the back by eroding the nation's will to prosecute the war in Vietnam to the fullest.[8]

The origins of press disaffection date to the early 1960s when, it is alleged, correspondents David Halberstam of the *New York Times* and Malcolm Browne of Associated Press, stepped beyond the bounds of 'objective journalism' to insinuate their anti-war and anti-Diem views into their news reports. This laid the groundwork for subsequent negative anti-war reporting. One of the most articulate spokesman for this viewpoint is none other than General William C. Westmoreland, as the following extracts from his memoirs indicate:

> Saigon in those early day was one of the world's less desirable assignments for newsmen. A faraway, alien place, it had little attraction for American readers, so that nothing short of the sensational was likely to gain space in the newsman's home newspaper. Finding fault was one way to achieve the sensational, and finding fault with an Oriental regime with little background in or respect for Western-style democracy was easy. Furthermore, newsmen were unrestrained by the bonds of official duty that affected American officials. If the regime of Ngo Dinh Diem collapsed, that removed what the reporters saw as an evil, and, unlike American officials, they bore no responsibility for whatever might ensue.
>
> In contradiction to their distinguished colleague Drew Middleton, of the *New York Times* who observed that a reporter's task is 'to report the event, not try to influence the course of events', other American newsmen in Saigon soon confused reporting with influencing foreign policy. When their peers back home rewarded two of them with a shared Pulitzer Prize

[Browne and Halberstam], the pattern for those who followed was set. To many of their successors, the young iconoclasts were folk heroes whose record demonstrated that the more criticism and the more negativism, the greater the possibility of recognition and reward.[9]

Later in his memoirs, Westmoreland observed:

With television for the first time bringing war into living rooms and with no press censorship, the relationship of the military command in South Vietnam and the news media was of unusual importance. Yet for all my efforts and despite the sympathetic support of many newsmen, relations were in large part strained, a legacy of the Diem days exacerbated by the length of the war and the questioning by many of what constituted the national interest.... .

Some newsmen in South Vietnam did 'come into camp, poke about among the lazy and pick up rumors and publish them as facts'. On almost any subject a reporter could find a soldier or a junior officer willing to criticize or complain, which for centuries has been a healthy feature of soldiering, but how expert is the opinion of the man in the ranks whose perspective is narrow?

One problem was the youth and inexperience of many correspondents. Having little or no knowledge of military history, having seen no other war, and, like most in the military, having no ability in the Vietnamese language, some reporters were ill-equipped for their assignments. Short deadlines contributed to inaccuracy and some freelance writers depended upon sensationalism to sell their wares. In general journalism appears to nurture the pontifical judgment.... .

A second problem was what may be called a herd instinct among the reporters. Everybody tended to view everything through the same pair of glasses. If it came to be generally accepted by the press, for example, that Thieu was corrupt or that his regime lacked popular support, seldom did anybody among the press elect to challenge the prevailing view....

Another problem was constant turnover in reporters. Even dedicated veteran correspondents seldom stayed beyond a year to eighteen months, and some served only brief stints .... . Providing the press with background and perspective was like trying to paint a moving train....

Television presented special problems. Even more than the telegraph during the Crimean War and the radio in World War II, television brought war into the American home, but in the process television's unique requirements contributed to a distorted view of the war. The news had to be compressed and visually dramatic. Thus the war that Americans saw was almost exclusively violent, miserable, or controversial: guns firing, men falling, helicopters crashing, buildings toppling, huts burning, refugees fleeing, women wailing. A shot of a single building in ruins could give an impression of an entire town destroyed.... Only scant attention was paid to pacification, civic action, medical assistance, the way life went on in a generally normal way for most the people much of the time.[10]

Westmoreland's views have been echoed by journalist Robert Elegant:

In the early 1960s, when the Viet Nam War became a big story, most foreign correspondents assigned to cover the story wrote primarily to win the approbation of the crowd, above all their own crowd. As a result, in my view, the self-proving system of reporting they created became ever further detached from political and military realities because it instinctively concentrated on its own self-justification. The American press, naturally dominant in an 'American war', somehow felt obliged to be less objective than partisan, to take sides, for it was inspired by the *engagé* 'investigative' reporting that burgeoned in the US in these impassioned years. The press was instinctively 'agin the Government' – and, at least reflexively, for Saigon's enemies.

During the later half of the 15-year American involvement in Viet Nam the media became the primary battlefield. Illusory events reported *by* the press as well as real events *within* the press corps were more decisive than the clash of arms or the contention of ideologies. For the first time in modern history, the outcome of a war was determined not on the battlefield, but on the printed page and, above all, on the television screen. Looking back coolly, I believe it can be said (surprising as it may still sound) that South Vietnamese and American forces actually won the limited military struggle. They virtually crushed the Viet Cong in the South, the 'native' guerrillas who were directed, reinforced, and equipped from Hanoi; and thereafter they threw back the invasion by regular North Vietnamese divisions. None the less,

the War was finally lost to the invaders *after* the US disengage-
ment because the political pressures built up by the media had
made it quite impossible for Washington to maintain even the
minimal material and moral support that would have enabled the
Saigon regime to continue effective resistance.[11]

In accounts critical of American press reporting, no incident looms
larger than the Tet offensive and its aftermath. Specifically, the
media's negative and erroneous coverage of the Tet offensive turned
an allied victory into defeat and contributed to undermining America's
national will to continue the fight. Press reporting on the Tet offensive,
then, marked a major turning point in the history of the media's impact
on the conduct of the Vietnam War. In an exhaustive study, Peter
Braestrup has demonstrated the inaccuracies and inadequacy of media
reporting of this crucial period which painted a clear allied victory as a
portrait of defeat.[12]

The Press and the Vietnam War

Objective Journalism

Critics of the role of the American press in Vietnam can cite a number
of individual stories which are wrong, unfair, or biased. These
instances, however, are not representative of American press reporting as a whole and generalisations made from these few examples can
be exceedingly misleading. The great bulk of war reporting by
American correspondents reproduced the official point of view. Tactics and strategy were criticised in early stages of the war, but never the
wisdom of the American presence. This was so because the ethics of
'objective journalism' and the ideology of the Cold War prevailed.
This case is made by Daniel Hallin in his study of *New York Times*
reporting mentioned above (pp.63–70).
    According to Hallin, American journalism was transformed from its
partisan beginnings into a profession as a result of the industrial
revolution and the rise of financially autonomous newspapers, which
were in fact profitable businesses. At the same time as the press
cherished its autonomy and independence from government
(guaranteed by the First Amendment), it grew closer to modern

government. In Hallin's view 'the professionalization of journalism in the United States has *strengthened* rather than weakened the tie between press and state' (p.64).

By 'objective journalism' Hallin means an ideological system based on the principles of 'independence', 'objectivity' and 'balance' combined with 'a set of routines and assumptions which allow them to be put into practice in concrete situations' (p.68). These three terms are defined as follows:

> *Independence*. Journalists should be independent of political commitments and free of 'outside' pressures, including pressures from government and other political actors, advertisers, and the news organization itself as an institution with economic and political interests.
>
> *Objectivity*. The journalist's basic task is to present 'the facts', to tell what happened, not to pass judgment on it. Opinion should be clearly separated from the presentation of the news.
>
> *Balance*. News coverage of any political controversy should be impartial, representing without favor the positions of all the contending parties.

'Objective journalism' thus unites the three principles of independence, objectivity and balance with the following 'set of routines and judgments': the use of official sources for 'the facts' (facts thus become 'the official facts); focus on the president (when he acts in public this overides all other priorities); absence of interpretation or analysis (no editorializing in news reports; this distinction was eroded in the early 1960s); and finally, focus on immediate events (news has priority over interpretation and analysis). David Halberstam's news reporting from Vietnam must then be placed in the larger context of reporting as it appeared in the *New York Times*.

Halberstam criticised the detail and specifics of US policy, relying on American officials in the field as his sources, but never attacked its rationale. Writing in 1965 he noted, 'I believe that Vietnam is a legitimate part of that global commitment. A strategic country in a key area, it is perhaps one of only five or six nations in the world that is truly vital to US interests'.[13] Even more significantly, Halberstam was reacting to the over-optimism of the US Mission in Vietnam. General Westmoreland has written that the chief US military officer, General Harkins 'was optimistic to the point of fault, which was the basis for his continuing difficulties with American reporters, who found his enthusiastic appraisals sharply different from the word they received from American advisers in the field'.[14] And later, Westmoreland noted, 'In those early days the newsmen were sometimes closer to the truth than were American officials, for there can be no question but that Paul Harkins was over optimistic'.[15]

With this as background, Hallin comments on press coverage by the *New York Times* in the mid-1960s by observing it was a period that

> is generally described, both by its critics and its defenders, as a first step in the process of domestic polarization that eventually led to US disengagement from Vietnam. And no doubt it was to some degree; no doubt the images of civil strife in South Vietnam (which shared the front pages with news of the conflict in the American South) and the contrasts that so often appeared between official optimism and reports from the field sowed the seeds of the 'credibility gap' that would later emerge. But those seeds were still buried and dormant when Lyndon Johnson came to office in 1964. More immediately, the legacy left by the Vietnam reporting of the Kennedy years was an image of Vietnam as a vital though shaky outpost of the Free World, one that could not be abandoned without the gravest consequences.[16]

Later, Hallin concluded his analysis of this issue with these words (p.58):

> It was this geopolitical view, in its Cold War adaptation, that dominated American thinking in the early 1960s. For the journalists covering Vietnam it had two important consequences. First, it meant that they started out with a presumption that the 'defense' of South Vietnam was vital to American interests, a presumption strong enough to stand up despite their considerable scepticism about the conduct of the war. Second, it meant that their coverage said little about those aspects of the conflict that might have provoked deeper doubts. The progress of military efforts to 'block Communist expansion' was considered more important than the grievances of peasants against their landlords; if it was a question of putting the conflict in context, the latest speech by Khrushchev was considered far more relevant than, say, the history of Vietnamese anticolonialism. Thus

for all the conflict over 'negative' Vietnam coverage, the consensus that in 1961 had made escalation in Vietnam something 'apparently taken for granted', as the *Pentagon Papers* put it, was intact when Lyndon Johnson came into office at the end of 1963.

The ideology of 'objective journalism' carried over to the Lyndon Johnson period. Press reports continued to be based overwhelmingly on the official view and the 'official facts' as provided by government spokesmen. Thus, even though the *New York Times* had known and published details about covert naval operations against North Vietnam in advance of the August 1964 Gulf of Tonkin incident, it did not question the official administration line at that time. In a similar vein, the steps leading to an escalation of the war, both in the air over North Vietnam and on the ground in South Vietnam, were reported at face value at the time as implying 'no change of policy whatever'. Where problems did arise, they were based on the gradual policies adopted by the Johnson administration and the contradiction between wanting to send a signal to Hanoi of American resolve and wanting to diffuse the war as a political issue between the American Right and the American Left.

The press reacted differently to the escalation of the Air War and the introduction of ground troops. In the former case, the Johnson administration, embroiled in internal debate, failed to exercise public leadership. What followed was an 'eerie silence', a vacuum of leadership into which the press stepped. The onset of the Air War 'produced visible alarm and scepticism, expressed strongly on the editorial page, and spilling at times into the news columns' according to Hallin (p.98–99). Later, when the ground war escalated quite dramatically with the introduction of US troops, the Johnson administration did exert leadership. As a consequence there was no 'leadership vacuum' and the press followed suit. Its columns reported these developments as 'straight' news, and in the editorial pages, including the *New York Times*, gave prompt endorsement to the administration's actions.

At the end of this period (1965), Hallin rounded off his review of newspaper reporting in this fashion:

> The liberal press, moreover, given the nature of the American political spectrum and its acceptance of the limits of that spectrum, found itself in the summer of 1965 with nowhere to go politically except to follow Lyndon Johnson into the 'big muddy'.

This is one of the most important consequences of the close connection between the modern media and government: the range of political discussion in the press is usually restricted to the policy alternatives being debated in Washington. In February [1965] most criticism of Vietnam policy had come from liberal Democrats. In June, however, many Republicans, seeing a potential Korea in the making, began to distance themselves from Johnson's policy, arguing that ground troops should not be sent unless Johnson was willing to relax limitations on the air war (these limitations were motivated mainly by fear of provoking Chinese intervention). As pressure from the Right increased, liberals, including columnists and editorial writers for papers like the *Times*, closed ranks behind their president, and no voice remained to question the Americanization of the war.[17]

During the remainder of the Johnson period, official spokesmen continued to receive favourable coverage, including Westmoreland's background briefings. This changed in 1967 when Westmoreland addressed Congress to support the view that President Johnson's policies were succeeding. Prior to this political intervention, Westmoreland's views were seen as credible and appeared in print unedited. Now Westmoreland was perceived as having crossed into the sphere of partisan politics.

Television and Public Opinion

Television became the most authoritative source of news for the American public in the mid-1960s. With each passing year an ever increasing number of Americans reported in surveys that they got their news from TV. In 1962, when asked which medium they would trust if there were conflicting accounts between TV and the press, 48 per cent said they would trust TV and only 21 per cent said newspapers.[18] Another survey indicated that the American public relied more on TV for coverage of the war than newspapers.[19]

In September 1963 CBS and NBC TV expanded their evening news from 15 minutes to a half hour, ABC followed in January 1967. Increasingly the role of the anchorman became important in American public life. However, it should be noted that during the Vietnam War period the American public put more confidence in governmental institutions, including the Executive and the American military, than it did in television news and newspaper reports. Public confidence in television and newspaper reporting fell continually during the period 1966 to 1972.[20]

As Hallin notes, there is a 'significant problem' with media studies that 'accept at face value what people say about television's impact on themselves'. Other data points to a different conclusion, that the impact of television may be overrated by the respondents themselves. For example, in 1968 comparatively few Americans watched any television news; just over one-half of the American public watched at least one network news program *a month*, approximately one-third watched *some* television news on any given evening, and fewer still, one per cent of all TV households, watched a major newscast four or more nights a week.[21]

The number of people actually watching television at the time when it was supposedly influencing public opinion against the war is arguable. One survey noted that in 1968, of 56 million television households present in America, fewer than half (25.3 million) watched the news on any given evening and that this rate decreased in subsequent years.[22] Did those who watched absorb the news? A survey in 1969 found that fewer than half of those who watched were paying attention. Of those asked what they could recall, 51 per cent were unable to recall a single story out of an average of 19 which had appeared. For example, of those who could remember, they ranked the final commentary by the anchorman (Harry Reasoner or Eric Sevareid) the least remembered item.[23] This was supposedly the most influential news segment in terms of public opinion!

Another study by Lau, Brown and Sears[24] found that longstanding commitments and habits of a lifetime had greater bearing on public opinion of the Vietnam War than even kinship ties. In examining attitudes of Americans who had relatives serving in Vietnam, they found that the families of soldiers paid more attention to the war than those who had few kin ties to it. The acceptance of official policy on the war, however, was more influenced by attitudes and preconceptions formed early in life, as expressed in political affiliations, degree of anticommunism, and a sense of confidence and support for the system of US government, than by their concern for kinsmen (loved ones) in Vietnam.

Quite simply, television coverage of the Vietnam War may have reinforced views already held. Walter Cronkite's famous about face on the war following Tet 1968 is an example. Licthy found in his 1968 survey of public opinion, that 75 per cent of those who favoured the war at the time Cronkite made his remark considered Cronkite (and other network anchormen) 'hawks'; while a majority of those who opposed the war considered Cronkite (and other network anchormen) a 'dove'.[25] And in a similar vein, a 1972 study by Hofstetter and Moore found to their surprise that '[t]he bivariate relationships between television news exposure and the two military variables ... reveal a positive correlation between TV news exposure and support for the military: those who watch TV news frequently express a higher regard for the military (69 per cent vs. 59 per cent) and greater support for defense spending (69 per cent vs. 58 per cent) than those who watch TV news infrequently'.[26]

The above discussion should serve as a warning that measuring the impact of television on public opinion is a complex affair. As Hallin notes,

> This is not to say that television should be assumed *not* to be a significant force in shaping of public opinion. Very few media researchers today accept the 'minimal effects' view that dominated academic media research in the 1950s and early 1960s. A growing number of studies confirm the commonsense idea that televisions – and other media[2] – can indeed, in certain circumstances and in certain ways, shape political perceptions very powerfully. But sweeping statements about the power of television, which have been a staple of most discussion of television and Vietnam, clearly need to be taken with a grain of salt. And the reader should remember, as we look at television's presentation of the war, that is is impossible to be certain how the news affected the audience.[27]

With this as background, we can now turn to the issue of American television coverage of the Vietnam War.

Television and the Vietnam War

Television coverage of war, which began with the Korean conflict, grew to maturity with the Vietnam War. Vietnam thus became the first truly televised conflict. Since Vietnam became one of America's most divisive and least successful foreign wars, critics argue, it would seem surprising if the two were not somehow related. According to Hallin:

> Those who have argued that the media played a decisive role in the defeat of American aims in Vietnam almost invariably focus on television as the principal cause of what they see as a national failure of will. And the view that, for better or worse, television turned the American public against the war is accepted so widely across the American political spectrum that it probably comes as close as anything to being conventional wisdom about a war that still splits the American public.[28]

Television news reporting in Vietnam carried on the tradition of 'patriotic journalism' characteristic of the Second World War and the Korean conflict and differed in significant ways from newspaper reporting. Hallin (p.109) boiled down these differences to two main categories: (1) television, as a visual medium, can show the raw horror of war in a way print cannot but, as a corollary, television is ill-equipped to deal effectively with politics and strategy; and (2) television focuses on the negative – especially in conflict – more than print. Hallin presents his analysis of the role of television and the Vietnam War by noting that the model of 'objective journalism' used as a framework in which to analyse the reporting of newspaper journalists is not applicable in the case of TV reporters. Hallin argues that 'the model of objective journalism ... does not apply: the television journalist presented himself, in this case, not as a disinterested observer, but as a patriot, a partisan of what he frequently referred to as "our" peace offensive [or "our war"]'. In 1966, when the Johnson administration launched a peace offensive, there was a stark contrast between the coverage in the 'prestige press' and on television. According to Hallin, 'The prestige press, for the most part, continued to practice the kind of objective journalism that lies just outside the Sphere of Consensus, though there has perhaps been a little movement outward within the Sphere of Legitimate Controversy ... Most press reports reported official statements at face value'. These were accompanied by front page reports of Congressional criticism. A greater diversity of sources were cited, invariably from within the administration or from Congress. But television was very different, as Hallin notes (p.118): 'On television, on the other hand, the peace offensive appeared as a kind of morality play: while the coverage of a paper like the *Times* had a dry and detached tone, television coverage presented a dramatic contrast between good, represented by the American peace offensive, and evil, represented by Hanoi.'

Figure 1 below sets out the realm of 'objective' reporting for the television reporter – it is the middle region labelled 'sphere of legitimate controversy'. This is the region of electoral contests and legislative debate on only those issues recognised as such by the major established actors of the American political process. The limits are defined by the two-party system and their relationship to the bureaucracy and Executive. 'Within this region', notes Hallin, 'objectivity and balance reign as the supreme journalistic virtue'.

FIGURE 1

SPHERES OF CONSENSUS, CONTROVERSY, AND DEVIANCE

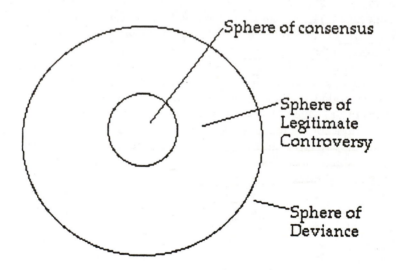

Source: Daniel C. Hallin, *The 'Uncensored War'*, p. 117.

The 'sphere of legitimate controversy' is bounded on one side by the 'sphere of consensus' and on the other by the 'sphere of deviance'. Within the former the television reporter deals with 'motherhood and apple pie' issues. As such, TV journalists do not present opposing views nor do they remain disinterested observers. As Hallin notes (p.117), 'on the contrary, the journalists' role is to serve as an advocate or celebrant of consensus values'. Within the latter, the 'sphere of deviance', are to be found political actors and views which the political mainstream of society rejects as being worthy of consideration. For example, it was written into the Federal Communication Commission's 'Fairness Doctrine' 'it is not the Commission's intention to make time available to Communists or to the Communist viewpoints'. Hallin notes that there are 'internal gradations' within each sphere and that the boundaries between them are 'often fuzzy'.

Space does not permit a more elaborate presentation of Hallin's quantitative content analysis of television coverage of the war. What follows below is a bald summary of his major findings.

Censorship and the Focus of War Reporting

There was no censorship imposed on the American news media in Vietnam, although they were expected to follow voluntary guidelines in order to protect military security (there were 15 categories of information which could not be reported without prior authorisation). There were only four reported cases after 1966 when accreditation cards had to be revoked for breaches of these guidelines. While direct censorship was not imposed, information was often withheld, embargoes were applied and access to the 'front' denied on occasion.

TV coverage of the war followed 'American boys' into action in the field and focused overwhelmingly on that one central story – American soldiers in combat. Contrary to views expressed by media critics, TV coverage did not dwell on graphic depictions of the horror of war. Hallin has determined that only about 22 per cent of all film reports from Southeast Asia in the period before Tet 1968 showed actual combat, and this was minimal. A similar percentage (24 per cent) showed film of dead or wounded, and these were usually brief. Less than 10 per cent of the pre-Tet 1968 sample of television reports included more than one video shot of the dead or wounded.

According to William Hammond, 'television tended to show combat from a distance ... soldiers moving into battle or firing at some vague target or pulling themselves together after an engagement. There was considerable commotion – rifles popping in the background, helicopters landing and taking off, smoke and dust – but little of the violence characteristic of Vietnam, in which a man stepped on a mine or fell into a booby trap'[29]. According to Lawrence Lichty, from August 1965 to August 1970, of some 2,300 reports shown on network evening news programmes, no more than 76 showed anything approaching true violence – heavy fighting, incoming small arms and artillery fire, killed and wounded within view.[30]

Why so little coverage of 'blood and guts' on television? First, the networks made a decision not to use certain pieces of film, such as identifiable American casualties (to protect the families from premature notice). Second, as Hallin notes, 'the major reason for the limited amount of bloody film was probably the simple fact that this was how the war was: most operations in Vietnam involved little contact with the enemy; for the average combat unit a bloody firefight was not an everyday occurrence' (p.130).

Hallin then raises another question 'not *what* or *how much* television showed of the war, but *how* it showed it: the point of view it employed and the framework of meaning into which it fit the incidents and images it reported'. Media critics argue that television did not show violence in a supportive framework, as was the case in World War II, but in a critical framework. Critics also hold that TV showed literally the destructiveness and frustration of war as if it had no meaning or purpose. Thus television coverage of war, regardless of its political context, would result in a decline of public support. Hallin argues that this view ignores 'the elementary facts of selection and editing' and 'the fact that television's visual images are extremely *ambiguous*'.

When television began its sustained coverage of Vietnam it periodically reported critical stories very different from what Americans had encountered in previous wars. They fell into four categories: civilian casualties caused by American action; corruption in the Saigon regime (Republic of Vietnam); US and ARVN killed in action by 'friendly fire'; and reports concerning frustration at fighting a war of attrition. According to Hallin's findings, 'these stories were by no means typical of television coverage in the period before the Tet offensive. They were minor currents in a general flow of reporting that was strongly supportive of American actions in Vietnam ... official statements about the war or positive images of the American role flew through the gates of journalism unimpeded ... television's most important sources in 1965–67 were American soldiers in the field; television reported the war from their point of view, and as long as they remained supportive of it, there would be a strong tendency for television to be so as well' (pp.133–34).

The Big Picture – Ideology and the Anchorman

As noted above, most television reports from the field gave a glimpse of one very small part of the war, saying little explicitly about its wider significance. The 'big picture' was provided by the TV network anchorman. According to Hallin, in terms of the ideology of TV coverage, there was little discussion of the global stakes. Television reporting 'was structured primarily by a different, much less conscious level of ideology: it was structured by a set of assumptions about the value of war – not so much as a political instrument, but as an arena of human action, of individual and national self-expression – and by images and a language for talking about it'. Hallin listed four set of unspoken assumptions: war is a national endeavour; war is an American tradition; winning is what counts; and war is rational.

In sum, Hallin concluded (pp.146–47):

> Eventually, one of the things that may have soured the American public on the war in Vietnam is the fact that it was a war of attrition, without fronts or fixed objectives, and therefore appeared irrational; it was never clear whether any given battle or operation should be considered a victory or defeat, or how it contributed to the achievement of more general strategic objectives. But this was not how the war appeared on television for the first two years. Here the role of the anchor is particularly important. The anchor's battlefield roundups ... gave Vietnam the appearance of structure Americans had come to expect from their wars, complete with 'fronts' and 'big victories' and a sense of driving, goal-directed energy. These roundups were based on the daily press briefing in Saigon ... and the claims of victory presented there were taken most of the time at face value. So this reporting, combined with reporting from Washington on optimistic statements by the administration and a fair number of upbeat reports from the field, meant that militarily the war appeared to be going very well for most of 1965, 1966, and 1967. Of all those battles or operations in the sample for the pre-Tet period for which journalists offered an assessment of success or failure, 62 per cent were presented as victories for the United States and South Vietnamese, 28 per cent as successes for the other side, and only 2 per cent as inconclusive. The United States and its allies were also generally reported as holding the military initiative ... It must have been very hard in this early period for

the average television viewer to imagine the possibility that American arms might not ultimately be successful in Vietnam.

Hallin rounded off his pre-Tet coverage by discussing how television portrayed the enemy – the North Vietnamese and Vietcong. Quite simply, 'television painted an almost perfectly one-dimensional image of the North Vietnamese and Vietcong as cruel, ruthless, and fanatical – clearly beyond the bounds of Legitimate Controversy' (p.148). To document this claim, Hallin analysed the issue of TV coverage of civilian casualties caused by both sides. Invariably enemy-caused civilian casualties were 'atrocities'– the direct result of a policy of terrorism. Hallin concluded:

> The theme of terrorism as an element of North Vietnamese and NLF [Vietcong] policy had the important effect of putting them outside the political realm, making them appear more as criminals than as a political movement or rival government. The language of law and order was common in television coverage: while a South Vietnamese government official taken by the Vietcong was 'kidnapped', an NLF political cadre – or any Vietcong, since television made no distinction between the political and military sides of the NLF – taken by the government was always a 'Vietcong suspect'. And with the imagery of gratuitous savagery television went a step further. Like most twentieth-century war propaganda, television coverage of Vietnam dehumanized the enemy, drained him of all recognizable emotions and motives and thus banished him not only from the political sphere, but from human society itself. The North Vietnamese and Vietcong were 'fanatical', 'suicidal', 'savage', 'half-crazed'. They were lower than mere criminals ... they were vermin. Television reports routinely referred to areas controlled by the NLF as 'Communist infested' or 'Vietcong infested'.

The Tet offensive and the Erosion of Public Support

Decline in American public support for the war in Vietnam preceded the 1968 Tet offensive. Press reportage paralleled the American public's shift in its view of the war.[31] Hallin notes (p.168) that 'early in

1966 a steady erosion in public support began – at a time, it is important to note, when television was still strongly committed to the war. Well before Tet, in October 1967, a plurality of the public believed the United States had made a "mistake" going into Vietnam. Considerably earlier, at least by the beginning of 1967, a plurality were saying they disapproved of Johnson's handling of the war'. Also, 'the first signs of a major shift in television's image of the war had appeared [in reaction to fighting for Hills 881 and 861 in April/May 1967]. The change would continue gradually through the rest of the year, as political divisions and the pace of fighting increased, and accelerate with the Tet offensive and the dramatic political events of 1968 [Johnson's decision not to stand for re-election]'.

What was the main reason for this shift in public opinion? Between 1966 and 1968 American acceptance of the Vietnam conflict declined consistently as American casualties rose in number. Support for the war fell some 15 percentage points each time the number of killed and wounded rose by a factor of ten.[32] In other words, when total casualties (all causes) rose from 1,000 to 10,000, public support for the war dropped by 15 per cent. This response occurred regardless of whether the war appeared to be going well or poorly and irrespective of favourable or unfavourable media coverage. A similar pattern prevailed during the Korean War where television coverage was minimal.[33]

The 1968 Tet offensive proved a major turning point. Peter Braestrup, as noted above, has painstakingly documented the negative impact of press and television coverage at this crucial juncture. Yet Braestrup's study should not be taken out of context. In his view, press reporting at this time was an aberation and should not be assumed to be the causal link which undermined American national will to continue the war in Vietnam. In his study of media reportage of this period, Hallin concluded:

> But Tet is also remembered as the event that shattered American morale at home; and it is Tet that is most often pointed to as the event that demonstrates the immense power of the media. 'It was the first time in history a war had been declared over by an anchorman,' wrote David Halberstam ... Tet appeared in the news as a dramatic and disastrous turn of events. But its impact on public opinion and on policy is more complex and less dramatic – though certainly not insignificant – than generally

supposed. Tet was less a turning point than a crossover point, a moment when trends what had been in motion for some time reached balance and began to tip the other way.[34]

Tet was certainly a period of exceptional journalistic activity, with an above-average outpouring of editorials and commentary by the working press. Media coverage of the Tet offensive emboldened political opponents of the administration to speak out; it was also clear that there was great concern among policymakers about the impact of the offensive on public opinion.

Post-Tet was also a period of silence by the administration as it became engulfed in an internal debate lasting nearly two months. The debate surfaced on 10 March when the *New York Times* reported that the Joint Chiefs of Staff had requested an additional 206,000 troops for Vietnam. At the same time, the Johnson administration was also subject to the humiliation of the *Pueblo* affair. The silence of this period was broken only in late March when Johnson announced that he would not seek re-election. According to Hallin, 'that announcement had a dramatic effect on public opinion, perhaps more significant than the effect of Tet itself' (p.170).

Media coverage of Tet generally accepted the official claim that the communist offensive was a military defeat, but press coverage also stressed the destruction caused and the casualties inflicted on American and ARVN soldiers. Tet was also the first sustained period during which it could be said that the war appeared on television as a really brutal affair (the 1972 Spring offensive would provide similar coverage of destruction and bloodshed). According to Hallin, the 'bottom line' was that press coverage convinced the public that the war was not under control (p.173). In his words:

> This was a perspective ... shared with much of the US mission in Saigon, which was divided over the significance of Tet, and with many in Washington, both in Congress and in the administration itself. This attitude developed so rapidly that it is perhaps best to see it, initially at least, as a coincidence of views, rather than as a product of mutual influence. It may be one of the many ironies of Tet coverage that it gave the public a more accurate view of the overall course of the war through the *inaccurate* view it gave of the outcome of one particular battle.[35]

There is little argument that press coverage became more critical after the Tet offensive. Hallin reported that prior to Tet, spokesmen for the war predominated over critics in television news reports by a ratio of 26.3 to 4.5 per cent, after Tet the critics achieved a rough parity of 26.1 to the supporters' 28.4 The change came because sources in the government used in previous reporting had switched sides. Forty-nine per cent of all domestic criticism of government war policy appearing on television now came from public officials of one sort or another, while only 16 per cent originated from reporters themselves in commentaries and interpretive digressions; 35 per cent of the remainder came from sources such as antiwar activists, soldiers in the field, and the man in the street.

As a result, television's portrayal of the Vietnam War changed dramatically as this summary by Hallin indicates (pp.175–78):

> *War is a National Endeavour.* Before Tet, Vietnam was 'our' war; after Tet, most of the time, it was simply 'the' war: as it entered the Sphere of Legitimate Controversy, journalists began to distance themselves from it and use of the first-person plural dropped off.

> *War Is an American Tradition – Invocation of the Memory of World War II.* Never, after Tet, did I encounter a television story that mentioned World War II; Vietnam was now cut off from that legitimizing connection with tradition.

> *War Is Manly.* The change here can be seen in the handling of war casualties. Never after Tet does one hear a phrase like, 'They were bloody but that was what they wanted'. There was increasing focus on the costs of the war to American troops. . . .

> *War Is Rational.* The image of the efficient American war machine moving inexorably toward victory was supplanted to a large extent by an image of war as eternal recurrence, progressing nowhere. . . .

> *Winning Is What Counts.* . . . it is here that we can get a better sense of why news coverage changed as it did after Tet . . . Winning, after all, was no longer what counted. When Lyndon Johnson was preparing his March 31, 1968, address on the war, aides persuaded him to change the opening line from 'I want to talk to you of the war in Vietnam' to 'I want to talk to you *of peace* in Vietnam'. And from that point forward, the message Americans heard was – to quote a 1968 cable sent by NBC News

to its correspondents in the field – 'We are on our way out of Vietnam'.

Conclusion

This paper has tried to present evidence that there is no simple direct connection between American media coverage of the Vietnam War and the loss of America's national will to persist and to win that conflict. Critics of the American media have been selective in their examples or have based their findings on flawed research methodologies. This paper has presented the findings of the US Army's official history (quoted below) as well as the most comprehensive scholarly study to be published to date. Hallin's study is all the more impressive as it focused on the *New York Times*, one of America's most liberal papers, and did not take into account pro-war dailies such as the *Daily News* (New York), *San Diego Union* and *Chicago Tribune*. Hallin also focused on the national broadcasts of the three major television networks. Here too, reference to local stations and their programmes may have produced a more conservative result concerning the impact of the media on public opinion. All of these studies, however, neglect to assess the impact of multiple news sources on public opinion, especially elite opinion.

Quite clearly, the American press relied on official sources for the bulk of its reporting. When official spokesman presented themselves in public, or offered 'background briefings' the press reported these views. The press also relied on officials in the civil bureaucracy and in the military. It would appear that linking media coverage directly to the loss of America's national will, is much like the reported practice of killing the messenger for bearing bad news. Halberstam's critical reporting in the early 1960s, it has now been revealed, closely paralled in-house assessments prepared by American officials.

It seems appropriate to conclude with the views of the US Army's official historian on this subject:

> In the end, what happened in Vietnam between the US Government and military on the one hand, and the news media on the other was symptomatic of what happened in the United States as a whole. At the beginning of the war, the main elements in American society moved in a direction that represented the greatest perceived good, toward containment of Chinese and

Soviet ambitions in Southeast Asia by taking a stand in South Vietnam. Although prone at times to believe the worst of officialdom the American news media both reflected and reinforced that trend, replaying official statements on the value of the war and supporting the soldier in the field if not always his generals. With time, under the influence of many deaths and contradictions, directions changed. Significant portions of the leadership in American society moved to repudiate the earlier decision. Cueing to that trend if not to sources within the elite, the press again followed suit but the US Government and military lacked the ability to do the same. Remaining behind in South Vietnam to retrieve whatever national face they could, those of their members most emotionally tied to the failed policy fixed their anger upon the news media, the most visible exponent of the society that appeared to have rejected them. The recriminations that we see today became the most inevitable result.[36]

NOTES

1. Geoffrey Mungham, 'The Eternal Triangle: Relations Between Governments, Armed Services and the Media', *Army Quarterly*, Vol.115, No.1 (1985), pp.7–21.
2. William M. Hammond, *United States Army in Vietnam, Public Affairs: The Military and the Media, 1962–1968* (Washington, DC: United States Army Centre of Military History, 1988).
3. Daniel C. Hallin, *The 'Uncensored War': The Media and Vietnam* (New York and Oxford: Oxford University Press, 1986); this was based on his doctoral thesis, 'The Mass Media and the Crisis in American Politics: The Case of Vietnam', The University of California at Berkeley, 1980.
4. Hallin notes the diversity of the American news media (pp.11–12), some sections of which were very 'pro-war'. He justifies his use of the *New York Times* in this way – 'the intent here is to deal with the best of American journalism'.
5. Ibid., pp.111–12.
6. Peter Braestrup, *Big Story: How the American Press and Television Reported and Interpreted the Crisis of Tet 1968 in Vietnam and Washington* (Boulder, CO: Westview Press, 1977), 2 vols. This was abridged and published as a single volume, with corrections to the original edition by Yale University Press in 1983.
7. Daniel C. Hallin, 'The Media, the War in Vietnam, and Political Support: A Critique of the Thesis of an Oppositional Media', *Journal of Politics*, Vol.46, No.1 (Feb. 1984), p.2.
8. Jeffrey P. Kimball, 'The Stab-in-the-Back Legend and the Vietnam War', *Armed Forces & Society*, Vol.14, No.13 (Spring 1988), p.433. See also Richard Nixon, *RN: The Memoirs of Richard Nixon* (New York: Grosset and Dunlap, 1978); Nixon, *The Real War* (New York: Warner Books, 1980), especially Ch.5; and Nixon, *No More Vietnams* (New York: Arbor House, 1985).

9. Gen. William C. Westmoreland, *A Soldier Reports* (New York: Dell Publishing Company, 1976), pp.82–83, see also pp.89 and 557.
10. Ibid., pp.553–55. In a later address Westmoreland asserted that 51 per cent of American reporters were under 29. Westmoreland's statistic is questionable. Of 110 US citizens accredited to report the war from Saigon in January 1966 (the only date when figures are available), 38 were below the age of thirty [34.5 per cent] and 72 above it, 37 were above the age of forty-one and 8 were fifty-one or older. Similar statistics prevailed among the 170 non-US correspondents present in Saigon at this time. The average mean age for all correspondents who served in Vietnam whose records survived in Army files was 35.83; see William M. Hammond, 'The Press in Vietnam as Agent of Defeat: A Critical Examination', *Reviews in American History*, Vol.17, No.2 (June 1989), p.314.
11. Robert Elegant, 'How to Lose a War', *Encounter*, Vol.57, No.2 (1981), p.73. Elegant covered the Vietnam War, in his own words, 'as correspondent and commentator ... from 1955 to 1975'. He wrote from Vietnam for *Newsweek* from 1955 to December 1962 and then returned in 1966.
12. Braestrup, *Big Story* (1977). Press reporting emphasised that the offensive came as a surprise; ARVN forces were ineffective; civilian loyalty to the RVN had been seriously eroded; the US employed massive indiscriminate firepower which caused widespread destruction; the US Embassy had been entered by enemy sappers; the battle for Hue typified the war and that the siege of Khe Sanh was comparable to Dien Bien Phu; and that the Tet offensive was a communist victory.
13. David Halberstam, *The Making of a Quagmire* (New York: Random House, 1965), p.319.
14. Westmoreland, *A Soldier Reports*, p.82.
15. Ibid., p.83.
16. Hallin, *'Uncensored War'*, pp.48–49.
17. Ibid., p.99.
18. Richard F. Carter and Bradley Greenberg, 'Newspapers or Television: Which Do You Believe?', *Journalism Quarterly*, Vol.41, No.1 (Winter 1965).
19. Peter Clarke and Lee Ruggels, 'Preferences Among News Media for Coverage of Public Affairs', *Journalism Quarterly*, Vol.47, No.3 (Autumn 1970).
20. United States Senate, Committee on Governmental Operations, *Confidence and Concern: Citizens View American Government* (Washington, DC: US Government Printing Office, 1973), p.79.
21. Lawrence W. Lichty, 'Video Versus Print', *Wilson Quarterly*, Vol.6, No.5 (1982), p.55.
22. 'The Alfred I. Dupont – Columbia Survey of Broadcast Journalism, 1971–72', in Marvin Barrett (ed.), *The Politics of Broadcasting* (1973), p.6.
23. Ibid.
24. Richard R. Lau, Thad A. Brown and David O. Sears, 'Self-Interest and Civilians' Attitudes Toward the Vietnam War', *Public Opinion Quarterly*, Vol.42 (Winter 1978), pp.464–83.
25. Lawrence W. Lichty, 'The War We Watched on Television: A Study in Progress', *American Film Institute Report*, Vol.4, No.4 (Winter 1973).
26. C. Richard Hofstetter and David W. Moore, 'Watching TV News and Supporting the Military', *Armed Forces & Society*, Vol.5, No.2 (Winter 1979), p.263.
27. Hallin, *'Uncensored War'*, p.108.
28. Ibid., pp.105–106.
29. Hammond, 'The Press in Vietnam as Agent of Defeat', p.315.
30. Lawrence W. Lichty, 'Comments on the Influence of Television on Public Opinion', in Peter Braestrup (ed.), *Vietnam as History: Ten Years After the Paris Peace Accords* (1984), p.158

31. John E. Mueller, *War, Presidents and Public Opinion* (New York: Wiley, 1973).
32. Hammond, 'The Press in Vietnam as Agent of Defeat', p.318.
33. John E. Mueller, 'Trends in Popular Support for the Wars in Korea and Vietnam', *American Political Science Review*, Vol. 65 (1971), p.358.
34. Hallin, *Uncensored War'*, p.168.
35. Ibid., p.173.
36. Hammond, 'The Press in Vietnam as Agent of Defeat', p. 321.

BIBLIOGRAPHY

Berman, Larry, *Planning a Tragedy* (New York: W. W. Norton, 1982).
Bishop, Capt. Donald M., 'The Press and the Tet offensive', *Air University Review*, Vol. 30, No. 1 (1978), pp. 84–88.
Braestrup, Peter, *Big Story: How the American Press and Television Reported and Interpreted the Crisis of Tet 1968 in Vietnam and Washington*, (Boulder, CO: Westview Press, 1977), 2 vols.
—— *Big Story: How the American Press and Television Reported and Interpreted the Crisis of Tet 1968 in Vietnam and Washington*, Abridged Edition (London and New Haven: Yale University Press, 1983).
—— (ed) *Vietnam as History: Ten Years After the Paris Peace Accords* (1984).
Browne, Malcolm W., *The New Face of War* (New York: Bobbs-Merrill Co. 1965).
Carter, Richard F. and Greenberg, Bradley, 'Newspapers or Television: Which Do You Believe?', *Journalism Quarterly*, Vol. 41, No. 1 (Winter 1965).
Clarke, Peter and Ruggels, Lee, 'Preferences Among News Media for Coverage of Public Affairs' *Journalism Quarterly*, Vol. 47, No. 3 (Autumn 1970).
Elegant, Robert, 'How to Lose a War', *Encounter*, Vol. 57, No. 2 (1981), pp. 73–89.
Gelb, Leslie H. and Betts, Richard K., *The Irony of Vietnam: The System Worked* (Washington, DC: The Brookings Institution, 1979).
Geyelin, Philip, 'The Role of the Press in an Open Society', *Naval War College Review*, Vol. 27, No. 5 (1975), pp. 23–7.
Grossman, Michael B. and Kumar, Martha J., 'The White House and the News Media: The Phases of Their Relationship', *Political Science Quarterly*, Vol. 94, No. 1 (1979), pp. 37–53.
Halberstam, David, *The Making of a Quagmire* (New York: Random House, 1965).
Hallin, Daniel C., The Mass Media and the Crisis in American Politics: The Case of Vietnam. PhD. Thesis, The University of California at Berkeley, 1980.
Hallin, Daniel C., *The 'Uncensored War': The Media and Vietnam* (New York and Oxford: Oxford University Press, 1986).
Hallin, Daniel C., 'The Media, the War in Vietnam, and Political Support: A Critique of the Thesis of an Oppositional Media', *Journal of Politics*, Vol. 46, No. 1 (Feb. 1984), pp. 2–24.
Hammond, William M., *United States Army in Vietnam, Public Affairs: The Military and the Media, 1962–1968* (Washington, D.C.: United States Army Center of Military History, 1988).
—— 'The Press in Vietnam as Agent of Defeat: A Critical Examination', *Reviews in American History*, Vol. 17, No. 2 (June 1989), pp. 312–23.
Hess, Gary R., 'The Military Perspective on Strategy in Vietnam', *Diplomatic History*, Vol. 10, No. 1 (1986), pp. 91–106.
Hofstetter, C. Richard and Moore, David W., 'Watching TV News and Supporting the Military', *Armed Forces & Society*, Vol. 5, No. 2 (Winter 1979), pp. 261–269.

Holsti, Ole and Rosenau, James N., *American Leadership in World Affairs: Vietnam and the Breakdown of Consensus* (Boston: Allen and Unwin, 1984).
Hughes, Capt. Wayne P., 'Guarding the First Amendment – For and From the Press', *Naval War College Review*, Vol. 37, No. 3 (1984), pp. 28–35.
Huston, Capt. J. E., 'Public Relations – The War Ahead', *Defence Force Journal*, No. 84 (Sept./Oct. 1990), pp. 32–34.
Jacobsen, Lt. Cdr. K. C., 'Television and the War: The Small Picture', *US Naval Institute Proceedings*, Vol. 101, No. 3 (March 1975), pp. 54–60.
Johnson, Lyndon B., *Vantage Point: Perspectives on the Presidency, 1963–1969* (New York: Holt, Reinhart and Winston, 1971).
Kaplan, H. J., 'With the American Press in Vietnam', *Commentary*, Vol. 73, No. 5 (1982), pp. 42–49.
Kattenburg, Paul M., *The Vietnam Trauma in American Foreign Policy, 1945–75* (London and New Brunswick: Transaction Books, 1980).
Keenan, George, 'Morality and Foreign Policy', *Parameters*, Vol. 16, No. 1 (1986), pp. 76–82.
Kimball, Jeffrey, P., 'The Stab-in-the-Back Legend and the Vietnam War', *Armed Forces & Society*, Vol. 14, No. 3 (Spring 1988), pp.433–58.
Knightley, Phillip, *The First Casualty: From Crimea to Vietnam: The War Correspondent as Hero, Propagandist, and Myth Maker* (New York: Harcourt, Brace, Javanovich, 1975).
Lau, Richard R., Brown, Thad A. and Sears, David O., 'Self-Interest and Civilians' Attitudes Toward the Vietnam War', *Public Opinion Quarterly*, Vol. 42, No. 4 (Winter 1978), pp. 464–83.
Lefever, Ernest W., *TV and National Defense: An Analysis of CBS News, 1972–1973* (Boston, VA: Institute for American Strategy Press, 1974).
Lewy, Guenter, *America in Vietnam* (New York and Oxford: Oxford University Press, 1978).
Lichty, Lawrence W., 'The War We Watched on Television: A Study in Progress' *American Film Institute Report*, Vol. 4, No. 4 (Winter 1973).
——— 'Video Versus Print', *Wilson Quarterly*, Vol. 6, No. 5 (1982).
Lunn, Hugh, *Vietnam: A Reporter's War* (St. Lucia: University of Queensland Press, 1985).
Mandelbaum, Michael, 'Vietnam: The Television War', *Parameters*, Vol. 13, No. 1 (March 1983), pp. 89–97.
McDougall, Derek, 'The Australian Press Coverage of the Vietnam War in 1965', *Australian Outlook*, Vol. 20, No. 3 (1966), pp. 303–10.
Mecklin, John, *Mission in Torment: An Intimate Account of the US Role in Vietnam* (Garden City, NY: Doubleday, 1965).
Migdail, Carl J., 'A Perspective of the Military and the Media', *Naval War College Review*, Vol. 28, No. 3 (Summer 1976), pp. 2–9.
Mitchell, Maj. Michael C., 'Television and the Vietnam War', *Naval War College Review*, Vol. 37, No. 3 (Summer 1984), pp. 42–52.
Mueller, John E., *War, Presidents and Public Opinion* (New York: Wiley, 1973).
——— 'Trends in Popular Support for the Wars in Korea and Vietnam', *American Political Science Review*, Vol. 65 (1971), pp. 358–368.
Mungham, Geoffrey, 'The Eternal Triangle: Relations Between Governments, Armed Services and the Media', *Army Quarterly*, Vol. 115, No. 1 (1985), pp. 7–21.
Nathan, James A. and Oliver, James K., 'Public Opinion and U.S. Security Policy', *Armed Forces & Society*, Vol. 2, No. 1 (Fall 1975), pp. 58–59.
Nixon, Richard M., *RN: The Memoirs of Richard Nixon* (New York: Grosset and Dunlap, 1978).

——— *The Real War* (New York: Warner Books, 1980).

——— *No More Vietnams* (New York: Arbor House, 1985).

Pontuso, James F., 'Combat and the Media: The Right to Know Versus the Right to Win', *Strategic Review*, Vol. 18, No. 1 (Winter 1990), pp. 49–60.

Rigg, Col. Robert B., 'How Not To Report a War', *Military Review*, Vol. 49, No. 6 (June 1969), pp. 14–24.

Schandler, Herbert Y., *The Unmaking of a President: Lyndon Johnson and Vietnam*, (Princeton: Princeton University Press, 1977).

Smith, Lt. J. Morgan, 'Wanted: A Responsible Free Press', *US Naval Institute Proceedings*, Vol. 110, No. 7 (July 1984), pp. 77–85.

Szafranski, Richard, 'Thinking About Small Wars', *Parameters* Vol. 20, No. 3 (Sept. 1990), pp. 39–49.

Taylor, Sandra C., 'Reporting History: Journalists and the Vietnam War', *Reviews in American History*, Vol. 13, No. 3 (Sept. 1985), pp. 451–61.

Thayer, Carlyle A., *War By Other Means: National Liberation and Revolution in Vietnam* (Sydney and Boston: Allen & Unwin, 1989).

Thompson, W. Scott and Frizzell, Donaldson D., *The Lessons of Vietnam* (St. Lucia: University of Queensland Press, 1977).

Turner, Kathleen J., *Lyndon Johnson's Dual War: Vietnam and the Press* (London and Chicago: University of Chicago Press, 1985).

United States Senate, Committee on Governmental Operations, *Confidence and Concern: Citizens View American Government* (Washington, DC.: US Government Printing Office, 1973).

Venanzi, Lt. Col. Gerald S., 'Democracy and Protracted War: The Impact of Television', *Air University Review*, Vol. 34, No. 3 (1983), pp. 58–72.

Westmoreland, Gen. William C., *A Soldier Reports* (New York: Dell Publishing Co., 1976).

——— 'Vietnam in Perspective', *Military Review*, Vol. 59, No. 1 (Jan. 1979), pp. 34–43.

Northern Ireland

DR MICHAEL McKINLEY

The history of Ireland is marked by many rebellions. On many occasions these have taken the form of a strategic surprise to the British government; certainly the current rebellion, or insurgency, in Northern Ireland took Whitehall unawares in 1969. The 'Troubles', as this re-emergence of the Irish Question in military and paramilitary form was soon (once more) described, appeared avatar-like, in dramatic reproof to apathetic British stewardship of the six counties of Northern Ireland which comprise the remnants of its first overseas colony. In their destruction of an illusion – that Northern Ireland apparently quiet was Northern Ireland apparently at peace – the final stanza of the early nineteenth-century Irish poet James Clarence Mangan's *Vision of Connacht in the Thirteenth Century* is well-recalled:

> ... behold – a change
> from light to darkness, from joy to woe!
> King, nobles, all,
> Looked aghast and strange;
> The minstrel group sale in dumbest show!
> Had some great crime
> Wrought this dread amaze,
> This terror? None seemed to understand ...
> I again walked forth;
> But lo! the sky
> showed fleckt with blood, and an alien sun
> Glared from the North,
> And there stood on high,
> Amid his shorn beams, a skeleton![1]

In this light it was also interesting that the Ulster historian, A. T. Q.

The writer wishes to gratefully acknowledge the research assistance of Ms Helen Wilson of the Strategic and Defence Studies Centre, The Australian National University in the preparation of this paper.

116

Stewart, writing in the late 1970s, should note the dysjunction which events were presenting to those with only a 'modern' cast of mind:

> At an early stage of the Ulster troubles, it became apparent that attitudes, words and actions which were familiar and recognizable to any student of Irish history, but which seemed hardly relevant to politics in the twentieth century, were coming back into fashion. This was not to be explained by the deliberate imitation of the past; it could be accounted for only by some more mysterious form of transmission from generation to generation. In many ways it was a frightening revelation, a nightmarish illustration of the folk-memory of Jungian psychology. Men and women who had grown to maturity in a Northern Ireland at peace now saw for the first time the monsters which inhabited the depth of the community's unconscious mind. It was as if a storm at sea had brought to the surface creatures thought to have been long extinct.[2]

In another passage he synthesised the condition of Ireland in terms of Dracula's Transylvania: '... much troubled by the undead'.[3]

The strategic surprise in these terms was both literally and metaphorically dramatic – striking, sudden, threatening, tragic, turbulent and charged with emotion. It was, therefore, an inauspicious moment in which to reach understanding and decisions; at the same time these could not be avoided. The further result, of course, is the rise of what the American poet Carl Sandburg so perceptively saw as 'the capacity of so many men, women, and children for hating and fearing what they do not understand while believing that they do understand completely and perfectly what no one understands except tentatively and hazardously'. And this, essentially, is the incubator of opportunistic politics – an atmosphere devoid of intellectual ideas and moral purpose.

The point here, though, is not just surprise and its consequences; it is also the distinct probability that the surprise itself is a consequence of a previous choice not to understand, or attend to a particular situation. The pretence to complete and perfect understanding, therefore, is only the denial of wilful ignorance and the protection of an injured *amour propre*. This is not to suggest that a free media would obviate strategic surprise so much as it is to assert that it would diminish the likelihood of surprise. A priori, openness to inquiry and availability of information militate against the state and the government not understanding, and hence being surprised; or the body politic not understanding, and hence being surprised, either because of the government's default or, in some cases, as a result of the government deliberately withholding information – in effect not trusting its citizens.

Presumptions, Observations and Conundrums

The existence of a free press, however, is but one of the presumptions with which this essay is riven. Nevertheless, it is one with an outstanding pedigree, no more eloquently proclaimed than by Thomas Erskine, Baron, Lord Chancellor of England, in his defence of Thomas Paine, author of *The Rights of Man*, nearly 200 years ago:

> ... liberty of opinion keeps governments themselves in due subjection to their duties. ... Let reason be opposed to reason, and argument to argument, and every good government will be safe. ... We must not think to make a staple commodity of all the knowledge in the land, to mark and licence it like our broad cloth and our wool packs. ... The Press, my Lords, is one of our great out-sentries; if we remove it, if we throw it in fetters, the enemy may surprise us.

Coupled with this presumption is its corollary, *informed consent*, honoured in the preamble of the US Declaration of Independence and the First Amendment to the Constitution, a quality of singular importance in time of conflict. In the context of this project, it makes possible both debate about choice, and choice itself on the matter of putting lives at risk, either of one's own security forces or of another nationality or community. And choice, moreover, is a necessary condition not only for politics to exist, but also for politics to be democratic in any meaningful sense. To this end it is also presumed that all seemingly significant events must be reported since ignoring them will not alter the reality of their consequences; indeed both require publicising if correction or improvement is to be attempted. All of which means that this essay, along with those it appears with, is centrally located within theories of democracy and political action.

Presumptions notwithstanding, it would be improper to proceed without acknowledging a certain analytical uneasiness and intellectual restiveness. Both are occasioned by my intention to write critically – to be honest, very critically – on the subject of Northern Ireland and the attendant relationship between the military and the media. In the interests of attempting to establish good faith in another relationship, that between the reader and this writer, it is necessary to make as clear as possible his (my) own position on the Irish Question, especially since the analysis which follows makes much of the location in which journalists conduct their practices. Six observations are offered.

The first is that, as my name might suggest, and the best of my knowledge supports, I am of Scotch-Irish descent; three of my grandparents held names that are commonly found in Ulster. Whatever their confessional affiliations were there (and there is a possibility that my paternal grandfather was a Protestant), they were Catholics in New Zealand. I was raised as one accordingly. I have, furthermore, lived in Ireland for extended periods of research and study and made many friends there. My interest in the country therefore is both intellectual and personal-spiritual.

Second, because of this attachment, I am (hopefully) more acutely aware of the need to exercise a rigourous undiscriminating scepticism in the pages which follow. If some readers might think that I have not always succeeded, it was not for the want of trying. Third, I have attempted to demand of myself a similar (moral) rigour with respect to the violence, and the talk, or reportage of violence, which at times seems to be all pervasive. Fourth, though somewhat ambiguously, my position in this: I dearly wish to see a united Ireland to which all Irish men and women, North and South, have freely given their assent. This, I know, is but the remotest of possibilities given the current state of affairs; perhaps it is even chimerical. Nevertheless, it is my instinct. (The ambiguity results from the fact that, for the time being, this wish is determined by the dominance of the nation state as the unit of political life at the international level, and the principal unit of organisation at the domestic level when, at the same time, this writer finds the current arguments in defence of this unit somewhat threadbare and discredited).

Fifth, there is the inescapable question of moral responsibility in relation to the ongoing violence, by some who seek to keep Ireland partitioned, and by others who would re-unify it. In brief my views on this are identical with those of Albert Camus, the French existentialist, who wrote that:

> I am not one of those who long for ... people to take up arms again in an uprising doomed to be crushed under the eyes of an

international society that will spare neither applause nor virtuous tears before returning to their slippers like football enthusiasts on Saturday evening after a big game. There are already too many dead in the stadium, and we can be generous only with our own blood.[4]

Sixth, and finally, any discussion of Northern Ireland in the closing years of the twentieth century is obliged to acknowledge the *seeming* inequality of the situation there in so many comparative contexts. By this, the 23rd year of the 'Troubles' the conflict in Northern Ireland has resulted in a death toll of somewhere around 2,500 deaths – approximately 120 per year – a relatively low figure considering the scale of natural and man-made disasters, and their attendant deaths, we have become accustomed to. In absolute terms it is dwarfed by the 60,000 who have 'disappeared' in Sri Lanka during that country's civil war of the last eight years; or the 60,000 casualties of the war in the Horn of Africa in 1989 alone; or the initial estimates of 100,000-300,000 Iraqi dead in just the 43 days duration of Operation 'Desert Storm'. And it is certainly paltry alongside the 23,300 (i.e., nearly 3 per hour) recorded killings in the USA during 1990.

But for all that it is also the case that, because the killing and the violence take place in such a confined space – what Sir Walter Scott termed 'the narrow ground' – the impression is one of carnage on a grand scale. It is an impression, moreover, which is so accurate in pro rata terms as to force Northern Ireland towards the forefront of current political tragedies. After only seven years of the 'Troubles' (i.e., by the end of 1975), Richard Rose provided the following perspective: 'The number of dead in Ulster is, proportionate to population, twice the losses that Britain suffered in the Boer War, and about twice the number of deaths suffered by US forces in the Korean and Vietnam wars combined.'[5]

By 1991, this corrected death toll had reached 100,000 for the United Kingdom and 500,000 for the United States. And this says nothing about other, directly-related indices of a society in turmoil, such as the high incidences of dead and injured in both the total population and families, houses searched, and families displaced as a result of political violence and its consequences.[6] In all, however, there is nothing to dispute the application of Christopher Hitchens description, *abattoir state*, to Northern Ireland, a term he thought appropriate to El Salvador and Guatemala.[7]

Interestingly and notably Hitchens is a journalist. In the two words of his description he captured, I believe, much, but certainly not all of what Northern Ireland is about – violence, destruction and death, committed by professionals of one type or another, so as to satisfy an apparently widespread and continuous need. In this there is a conundrum, or rather two conundrums. The first is occasioned by the transnational nature of the Irish Question. Specifically, the relationship between Defence and the Media involves relations between at least two security forces, the British Army and the Royal Ulster Constabulary, and the media of both the United Kingdom and the Republic of Ireland. And even this is incomplete because, with regard to the print medium, Northern Ireland's newspapers – in particular the *Belfast Telegraph* – a third dimension must be acknowledged. Effectively, this is to recognise the analytical need sometimes to regard Northern Ireland as 'a place apart' from the United Kingdom and the Republic of Ireland, a unique place which mocks the disciplinary borders which many scholars (in the main, political scientists and lawyers) attempt to impose on the world out of administrative convenience rather than intellectual imperative.

The second conundrum is also an irony. This critical analysis of the defence – media relationship and of the deficiencies in the latter which will be addressed later, have themselves frequently been informed, and made possible by certain positive contributions of the media. I am, for example, in the debt of, and grateful for the penetrating reports offered on Ireland by Robert Fisk, late of *The Times* and currently with the *Independent*; Conor O'Clery (then of the London bureau of the *Irish Times*, and Vincent Browne of *Magill*. Ultimately, I am acutely aware of the need to avoid the synecdochical error of covering all journalists with the critique of most journalists while at the same time saying something material, and hopefully interesting.

My response is, in the circumstances, contradictory inasmuch as it observes Edmund Burke's disclaimer that he knew of no method of drawing up an indictment against a whole people (for which read journalists as a class); and adapts Winston Churchill's conclusion that tendencies are now more important than episodes. The result is that a generalised critique will be mounted but always in the spirit of that befitting humility which Oliver MacDonagh mandated as early as 1977 for 'academics' writing on Northern Ireland:

In black hours, it appeared that there was nothing left for any rational inhabitant of the island but to write Yeatsian poetry à la 1919–21, if only he had the talent. Moreover it was the day of the instantaneous. The course of events so twisted and darted, at times, that yesterday seemed irrelevant by midday and tomorrow unknowable at nightfall. The babble of explanation was too loud for thought, and, *in immediate exposition and analysis, the best of journalists proved themselves superior to the scholars* (emphasis added).[8]

Methodological Issues

As if the presumptions, observations and conundrums noted to this point were not barriers enough to writing, it has to be said that they pale in magnitude alongside five methodological issues which accompany this project. The first of these is the need to proceed with analysis in the face of a dominant epistemology – in journalism and academia (for in this the two are inextricably linked) – for establishing and producing 'truths'. By this is meant that journalists and academics share a common enterprise because they are engaged in the production of knowledge or, as it is sometimes called, 'productive truths'. Within this enterprise they also share something even more fundamental – a common epistemology (theory of knowledge) – which in many ways, is impoverishing, incomplete, inadequate and alienating.

Briefly, indeed very briefly stated, this is the result of the fact that, for the most part, the modern Western university and its modes of inquiry (which also dominate inquiry and explanation in general) are embedded in seventeenth century scientific thought and philosophy. In sum, these are riven with hierarchical and totalising Cartesian dualisms many of which are now so commonly accepted as to have acquired the status of 'givens': subject-object; mind-body; self-other; now-then; culture-nature; male-female; and weightless *material body*-material mind.[9] Hierarchical here refers to the first-stated ember of the pair being 'thought to be superior to its companion', and totalising because 'they are thought to exhaust the alternatives within the parameter in question'.[10]

Missing from this state is 'any sense that anything is missing' when, in fact what is missing is the understanding of relation – what the American philosopher John Dewey warned of when he wrote: 'The world seems mad in preoccupation with what is specific, particular, disconnected.' Or the Jewish scholar Martin Buber expressed in positive terms: 'Inscrutably involved we live in the currents of universal reciprocity.'[11]

Yet there is still more than reciprocity; there is the need to acknowledge, as have thinkers apart from Buber and Dewey, as ostensibly disparate as Albert Einstein, the English philosopher Alfred North Whitehead, the American William James, and the Italian anti-Fascist Ignazio Silone that 'reality' is always observed contingently by a man or woman 'of a certain region, a certain class, and a certain time'.[12] What this hints at, even if it does not require, is the 'formation of identity of self' which occurs 'largely at an archaic level of engulfment in the moody background world of everyday experience'. Within this condition, for which Wilshire's description is 'mimetic engulfment', people are typically but 'undeliberately modeling themselves upon others around them' to the extent that individuation is only ever a compromised quality.[13] In a special way consistent with these professionals (academic and journalists as separate examples) are recognized and authorized within their 'purified' (vocational) group at the same time as they phobically exclude those that would pollute them.[14]

And what does all this signify? In a line: there exists no objective reality independent of the observer's understanding of it. It means, also, as per Werner Heisenberg and others, that the very act of observing is simultaneously the act of participating. The need exists, therefore, to admit Whitehead's 'withness of the body' which, as William Irwin Thompson argues, allows observers to 'at least comprehend [history] through the relevance of (them) selves'.[15] In so doing the conclusion is inescapable that, despite urgings and inclinations to the contrary, the world is never meaningfully experienced by way of a series of confrontations directly with nature or events, but rather, these experiences are mediated by the science of nature.

In the case of Ireland in general and Northern Ireland in particular, Britain's mimetic engulfment and, indeed, what Hitchens has come to call, ironically, its 'bleeding lack of introspection',[16] has been well evidenced by writers on both sides of the Irish Sea. In the late eighteenth century John Fitzgibbon (later Lord Clare) expressed himself of the view that British statesmen were 'more ignorant of the affairs of Ireland than of any other country in the world'.[17] Less than one hundred years later T. P. O'Connor advanced the following view on the record of Britain's stewardship of Ireland: 'To any Englishman, whatever his party, such a record ... by any other people but his own, and in any other country but in Ireland, would bring prompt condemnation and swift resolve'.[18]

The nineteenth century also provided interesting material for those with an eye to the historical origins of many of the stereotypes applied to late twentieth century Ireland, including Northern Ireland. According to Richard Ned Lebow the prevailing theme was one in which the Irish were lazy, complacent, superstitious and violent, and moreover, government policy reflected these stereotypes. When reformist and nationalist movements challenged them, so deeply were they embedded that recognition of the true and popular nature of the protest was impossible because of what Lebow terms the 'perceptual prison' in which policy-makers operated.[19]

Nothing much changed in certain elite circles if the account by Sir John Peck, British Ambassador to Ireland for three years in the early 1970s, is to be believed. He recalls the 'nonsense' which was conveyed to his wife and himself, 'in and around London and the Home Counties in the year 1970 AD [sic]':

> We had not been long in Ireland when the wife of a very distinguished British ex-soldier, retired from public life, said to Mariska, 'Tell me, my dear, what is it like now, living in Government House?' 'I'm afraid I wouldn't know', Mariska answered very gently. 'The President moved in before we came here.'
>
> Unofficially, from friends, acquaintances and comparative strangers who had heard I was going to Dublin, I was told all about Ireland. I learned how lucky I was to be given that nice quiet Embassy where, traditionally, old faithfuls were put out to grass. There would be wonderful riding, racing, hunting, shooting, fishing and golf. I would not need to worry much about the Irish and there really were some nice ones, some people said. But London seemed to be well stocked with the nephews and nieces of somebody or other whose place had been burnt down in the Troubles, and they were able to warn me that the Irish were untrustworthy, idle and irresponsible. They kept hens in the kitchen. Irish women never cleaned their jewellery.
>
> I was told, too, about the Anglo-Irish, or the Ascendancy, sometimes referred to as the West Britons. These, it appeared, were rich and Protestant, pillars of the Church of Ireland, living in large properties surrounded by high walls. They did not mingle

with the native Irish and generally conducted themselves as though Independence had never happened. Provided the natives were not actively hostile, the British Ambassador could have a most agreeable time in their company.[20]

The fulsomeness of this quotation, hopefully, absolves the writer from continuing with a catalogue of similar accounts, either by writers as equally dumbfounded as Peck and recalling in similar vein, or excerpted from original sources containing views remarkably consistent with those who 'informed' Peck. Finally, suffice it to say that when James Callaghan was Home Secretary in the late 1960s he quickly reached the opinion that 'Members of Parliament knew less about [Northern Ireland] than [they] knew about our distant colonies, on the far side of the earth',[21] a hardly surprising fact given his earlier discoveries in, and attitudes towards that part of his portfolio:

... Northern Ireland was crammed into what was called the General Department, which was responsible for anything which did not fit into any of the major departments of the Home Office. It covered such matters as ceremonial functions, British Summer Time, London taxicabs, liquor licensing, the administration of the state-owned pubs in Carlisle, and the protection of animals and birds. One division also dealt with the Channel Islands, the Isle of Man, the Charity Commission and Northern Ireland, and this group of subjects was under the control of a staff of seven, of whom only one was a member of what was called the Administrative class .... There seemed to me at that time no reason to disturb the arrangement I found on arrival. Besides, there were many other things to preoccupy me.[22]

The second methodological issue arises out of the nature of the relationship between defence and the media. In practice it is a sub-set of the relationship between the state and the media. The literature, research materials and evidence all point in this direction. Thus, in Northern Ireland, Defence (or the Military) itself is frequently associated with the Home Office, the Northern Ireland Office, and sometimes even the Foreign and Commonwealth Office. As a result the defence-media relationship is a multitude of relationships between, ultimately, a great many individual journalists and several government authorities.

At the same time the functional relationship between the two overarching categories is one between antagonists: while the defence constellation practises conformity and secrecy, and articulates national interest and patriotism, the media's prerogatives, are criticism and discovery. In the normal course of events this induces a defensive disposition on the part of the state and an offensive disposition on the part of the media. Thus to the extent that the Northern Ireland situation is defined as a security question by the British government it is less inclined to openness in the name of national security – a cover not quite so readily available if it is defined as a political situation. The antagonism, then, tends towards the polarized and the rigid even when the 'security situation' is seen by the media as an accurate formulation, and incomprehension and frustration when it is not. In the final analysis understanding the defence-media relationship might be confounded by something as basic as the mutual exclusivity of the definitions employed.

Related to this is the un-feasibility of analysing comprehensively the defence-media relationship over the last 23 years. To this writer's knowledge, such a study has not been done and, needless to say, this particular essay in this particular project is not the place to do it, nor could it be given the questions it would raise and the length of account they would require. Additionally, the criteria by which that relationship would be assessed are themselves problematic: who, for example, would define them? And by what right? In this light all that can be offered here is a fragment, a conversation according to the writer's position and intentions mentioned earlier. Even this somewhat truncates the unfeasible nature of the problem since, more fully, it has also to be seen against a background of official (state) structures – such as justifiable confidentiality and secrecy, legal constraints on reporting, and official deceit and black propaganda operations.

Third among the methodological issues is the definitional problem raised by the term 'terrorism'. The Northern Ireland situation, if the media is to be believed, is defined as a 'terrorist problem', a conflict between the 'terrorist' violence of (predominantly) the Provisional Irish Republican Army and the security forces. A difficulty arises, however, when acts manifestly not 'terrorist' are nevertheless described as though they were. In the final analysis the currency of the term is debased and reportage of events distorted. The term, then, needs to be approached sceptically.

Hitchens practises this analytical virtue by suggesting that, since the

English language is rich with words which describe individuated acts of violence, writers in that language might, with advantage use them and offers the following examples:

1. One who fights a foreign occupation of his country without putting on a uniform: guerrilla or *guerillero*; partisan; (occasionally) freedom fighter.
2. One who extorts favours and taxes on his own behalf while affecting to be a guerrilla: bandit; brigand; pirate.
3. One who wages war on a democratic government, hoping to make it less democratic: nihilist; (some versions of) fascist, anarchist, Stalinist.
4. One who gives his pregnant fiancée a suitcase containing a bomb as she boards a crowded airliner: psychopath; murderer.
5. One who cuts the throat of an unarmed civilian prisoner while he lies in a shallow grave and buries him still living after inviting an American photographer to record the scene: Contra.
6. One who directs weapons of conventional warfare principally at civilian objectives: war criminal.
7. One who believes himself licensed to kill by virtue of membership in a religious or mystical fraternity: fanatic; (traditionally) assassin.[23]

The advantage, of course, would derive from the fact that distinctions obliterated by the convenience of 'terrorism' would become more apparent and perhaps even facilitate an increased understanding of the practice of violence in Northern Ireland, no matter by whom committed. To date, it has to be said, language, thought, and as a result, understanding, have been economised upon.

What is sometimes called the 'political economy of the mass media' provides the fourth methodological issue inasmuch as it problematizes the conventional wisdom concerning the role of the press in democratic societies. Especially important in this regard is what Walter Lippmann, writing in the early 1920s, referred to as the 'manufacture of consent'. Essentially Lippmann had in mind the propaganda function which, among others, he and many writers on public opinion, saw the media fulfilling on behalf of popular government. Obviously, this is a function contrary to the image of the media as dedicated searchers for truth, yet one difficult to dismiss in view of studies of how elite consensus largely structures all facets of the news. In scope and explanation Edward S. Herman and Noam Chomsky's 1988 institutional critique of the media outlines the extent of the challenge to commonly-held (mis) perceptions:

> Most biased choices in the media arise from the preselection of right-thinking people, internalized ownership, organization, market, and political power. Censorship is largely selfcensorship, by reporters and commentators who adjust to the realities of source and media organizational requirements, and by people at higher levels within media organizations who are chosen to implement, and have usually internalized, the constraints imposed by proprietary and other market and governmental centres of power.
>
> There are important actors who do take positive initiatives to define and shape the news and to keep the media in line. It is a 'guided market system' that we describe here, with the guidance provided by the government, the leaders of the corporate community, the top media owners and executives, and the assorted individuals and groups who are assigned or allowed to take constructive initiatives. These initiators are sufficiently small in number to be able to act jointly on occasion, as do sellers in markets with few rivals. In most cases, however, media leaders do similar things because they see the world through the same lenses, and subject to similar constraints and incentives, and thus feature stories or maintain silence together in tacit collective action and leader-follower behaviour.[24]

The general implications for this project are twofold: first, easy analytical access is afforded by the media consensus; and second, alternative or different views will be marginalised, even where they might more closely accord with the events they are describing. In both instances the ostensible democratic character of the media is compromised.

Given the nature and scope of the fourth problem, the fifth problem may be regarded as of no great consequence in terms of the press but a cause for something approaching despair in terms of the informed consent on which popular government is based. In brief, the fifth issue concerns both literacy and the discursive economy of television news presentations. At a more basic level the former translates to the ability to read, understand and reflect upon complex happenings and ideas, while the latter refers to the packaging of these same phenomena within sound and vision bites seldom of more than two minutes duration.

In so far as literacy is a prerequisite for informed consent the indications in the United States are that its absence – illiteracy, and its adjunct, alliteracy – is increasingly the norm. To be sure, the United States is not the rest of the world, nor is this writer attempting such a juxtaposition. But since it is the case that US society prefigures many if not all of the social pathologies which accompany intellectual, social and economic life in advanced, Western, industrialized societies, then it will be asserted here that the rise of illiteracy in the US holds considerable significance for the societies which are interested in this overall defence-media project. And since, also, this essay foreshadowed its reliance upon tendencies at the outset, it is no less legitimate at this point to observe a particular, debilitating proclivity than at any other.

If such an approach is indeed conceded as legitimate, then illiteracy has the most profound implications for the ways in which the 'informed consent of the governed' is at all meaningful. Literally dozens of studies have been conducted on illiteracy in the US over the past 20 years; many of the findings in these are summarised in Jonathan Kozol's *Illiterate America*, a truly devastating account of that country's malaise. Depending on the level of competence examined, but at all times relying on the most cautious of estimates, *no less than 34 per cent of the adult population of the US are functionally illiterate*. Some estimates, also careful in their bases for calculation, put this figure at 48 per cent.[25] And to this must be added the alliterate (those with the ability but without the inclination to read) in the population which Neil Postman reports the Librarian of Congress suggests is equal to Kozol's conservative estimate of illiteracy.[26]

Translated into effect: in 1988, when the US Navy was deployed in the Persian Gulf and the Iran-Iraq War had been under way for eight years, and hence the area had appeared almost daily in the news, survey data indicated that fully 75 per cent of adult Americans did not know where the Gulf is. In addition, despite the fact that the Nicaraguan Contras had received hundreds of millions of dollars of US support and figured in a presidential scandal, 45 per cent of adult Americans surveyed could not identify Nicaragua on a map. (But then over 14 per cent could not even identify the United States on a map of the world, with country names removed). In this context of knowledge about the world the USA vied for sixth place (with the United Kingdom) of 13 countries surveyed.[27]

If the illiteracy figures are accurate, and their consistency over time regardless of the organisation conducting the survey indicates almost irrefutably that they are, then the role of the press is relevant to only a small 'reading elite'. More, to the extent that the non-reading remainder obtain information at all about affairs in general and limited conflict in particular, it is obtained from the electronic media, most probably television. In which case, the discursive economy which operates therein will have the effect of maintaining the high levels of ignorance already documented.

If it is accepted that the media are, *inter alia*, part of a consensus-manufacturing process, that the press is not widely read, and that the high levels of documented ignorance probably have something to do with *what* news, and the *way* that news is presented on (predominantly) commercial television, then Hitchens is also probably close to the truth when he writes of US network television's mini-seminars on current political issues: '. . . they are indistinguishable in style, supplying three identical brands of audio-visual chewing gum for the vacant mind.'[28]

Hitchens, moreover, is not alone: Postman, Russell Baker and David Halberstam, just to name three other prominent commentators, have pointed to the same travesty as it effects the transmission of news and affairs.[29] Collectively, though Halberstam will be cited more than the others here, their analyses are relevant to any society in which entertainment, and the need to entertain has come to dominate politics (including, of course, the distinct possibility that politics has become, or is perceived to be a form of entertainment). News must, therefore, *never bore*. Since boredom has consequences for ratings (i.e., profits), news must, therefore, attract viewers and it does so, across the networks on the principle: If it bleeds, it leads.[31]

Accordingly, Halberstam concludes news and current affairs are not only presented by 'anchors' who are 'stars', but such status as a news item or news programme has is significantly determined by the personality profile of the presenter.[32]

The results are distressing and ironic. Distressing because news and current affairs are trivialised, foreshadowing logically, the trivialisation of politics which constitutes, one way or another, much of what news and current affairs is about. Brief sound/vision bites dominate presentation in such a way that those who appear on television know they must simplify their positions in order to appear in control of the issues at hand and to satisfy the temporal economy of programming. In the end this simplification becomes such an habitual denial of complexity that thought, overall, is the object of ritual abuse. And ironic because, within the process described, the most available and critical means of communication in a mass democratic society is blocked; and because no matter how constitutionally free the TV journalists might be, their form is not free. As Halberstam points it: 'Form dictates function.... what is lost is thoughtful civility of discourse.'[33]

Predictable Consequences in the Case of Northern Ireland

Deductively, three effects or outcomes may be anticipated on the basis of the analysis above. They are that the defence – media relationship would lead to:

1. a deformed character of reporting by the media on Northern Ireland;
2. the inscription of certain 'myths' concerning the nature of the issues subsumed under the heading of the 'Northern Ireland Question', and
3. the presence of 'silences' – questions, issues or problems not addressed – in media accounts.

By the same method of argument a justification in law which required or buttressed such practices might also be expected although this condition would not be mandated.

A survey of the literature supports the logic of this approach. Indeed, when informed by the work of, *inter alia*, Michael Bromley,[34] Liz Curtis,[35] John Kirkaldy,[36] Ed Moloney[37] and Philip Schlesinger,[38] a particularly compelling case emerges in respect of the deformed character of reporting on Northern Ireland. From the vantage point of 1988, Moloney, for example, identifies three phases in the British, Irish, and international media's coverage of events there. Of the first of these, the period 1968–74, he finds the coverage characterised 'by all the healthier aspects of journalism – curiosity, indignation, scepticism, and a wish to inform and explain'. In short, he continues, it was a time in which 'many journalists felt it obligatory to question all assumptions, particularly those handed down by the people in power'.[39] And the events in question, of course, were of a type which could catalyse this disposition – the use of British troops in aid of an increasingly bankrupt civil power; violent civil unrest; the re-emergence of para-military organisations; anti-Catholic pogroms by elements of the local security forces; incipient civil war; internment of suspects without trial; presumptively unlawful killing by the military ('Bloody Sunday'); and, eventually, the suspension of the Northern Ireland Government by the United Kingdom Parliament at Westminster.

The second period he dates from the 1974 success of the Ulster Workers' Council strike which broke the power-sharing Northern Ireland Executive. This event, to many a neo-Fascist putsch, served to emphasise a common theme in much of the writing on the Troubles: '. . . the hopelessness of the problem, underlining what appeared to be an essential truth – that there was no solution.'[40]

From 1974 until the early 1980s this 'weary belief' imbued accounts of a Northern Ireland returned to what was, and still is known as Direct Rule (by and from Westminster). Stereotypes of the protagonists and descriptions of the relations between them which implied analytical closure were dominant. Both intentionally and inadvertently Northern Ireland, with all of its complexities, was being 'forgotten' out of understanding in favour of a more simple formulation. The parties to the conflict were recalled, according to previous habits, as 'incompatible Paddies', the violence was 'mindless' and, once again above all, the problem 'insoluble'.[41] Caricatures not only abounded but in some cases were encouraged from unlikely sources. One was Ireland's brilliant, enigmatic man of letters and affairs, the iconoclast Dr Conor Cruise O'Brien. In his 1972 work (published in paperback in 1974), *States of Ireland*, a part autobiography, part history, part diary, part political analysis, he had recourse to the Old Testament for a metaphor to explain what he saw as the *tribal* dimension to the Troubles: 'One could say that Ireland was inhabited, not really by Protestants and Catholics but by two sets of imaginary Jews.'[42] The point here is not Dr Cruise O'Brien's scholarship (or the literary bases upon which he developed this theme); on the contrary, and as usual, it was formidable. It is, however, to suggest that, in explaining one of Europe's most intransigent political and religious problems in terms of one of the Levant's most intransigent political and religious problems, he might actually have been contributing to its mystification. His views are also of significance in the light of his subsequent cabinet position in the Fine Gael-Labour coalition government (1973–77) as Minister of

Posts and Telegraphs and his appointment in the late 1970s as Editor-in-Chief of the *Observer* in London.

In the prevailing mood, and given the prevailing simplifications, Northern Ireland became a subject for decontextualised reporting. Contemporaneous violence, for the most part devoid of analysis, was recounted in both the British and Irish media in a desultory fashion. In all, it is difficult to disagree with Moloney's view that boredom had effectively seized the public mind in all relevant constituencies outside the Six Counties.[43]

Then, in 1981–82, a third phase of media coverage was made imperative by developments once more deemed to be more dramatic than those of the previous seven or so years. Initially, with the prison hunger strikes of 1981, and then Sinn Fein's relative popularity at the ballot box in the following year, a reappraisal of Northern Ireland was deemed imperative. For seven years (at least) the Northern Ireland Question had, as a result of British Government and Loyalist insistence, been presented as a security question; yet, after seven years there was not only no sign of a victory over the IRA, but there were even undeniable indications that the Provisional movement was a moral polity. Questions of the type asked in the first years of the Troubles once again, therefore, appeared in the media, as did analysis. By the mid-1980s, the media it seemed, had rediscovered its role:

> For the first time in over a decade journalists and politicians were forced to question why so many people supported organisations like the IRA. What was there about British policies in the security and economic fields, in the behaviour of the British Army, the RUC, the UDR, the courts and the Unionists that led thousands of normal and otherwise peaceable people to believe that the only way to deal with them was through the bomb and the bullet? Was this a new phenomenon brought about by British handling of the hunger strikes or something that had been there all the time – hidden, camouflaged, festering, and wished away or deliberately ignored?[44]

This third phase, however, only arguably exists in 1991. Indeed, it is doubtful whether it survived intact beyond the mid- 1980s when London and Dublin signed the Anglo-Irish Agreement in 1985. Agreements, it also, seems energised the media – as though they represented a 'solution', and thus a rationale for diminished curiosity. Moloney, in 1988 raises this possibility in regard to 1985 and this writer suggests that he was right to do so, particularly with regard to the media's analyses of the Brooke initiative of early 1991. The reflex to welcome a negotiated settlement, perhaps *any* negotiation, as though it was a panacea, though understandable, appears now to be a feature of media coverage of Northern Ireland. In truth, however, it contributes to the on-going tragedy of the province since it constructs a 'reality' which just encourages – by not challenging – propositions that are frequently bankrupt or seriously flawed.

The BBC is deserving of special consideration in this regard because of its internationally respected status as an independent broadcaster. Significantly, a most thorough and meticulously documented account of its performance accords with Moloney's depiction of the second phase of media coverage of Northern Ireland – that marked by dereliction. In Philip Schlesinger's reconsideration of his 1978 study of BBC News, *Putting 'Reality' Together*, he details state intervention, ahistorical and decontextualised reports of violence, and superficiality as characteristics of that organisation's (and most of the rest of the British media's) coverage of Northern Ireland.[45] He writes of 'a decline in both the frequency and quality of debate' in the period since the early 1970s and that a 'general indifference has reigned', increasingly tolerated by the public.[46]

With this study in mind it is, perhaps, not surprising that, in the period 1968–83, 45 television programmes on the North of Ireland, scheduled for BBC and other outlets, were subject to state inter- ference by way of being banned, censored, or delayed.[47] In the period since then, the trend at least is continuing, as witness the furore which attended Thames Television's documentary, 'Death on the Rock'.[48]

In Northern Ireland itself, a combination of tendencies produced virtually the same effect, noted earlier in relation to the post-1974 coverage, in the *Belfast Telegraph*. As Michael Bromley explains, this newspaper had, for the previous decade and a half, been unique:

> At the height of its popularity the paper probably penetrated virtually every household in the province; as commonly read by Protestants as by Catholics, and was from 1960 the only paper generally circulating in Northern Ireland without an overt, direct connection with one of the major national political or religious groupings.[49]

As well, it was seen as standing apart from 'the all-pervading tribal attitudes' which beset Northern Ireland.[50]

Within its structural orientation to its circulation area it adhered to an ethic which emphasised Ulster's positive aspects (so as to promote investment and commercial development) while simultaneously disavowing violence on both sides of the sectarian divide.[51] Yet, as the Ulster Workers' Council strike progressed towards toppling the Catholic-Protestant power-sharing Executive in mid-1974, the *Belfast Telegraph*'s voice become confused and its ethic compromised. Within a short time it was supporting, as the best of available options, a return to Direct Rule from Westminster.[52]

Two coincident factors accounted for this transformation – commercial difficulties occasioned by a falling circulation and a readership which, whatever its various views, did not support the progressivist views of the *Belfast Telegraph*.[53] Its response was also twofold. It deemphasised the political (even abolishing the post of political editor!) and emphasised the 'human interest' and the 'professional'.[54] It became, essentially, a vehicle for entertainment and 'ephemeral interests' ('non-political populism').[55] Sacrificed in the process, however, was the political ethic which guaranteed its uniqueness: '... the central core of liberal unionism: the commitment to devolved community government, and the acceptance therein of the fundamental legitimacy of nationalist aspirations in Northern Ireland'.[56]

Reinforcing, but by no means causing the state of affairs outlined by critics of the media canvassed to this point, are certain legal controls exercised by both the British and Irish governments. As regards the former, and in brief, their effect is to require the media (in terms of the Prevention of Terrorism Act and the Emergency Provisions Act) to inform the police before interviews with, or witnessing the activities of paramilitary volunteers. Not to do so can result in charges being laid as can also happen if journalistic contacts are not identified.[57] In Ireland, Radio Telefis Eireann (RTE) is subject to such strict controls that it is effectively prohibited from interviewing, or reporting interviews with members of proscribed organisations (including Sinn Fein). Similarly, the press, though not subject to the same controls, are prohibited from publishing or printing 'incriminating', 'treasonable' or 'seditious' documents – effectively by the same proscribed organisations denied to the electronic media.[58]

The second predictable consequence foreshadowed earlier was that of 'myths' – extravagant propositions concerning nearly every dimension of the Northern Ireland conflict. Indeed, the study of the Troubles, including its reporting at times, has proved to be such a fascinating and seductive enterprise that many of those who have undertaken it seem to have done so with a somewhat perverse sense of openmindedness. Their assertions and conclusions have been arrived at unprejudiced by inquiring and unqualified by evidence to the contrary.

With the elapse of time a vision composed of a great number of elements which, in their repetition and publication, reinforced the whole so long as care was taken not to examine it for internal consistency or historical accuracy, the Provisional Irish Republican Army (IRA) is seen as an organisation lacking in grassroots or popular support which, nevertheless, persists in a bungling way in the conduct of its operations. So without appeal is the IRA that its meagre internal or domestic resources are insufficient; it is, therefore, involved with organised crime, including the drug trade, and is heavily dependent on foreign financial backing. It follows that the adoption of Marxism and Soviet influence over the IRA are viewed as logical consequences of this state of affairs. It also follows, again according to much of the literature, that the British government would never negotiate with the IRA; rather, the assured defeat of the terrorists would be pursued through a combination of firm political and military measures.

As has been argued elsewhere, in fact, however, the IRA is substantially different from some of the popular beliefs that are held about it. In fact, too, it is also the opposite of the type of organisation it is held to be according to fictional but popularly-held views. It needs to be seen, therefore, as a political and paramilitary movement which enjoys a considerable level of domestic support and is, in addition, well-endowed with its own resources. In so far as links with the criminal underworld are concerned the IRA not so much has links with organised crime, in some of its guises it *is* organised crime, but exercises a certain self-denial in the matter of drugs. Furthermore it is obliged to no foreign party for its continued existence; nor is its thinking dominated by alien ideologies. It exists, therefore, as an autonomous organisation, at times a peculiarly Irish state-within-a-state. That this description is appropriate is confirmed by the fact that London not only has seen fit, but seen it as necessary to negotiate with the IRA. But above all, it has proved resilient to the point where it is impossible to imagine Northern Ireland without the IRA.[59]

Where the third consequence – the presence of 'silences' – is concerned, the list is truly a lengthy one. At the community level Kirkaldy cites religion or religious issues such as censorship, contraception, church-state relations, divorce, education, mixed marriages, papal infallibility and the Orange Order. And more directly related to the violence and those who commit it, he names the relations between paramilitary protection rackets, illegal drinking dens, Protestant paramilitary links with the UDR and RUC, and IRA bank robberies. He also mentions 'black' propaganda operations and illegal intelligence activities by the state's security forces, as well as state pressure and harassment of journalists whose diligence was embarrassing to the government.[60] To these Moloney provides a further catalogue of unaddressed, or scantily addressed questions which have to do with understanding the motivation, sociology, recruitment, and survivability of the IRA and its manifest levels of support in the republican community. Not to address these, he implies, is wilfully to misunderstand a phenomenon now in evidence for some 23 years.[61]

From other perspectives still more pressing issues have been 'dealt' with by the same discursive practice. The patterns or cycles of Anglo-Irish relations and, within these, the Torture Case which ran from 1971 to 1978, were seldom seriously confronted by the British media. Despite the fact that British media reports had provided a substantial contribution to publicising the matters which led to the case originally, the extended time over which the case was heard stretched well into the post-1974 period and so it, too, became a casualty of the prevailing indifference.[62] And this leaves to one side the almost complete ignorance of the patterns of and motivations for the IRA's attacks in mainland Britain and Western Europe, both of which point to a doctrine of limited conflict beyond the borders of the Six Counties.[63] And it certainly 'forgets' the efficacy of violence – that as a result of violence, and nothing but violence – the British government has been obliged to think about Northern Ireland more seriously since 1968 than at any other time since partition.

The point here, it is probably necessary to repeat, is not to indict gratuitously the media but it is definitely to establish that the relationship between it and the state has been one in which much of substance has been left untouched. Moreover, to the extent that deformations, myths and silences operate at the level of popular belief (and disbelief) government remains above accountability and responsibility; the state, as the repository of the right and resources to legal violence, remains unchallenged, and the governed remain not only ignorant but also incapable of giving voice to an informed demand and consent.

Conclusion

If the media's project is to advance understanding as well as 'factual' knowledge (and the distinction between the two is frequently tenuous) and if, in a declaratory sense at least, the state acknowledges this project, then this essay points to a need for self-consciousness. If at the same time understanding is sought so as not to be strategically surprised and all that that implies, then it is essential that all parties to the defence-media relationship become aware of the problematic nature of their respective positions within structures which are culturally, socially, economically, politically, linguistically and historically determined or mediated. No aspect of the relationship, in these terms, is innocent or neutral; on the contrary all carry portents which, almost certainly, under certain circumstances, will be realised and thus find expression as 'observation' when they are, in fact, more implicated than that.

If these connections are themselves understood and made explicit in a manner not common at present, then in the case of Northern Ireland a better appreciation of the Troubles would eventually follow. Given that Northern Ireland is held to be a problem essentially within the domestic jurisdiction of the United Kingdom, such a critically aware disposition would, again almost certainly, engender a greater tension between defence and the media because the situation generally lacks an external 'Other' which initially provides a focus for unity. In time, however, the 'Other' would return because understanding guarantees it. Understanding would establish one thing beyond doubt, known to students of revolution but somehow lost in the day-to-day discourse on 'terrorism'. Oppressed men and women do not rebel – kill, fight, suffer and die – on a whim, or frivolously. They are not extras in a play with nothing better to do at a particular historical moment. They have, above all, a sense of grievance which is experienced so strongly that they would abrogate the norms of otherwise orderly and law-abiding lives to redress it. This, really, was the theme running through so many of the analyses which pointed to the deformations, myths and silences. Until such time as they are seen in this light, and until such time as they are no longer the prevailing language emerging from the defence-media relationship on Northern Ireland then, to borrow from Michael

Walzer, the critical role of the media will have been usurped by the promotional role of the apologist: 'defending with eyes resolutely closed what can no longer be defended with eyes open.'[64]

NOTES

1. I am grateful to Professor Oliver MacDonagh for first making me aware of this poem and also for suggesting, in two of his works, its relevance to the contexts of modern Ireland; see his *Ireland: The Union and its Aftermath* (London: Allen and Unwin, 1977), esp. pp140–41 (hereafter cited as MacDonagh, *Ireland*); and *States of Mind: A Study of Anglo-Irish Conflict 1780–1980* (London: George Allen and Unwin, 1983), esp. pp.13–14 (hereafter cited as MacDonagh, *States of Mind*).
2. A. T. Q. Stewart, *The Narrow Ground: Aspects of Ulster, 1609–1969* (London: Faber and Faber, 1977), p.16.
3. Ibid., p.15.
4. Albert Camus, *Resistance, Rebellion, and Death* (New York: Vintage, 1974), p.157.
5. Richard Rose, *Northern Ireland: A Time of Choice* (London: Macmillan, 1976), pp.26–27.
6. For these figures in the period 1969–75 see ibid., pp.24–25.
7. Christopher Hitchens, *Prepared for the Worst* (London: Hogarth, 1990), p.167 (hereafter cited as Hitchens, *Prepared for the Worst*).
8. MacDonagh, *Ireland*, p.142.
9. The ideas raised in this paragraph and elaborated upon subsequently, are derived from Bruce Wilshire's seminal work, *The Moral Collapse of the University: Professionalism, Purity, and Alienation* (Albany, NY: State Univ. of NY Press, 1990), esp. pp.xx and 255–56 (hereafter cited as Wilshire, *Moral Collapse of University*).
10. Ibid., pp.255–56.
11. Ibid., p.175 (for Dewey), and p.187 (for Buber).
12. Ibid., pp.190–91 (for all except Silone). For Silone see Michael Walzer, *The Company of Critics: Social Criticism and Political Commitment in the Twentieth Century* (London: Peter Halban, 1989), pp.101–16, and p.230 (hereafter cited as Walzer, *Company of Critics*).
13. Wilshire, *Moral Collapse of University*, pp.41–43.
14. Ibid., pp.42–43.
15. William Irwin Thompson, *The Imagination of an Insurrection: Dublin, Easter 1916* (New York: Harper & Row, 1972), pp.235–36.
16. Hitchens, *Prepared for the Worst*, p.345.
17. MacDonagh, *State of Mind*, pp.132–33.
18. T. P. O'Connor, *The Parnell Movement, With a Sketch of Irish Parties from 1843* (London: Kegan Paul, Trench and Co., 1886), p.557.
19. Richard Ned Lebow, *White Britain and Black Ireland: The Influence of Stereotypes on Colonial Policy* (Philadelphia: Institute for the Study of Human Resources, 1976).
20. John Peck, *Dublin from Downing Street* (Dublin: Gill and Macmillan, 1978), p.18.
21. James Callaghan, *A House Divided: The Dilemma of Northern Ireland* (London: Collins, 1973), p.117.
22. Ibid., p.2.
23. Hitchens, *Prepared for the Worst*, p.301.

24. Edward S. Herman and Noam Chomsky, *Manufacturing Consent: The Political Economy of the Mass Media* (New York: Pantheon, 1988), p.xii.
25. Jonathan Kozol, *Illiterate America* (New York: Anchor/Doubleday, 1985), pp.2–12.
26. Neil Postman, *Conscientious Objections: Stirring Up Trouble About Language Technology and Education* (New York: Knopf, 1988), esp. pp.64 and 111 (hereafter cited as Postman, *Conscientious Objections*).
27. Kelly Griffin, 'American Know-how: 1-in-7 lost in space', The *Australian*, 29 July 1988, p.7.
28. Hitchens, *Prepared for the Worst*, p.320.
29. See Postman, *Conscientious Objections*, pp.72–81; Russell Baker, *So This is Depravity and Other Observations* (New York: Congdon and Lattes, 1980), pp.112–114; and David Halberstam, *The Next Century* (New York: William Morrow, 1991), pp.99–108 (hereafter cited as Halberstam, *Next Century*, p.104).
31. Ibid., p.105.
32. Ibid.
33. Ibid., pp.106–7.
34. Michael Bromley, 'War of Words: The *Belfast Telegraph* and Loyalist Populism', in Alan O'Day and Yonah Alexander (eds.), *Ireland's Terrorist Trauma: Interdisciplinary Perspectives* (New York: Harvester Wheatsheaf, 1989), pp.213–223 (hereafter cited as Bromley, 'War of Words').
35. Liz Curtis, *Ireland: The Propaganda War* (London: Pluto, 1984), hereafter cited as Curtis, *Propaganda War*.
36. John Kirkaldy, 'Northern Ireland and Fleet Street: Misreporting a Continuing Tragedy', in Yonah Alexander and Alan O'Day (eds.), *Terrorism in Ireland* (London: Croom Helm, 1984), pp.171–200 (hereafter cited as Kirkaldy, 'Northern Ireland and Fleet Street').
37. Ed Moloney, 'The Media: Asking the Right Questions?', in Michael Farrell (ed.), *Twenty Years On* (Dingle, Co. Kerry: Brandon, 1988), pp.134–46 (hereafter cited as Moloney, 'Asking the Right Questions?').
38. Philip Schlesinger, 'Terrorism, the Media, and the Liberal-Democratic State: A Critique of the Orthodoxy', in Alexander and O'Day work detailed in preceding note, pp.213–32; and *Putting 'Reality' Together: BBC News* (London: Methuen, 1987), hereafter cited as Schlesinger, *Putting 'Reality' Together*.
39. Moloney, 'Asking the Right Questions?', pp.142–43.
40. Ibid., p.143.
41. Ibid.
42. Conor Cruise O'Brien, *States of Ireland* (St Albans, Herts: Panther, 1974), p.287–88.
43. Moloney, 'Asking the Right Questions?', pp.143–44.
44. Ibid., p.146.
45. Schlesinger, *Putting 'Reality' Together*, p.243.
46. Ibid., p.xxi.
47. Curtis, *Propaganda War*, pp.279–90.
48. See Roger Bolton, *Death on the Rock and Other Stories* (London: W.H. Allen, 1990), and *The Windlesham/Rampton Report on 'Death on the Rock'* with a foreword by Sir Ian Trethowan (London: Faber, 1989).
49. Bromley, 'War of Words', p.213.
50. Ibid.
51. Ibid., pp.215–18.
52. Ibid., pp.220–24.
53. Ibid., pp.224–25.
54. Ibid., pp.226–28.

55. Ibid., pp.227–29.
56. Ibid., p.229.
57. Gerard Hogan and Clive Walker, *Political Violence and the Law in Ireland* (Manchester: Manchester University Press, 1989), p.158.
58. Ibid., pp.267–69.
59. For an analysis and rebuttal of these myths see Michael McKinley, 'Matters of Fiction and of Fact: Reading and Misreading the Contemporary IRA', *Journal of the Royal United Services Institute of Australia*, Vol.8 (Dec. 1985): pp.23–33 (hereafter cited as McKinley, 'Matters of Fiction and of Fact').
60. Kirkaldy, 'Northern Ireland and Fleet Street', pp.192–94.
61. Moloney, 'Asking the Right Questions?', pp.144–45.
62. For an account of the Anglo-Irish Politics of this issue see Michael McKinley, 'Ireland, Britain and the Strasbourg Torture Case', *Conflict* Vol.7, No.3 (1989): pp.249–83.
63. McKinley, Matters of Fiction and of Fact, pp.26–27.
64. Michael Walzer, *The Company of Critics*, p.227.

The Falklands War: A Commander's View of the Defence/Media Interface

MAJOR-GENERAL SIR JEREMY MOORE, RM (RETD)

In early autumn 1982 our Chief of Defence Staff sent me to Washington for a couple of days to address various governmental and other bodies on the subject of Operation 'Corporate' and the repossession of the Falkland Islands after the Argentine invasion on 2 April that year. As I recall it, I gave some five talks, and in the question periods following these, as well as on half a dozen other occasions, was repeatedly asked how it was that we (the British) had so successfully managed our media relations that our PR policy at least appeared to have had a positive effect on the outcome of the conflict – though even at the time I thought that what was really in the mind of the questioner was 'had avoided a negative effect ...'.

From this visit I returned overnight to Heathrow in order to make my way to London, to join up with my colleague the then Rear-Admiral Sandy Woodward, so that we could appear before the House of Commons Select Committee on Defence, to give evidence as part of their investigation into how it had come about that we had made such a disastrous mess of our handling of publicity and the media during the campaign. Well, that is what we thought we were appearing for, and I am quite certain it is what the majority of our national media thought we were appearing for. I am not now quite so sure that that is the way the Committee saw it. It may be interesting to wonder why we were so sensitive on the subject. Possibly you may conclude that something further may have emerged upon that by the time my address is over this afternoon. The point just now is, of course, to stress how different the view may appear depending upon the vantage point from which it is seen.

The second point I would like to make by way of introduction is that, because we are all, as everyone is aware, the prisoners of our past, my own past now inevitably includes the electrifying events in the Gulf in January and February just past. I was concerned, when first thinking about this, that they might divert me from what I was invited to come here to talk about. Well; that may be the case, for my invitation to this conference came early last July, but, after further thought, I have concluded that my reactions to the more recent events, in the light of my earlier experiences, are relevant to the conference theme and I will therefore devote a few minutes to them after giving you some views on the Falkland episode itself.

My preparations for this talk were, indeed, much easier; certainly very much more straightforward; before last August. My materials, were mostly assembled by the end of July, I had the papers I needed, I had a pretty good idea what I wanted to say; and there were five months before the end of 1990 in which to go through it all. I even allowed myself to think that perhaps I might make a nicely rounded case to show how I thought things could go, and how I would react to events, next time round. Naturally they didn't; and I didn't!

I now have, later by a war of wholly different dimensions, and of even shorter duration; by a score or so of broadcasts on the UK media; and a dozen rethinks; considerably recast my thoughts. I am not sure that most, indeed many, of my conclusions are that radically different, but how one arrived at them has often been markedly complicated.

The Practical Difficulties for a Soldier in 1982

I think the first thing that needs to be said about this war is to remind ourselves that it was not only a very short war – the whole period of operations was some six and a half weeks, of land operations about three and a half – it was also a very remote war, without any facilities for flying correspondents or Service people in or out over the last 4,000 miles. It was mounted at great speed and without any serious belief among many of those involved when the Task Force sailed, that it really was going to come to serious fighting. Brian Hanrahan, who was after all *the* television presenter for the national broadcasting corporation, was not even a defence correspondent; he just happened to be the general reporter who was on duty that weekend.

This situation was bound to lead to a fair degree of frustration among editors and media people in general back at home. The operation was being conducted using what were inevitably limited shipborne communications systems, shared between the media and the military who, hardly surprisingly, were inclined to give a higher priority to operational messages than to media coverage. There were of course no host country civilian systems available to correspondents; at least not until we got into Port Stanley; further causes of frustration for both correspondents and their editors, who were inevitably stuck with what they had, and were unable to react to developments when things got under way. Add to that the serious lack of movement facilities, i.e., helicopters – especially after the loss of *Atlantic Conveyor* with three quarters of our medium/heavy lift support transport, and a fair quantity of our other administrative lift capability before the ground forces even moved forward from the beachhead area.

The correspondent's only other means of transport was, like the soldier's, his feet. Some correspondents like Max Hastings, then of the *Evening Standard*, now Editor of the *Daily Telegraph*, presented pretty unlikely looking figures when it came to tramping about the hills and bogs – and as you would expect one or two sergeants-major let them know of this! On the whole, however, they made a very fair fist of getting to the best, or at least the next best, vantage points.

Before my next observation it is worth pointing out that as the operation developed I found myself acting in several quite distinct capacities. Once the amphibious force had been mounted out from its home ports I served for the next six weeks as the Land deputy to the Commander-in-Chief Fleet (Admiral Sir John Fieldhouse), who was the overall commander (the Commander Task Force) of Operation 'Corporate', at his Headquarters in Northwood, a few miles west of London. Only later did I travel south and take over command of the land forces ashore in the islands in time for the arrival of the second brigade at the end of May.

In these early six weeks I was of course near the centre in Whitehall and Westminster. I was thus reasonably close to the political developments as well as the military conduct of operations. It is interesting, I think, to compare the reaction, and the readiness for the type and scale of media attention which would focus upon matters, of those of us coming from different backgrounds.

For instance the Royal Navy clung still, I think (and remember that though a soldier I do speak as a member of the Senior Service) to a tradition of being 'the silent Service'. Other than a fair amount of attention (most of it as I recall not very helpful to our case) over the

Cod War in the 1970s, it had conducted its affairs largely out of the limelight. Admiral Woodward, as he has subsequently said, and particularly because he was by specialisation a submariner – as was the Commander-in-Chief – had not previously been subject to much media attention. This he has told me, led him to an at times rather naive – I think he would say – approach, and to a number of statements which subsequently caused him some embarrassment.

We soldiers, on the other hand, had been accutely aware of the important place public information must take in our thinking at least since the current round of Troubles in Northern Ireland blew up in 1969. I myself had served in the Province as a Commanding Officer in 1972 and 1973. All of us had given serious thought and study to the matter and undertaken training. This training had not merely been in interview techniques; though I think that does play a greater part in the development of full understanding of the problem than its immediate objectives might suggest; but also in the whole history and development of the public image of our role and conduct of affairs. I had had practical experience of the matter in some pretty sensitive situations on the streets of Belfast, and, subsequently as the commander of a Joint International Brigade which often exercised in areas where there were strong anti-military or anti-foreigner local feelings. I'm not sure I'd claim this experience made me any less concerned about the matter than my bluewater colleagues, but I do think my formation (the Land Forces) was better prepared to cope at almost all levels.

In our war, while they always preferred in any case to deal with servicemen rather than civil servant PROs, I think that our small press corps would have said almost to a man – most of them have – that they would always have sought out my Public Relations Officer where they could. At that time, I think we in the Land Forces were better prepared to cope with the problems at all levels than our Naval colleagues. I do not though suggest that the difference still exists.

There was another difference which I observed between my time in Northwood and the way things were when I got down to the operational area. As Land Deputy to the Commander-in-Chief, I was always reasonably content, in principle, with appearing on the media to give any briefings on matters in my field of responsibility which might be appropriate, despite the added strain and consumption of valuable time involved. We were certainly clear on the considerable advantages to be gained by having briefings given by as senior a commander as could be made available to do so.

For instance, after the successful recapture of South Georgia at the end of April, it was our intention that I would myself give the definitive brief on the operation at a major press conference in the Ministry of Defence. However, for reasons which were never explained, we received instructions that no-one above the rank of Lieutenant-Colonel in the Northwood HQ was to appear on television. One can only surmise as to the reason for this – to me – quite extraordinary order, but I find myself inevitably concluding it was political.

Incidentally this particular brief was most successfully, indeed in my view most impressively, given by a lieutenant-colonel from my staff, and we were shortly afterwards told that in future no Service officers were to appear on television. Thereafter all Ministry of Defence briefings were given (under instruction) in a deliberately deadpan manner by a civil servant, whom someone unkindly – but not entirely inappropriately – christened 'The Humanoid I-speak-your-weight Machine'.

Once I had moved to the South Atlantic and taken over the command of the Land Forces, I was of course once again in control of my own destiny. I did not in fact conduct any regular series of briefings for our small press corps (they totalled only 29 souls), but that, I think, had less to do with any deliberate policy than with the practicalities in the circumstances (which I have already mentioned) of gathering them together.

I did of course meet several of them quite early on – including a most awkward interview with Brian Hanrahan on board the flagship, at which I appeared enveloped in a vast fluorescent orange immersion suit (while Sandy Woodward, dammit, looked as spic and span as could be!). I felt I was portraying more the image of a wounded duck – Donald Duck at that – than a vigorous, thrusting commando general.

What I missed was an opportunity for a reasonably full, off the record, discussion with the journalists to make plain to them what my policy would be. I did try to make sure they knew, as opportunities arose to make the point, that I would always be prepared to seek time to talk with them about what was going on. I like to think that they accepted, in return, that if I said 'Not now', that was because I really did judge there were even more important things I ought to be doing at that moment, and was not just a ploy to avoid awkward questions.

I think we did on the whole establish a pretty good rapport, though perhaps that was not too difficult while we were seen to be winning. Maybe it would have been different if we had been losing, or have been thought to have been losing. The relationship did however take rather longer to establish than I would have liked.

And now I will move on to a short discussion of the principal matters which concerned me with regard to the effects of the media coverage on our war and its prosecution, as opposed to the practical enabling measures so far addressed.

I think I would be justified in describing my understanding of the role of the press, even in time of conflict, as reasonably liberal. I joined the Service just after the end of the Second World War, so had spent virtually the whole of my 35 years' service, as I saw it, defending the public's right to be informed about what was going on, and what was being done in its name. Naturally I was also aware of the necessity to maximise the government's reasonable freedom of manoeuvre, and this was made even more apparent by my observation of the working of the War Cabinet while I was still at Northwood.

I do not subscribe to the view that once the public has been told that it has gone to war it then only has the right to be informed when it has won. I do believe in the dissemination of information as soon as it can be given; in adhering, as far as is possible, to the truth; and in being blunt about what one is not prepared to discuss. But at the same time I know all too well that in war very little is ever as straightforward as journalists would quite reasonably like it to be.

Nevertheless, it is I imagine no surprise that my main concerns in 1982, or at least the first three of them, reflected my own responsibilities as an operational commander. These three matters were:

1. The danger of the revelation of information which might be useful to the enemy.
2. The maintenance of the morale of the troops for whom I was responsible.
3. The positive use of media coverage to aid my operations by judicious use for the purposes of deception.

I will now take each of these three areas in turn and will then move on to a matter of a more personal nature.

1. The Revelation of Information to the Enemy

The danger of information being revealed to the enemy came in several guises. One of the most interesting features to me, during April and May, was the number of interviews conducted on television with my former seniors, in which they were asked, and it seemed to me explained in some detail, just how I would be likely to operate, and what were our Standard Operating Proceedures for the conduct of an amphibious landing. One, I have been told, also gave a run down of the possible landing areas in the Islands and explained the merits and drawbacks of each. 'If only I could watch a series of programmes like these on General Menendez and his subordinates,' I thought, 'how very much more useful it would be than the less than one page document on him which my intelligence staff has been able to dig up!'

In the event I never did hear that any, let alone all, of this material did reach my opponent; but that did not prevent it causing me a lot of concern at the time. I shall return to this theme later on

The second area of concern under this heading is the danger of reporters picking up information and using it in their copy so that details of our plans, or parts of them, are compromised. There is I think little danger of such compromises occurring where all the correspondents are from one's own country, and even more so where they are attached to particular units. And I would point out that that last is less a cynical remark about self-preservation than a comment upon the very close sense of identity which will be transmitted by any good military unit even to outsiders serving with it. Certainly we did not suffer from this problem as a result of any reports made by any of our press representatives in the South Atlantic. A case did occur when an announcement was made on the BBC World Service news that 2nd Battalion the Parachute Regiment were about to capture Goose Green before the Argentine garrison had become aware of their approach, and it was reinforced – though not in the event effectively – at the last moment.

This infuriating announcement was I believe the result of some piece of ineptitude in London. It is arguable whether the most enraged man in the Falklands was the Commanding Officer of 2 Para or Robert Fox, the BBC Radio correspondent who was attached to him.

Finally there is the danger that in what is to him some perfectly normal activity, a journalist may in his ignorance and general lack of awareness of the imperatives of military security, give something away. We had a case in which one young reporter 'rang up' on the local telephone from one farm on the north side of the island well behind our lines for a chat with a fellow journalist at another farm on the south coast, and had a discussion referring to the units they were with, happily unaware that the telephone exchange which had put the call through was, in fact, in enemy-occupied Stanley. Five minutes with a quiet but exceedingly angry brigadier advanced his education quite a lot.

2. Maintenance of Morale

It is well enough known that considerable strength is to be drawn from good positive coverage of troops' activities. Having spent a good three-quarters of my service either at training establishments where 'leadership' was part of the everyday menu, or in operational appointments, I was of course well aware that one does nothing for morale, even in the worst circumstances, by trying to conceal the truth from troops. I believed that on the whole our public too was a robuster animal than it has often been given credit for. I have to admit that that may have been helped by a degree of feeling that it was a bit of the home country which had been invaded – even after it had become clear to one and all that the Falkland Islands were not merely a couple of the remoter members of the Shetland group, but were on the far side of the world and in the opposite direction. This jingoism was also quite strongly reinforced by certain cheaper sections of the press, and fitted in with a strong lead from a powerful personality in Downing Street.

The field in which I felt some cause for concern over how the media might impinge on the morale of my troops was over the stress caused to families; which stress could then of course be transmitted to the troops themselves. In a war as short-lived as the one we are considering there was no time for the factor to have any serious bearing, but there were a number of cases of the grossest intrusion into privacy and of the most thorough bad taste, which did no good at all for the blood pressure of the Commander of the Land Forces. On the whole though, I would judge the media coverage of the war had quite a strong positive effect for the troops involved.

There is though also another matter which may be thought to have an effect upon morale in the aftermath of any war. This is the exploitation, it often seems to those affected simply for the sake of scandalmongering, of incidents which can be made to seem blameworthy, or even if enough hyperbole is used positively criminal, but which are as much a part of the battlefield as is the death of a fieldmouse in the talons of a bird of prey.

I shall refer again to such matters under another heading shortly, but I do not believe that, beyond a certain amount of short-term anger, largely directed against the media itself, I have come across any cases where I would judge there has been any longer-term effect upon morale.

3. Deception

Now we come to the exercise of a degree of control over the release of information for the purposes of deception. An excellent example was the expectation of an amphibious landing in the recent operations in the Gulf, but I would like to illustrate the matter by describing a particular plan of my own during the Falklands War, and the attempt made to exert this sort of control

I am afraid I must start by briefly setting the scene. From my assessment of the Argentines' background and what little I knew of their training in amphibious warfare, backed by the facts of their own landing and what intelligence we had managed to assemble of their subsequent defensive positions, I assessed that they expected us to make our main landing in the area to the south and south-west of Stanley. Even after it had become plain to them that we had made a substantial lodgement at San Carlos it seemed clear that they still expected another major landing much nearer and to the south of Stanley. If therefore I could keep them thinking this way I should be able to make life a whole lot easier for the troops making their actual attack from the mountains to the west and north west.

While 3rd Commando Brigade, who were already getting established in the mountains carried out their reconnaissance and made their plans, I aimed to keep attention focused the way it was by pushing 5th Infantry Brigade along the southern coastal strip, which also contained what was occasionally flatteringly called the only road. For reasons which there is no purpose in going into detail here, but which clearly centred on the lack of any other means, this move was largely made by sea; and it was near the end of this process that, in Port Pleasant at a settlement called Fitzroy, a flight of enemy aircraft caught the last half battalion still on board one of the landing ships and caused us over a hundred casualties.

When I discussed the incident with the Commander-in-Chief that evening I asked, I thought entirely justifiably – and he agreed – that the extent of the casualties we had suffered be withheld from publication for a couple of days (the next-of-kin would of course be informed as soon as possible), because I feared that if the enemy realised the full extent of the damage he had managed to cause he might feel able to withdraw one or more battalions from their present, southward-facing deployments to reinforce his positions in the mountains, for these were now being increasingly dominated by the vigorous patrolling of the commandos and parachutists in preparation for their attack. As far as I can recall I asked for about a two-day delay.

War being war, things did not work out like that! In the event the news was released in London; the enemy breathed a sigh of relief, and decided we could not be ready to mount an attack for at least another ten days; my logisticians did another of their wonders and halved the delay I expected. Two nights later 3rd Commando Brigade launched the night attack which carried all the Argentine outer ring of positions in the mountains and began the collapse of the Stanley defences.

The last experience I would like to tell you about from the Falklands is of a more personal nature. It is about stress. All commanders know that their responsibilities will bring stress; training and career structures are designed, as well as they may be in peacetime, to prepare them for it. In my own case, I had first had to cope with one of my men being killed when I was 22, one had experience of action at platoon, company and battalion level and was as well prepared for that element of stress as one could have been. I have also already explained about the build-up of experience I had been fortunate enough to have in coping personally with the importunities of journalists.

The one who was not was my wife, and neither, except in rare cases were the other wives; and their distress in being subjected to the attentions of tactless, tasteless and tendentious invasions of their privacy on the telephone or personally, transmitted itself to me. My own wife developed something of a siege mentality, and ended up thinking she was about to be invaded in her own home when reporters came beating on her door in the middle of the night, and told her she must have a statement to make. Her distress was not one whit the less because the most intrusive attacks (which is what she saw them as) came in relation to the good news – the surrender.

Our war, I remind you again, was a short one and there was not a lot of time for these pressures to transmit themselves to the husbands, but I wonder whether consideration ought not to be given to preparing the wives, at least of commanders, to cope with the problem. Given my time again, I would certainly have found a means of helping my own wife.

The other aspect of this pressure is in the aftermath of war. For myself, I found that coping with the too common desire of too much of the media to find something discreditable about someone to uncover, caused me almost as much anguish as anything that had occurred during the campaign itself. Though for some reason I have never been able to fathom, I myself was never the target of such attacks. My flight home in July 1982, which one might have thought would have been largely taken up with the pleasure of getting back to my family, was mostly occupied with agonising over what discourteous questions I was going to be targeted with at the airport press conference I knew was being arranged, and how to avoid being tricked into letting someone down.

The Experience of an Ex-soldier in 1991

In my section on the dangers of the revelation of information potentially useful to an enemy, I referred to the appearances on television in 1982 of a number of armchair generals and the concerns which this caused me at the time. It is therefore salutary that I reflect for a moment upon the fact that I have now become such a one myself, and I would like to describe to you the development of my thinking over these nine years.

My assessment of the impact of this factor in 1982; once the dust had had time to settle, and we had learned more about the Argentines' view of things, was that the appearances had probably been of no actual help to the enemy, but that they certainly could have been if they had been carefully studied by the Argentine intelligence staff and commanders. They did however, or rather some of them did, cause additional and perhaps unnecessary stress to our own commanders; or at least to this one.

In the following years therefore I gave some thought to what might be a proper reaction to events if another similar sort of event should arise. First reaction was simply to decline to appear on television or radio at all, but further thought led me to conclude that I might do better than that. If I were to take an opportunity to point out publicly the dangers and effects of giving explanations of the way our forces think and work, I hoped I might inhibit unhelpful discussion, and possibly even help to turn it in a more helpful direction. An arrogant thought maybe, but it did seem reasonable to assume that some at least of the media would be keen to get me on air.

And then came the Gulf Crisis; so how did I react in the event? I did indeed receive many approaches from all branches of the media. In the early days I (and, incidentally, my 1982 colleague Brigadier, now

Major–General Julian Thompson) declined to take any part in any speculation, on sand-table models etc., on the form any allied operations might take.

As 15 January 1991 approached I did begin to make some appearances and to give some interviews. For this purpose I had a fairly simple set of personal 'Rules of Engagement', which I invariably made clear to all producers and programmers who approached me, and which I also reiterated in the studio before each broadcast. I pointed out to the broadcasters that, hardly surprisingly, I identified with the soldiers and service people on the ground, and that therefore I chose only to appear in cases where I thought my doing so might be helpful to them, either directly or, more often, through their families and the public by informing the latter of, and explaining, the things which they would wish to have explained. I made clear that I would retain my freedom to reject any line of questioning I found unacceptable, and to explain in public why I found it so. One interviewer did ask such a question, I think knowingly, and I welcomed the opportunity this gave me to point out on air why it would be wrong to answer it. All of them, I think without exception, readily accepted my rules.

I think my sort of approach was not uncommon, and I also think the coverage, at least in the British media, was more balanced this time round.

Conclusion

My conclusion is brief.

I think that the two most recent incidents with which I have had any connection have both been too brief for the media to have had any unduly deleterious effect upon operations, though some of the political decisionmaking – which is of course outside my field – may have been more or less seriously influenced.

I remain sometimes astonished at the ability of even the so-called responsible media, while claiming not to have any political axe to grind, to smell the rat of conspiracy down the pipe of the sort of simple cock-ups which are so observably the normal and natural outcome of the simple human ineptitudes to which we are all subject – even when we are not under stress.

To try to ensure that this particular Pom does not get caught whingeing too much, I try to keep my sense of proportion alive with two maxims. Both of them, poor things though they may be, so far as I am aware, are mine own:

First, in *Decline and Fall*, Gibbon described corruption as '... the most infallible symptom of constitutional liberty'. I am inclined to steal the thought to suggest that a degree of the most abysmal bad taste may not at least be '... the most infallible symptom of a free press'. And that, God help me, is one of the principles I have spent a fair proportion of my life fighting to protect!

Second, it has occurred to me that an interview with the press might be described as like a passport photograph; no one seriously doubts that it is the result of a confrontation between the subject and a camera, but did you ever see one that was recognisable?

The Falklands War: A Critical View of Information Policy

DR KEVIN FOSTER

It is my assertion here that the Ministry of Defence's (MoD) information policy during the Falklands War, fostered in part by the military and sanctioned by the government, was a policy of propaganda. Sustained by censorship, it underpinned the government and the ministry's official line on the conflict. It will be the aim of this paper to explore why and how this policy was instituted, enforced and maintained, and to consider some of the lessons that the military and the media can take from their dealings with each other during the Falklands War.

When news of Argentina's invasion of the Falkland Islands broke on the morning of 2 April 1982, a bemused press corps besieged the MoD. Where were the Falklands? What had led Argentina to invade them and how would Britain respond? Service and civilian PR officers remained tight-lipped pending the arrival of policy guidelines on what they could and could not tell the media about the composition of the task force and its objectives. In the confusion, the most recent MoD brief on Information Policy in the event of armed conflict, prepared by ministry officials in 1977, was entirely forgotten. The MoD's acting Head of Public Relations at the time, the man charged with co-ordinating and implementing the ministry's information policy, was Ian McDonald.

A career civil servant, McDonald had been assistant secretary in charge of the ministry's pay and recruitment section until 1979. He had no professional experience of public relations. McDonald devised his own policy. He cancelled the unattributable briefings through which the military conducted its political battles, promoted itself and provided defence correspondents with the flow of information which sustained them. All news was now to be distributed in a daily communiqué delivered, usually, by McDonald himself. He later told the House of Commons Defence Committee's Enquiry into the Handling of Press and Public Information during the Falklands Conflict

(HCDC) that he had 'closed the door of my office and locked it and sat trying to think it out for five minutes'.[1] Plenty of time to boil an egg but hardly enough to resolve the competing demands of news and security.

McDonald claimed that by cancelling unattributable briefings he was denying useful information to the Argentines:

> There was a very strong feeling that in fact to talk about where the Fleet, the Task Force, was, how it was being split up as it sailed to the Falkland Islands, would be to give information to the Argentines about possible intentions. I did not see how, talking unattributably off the record, we would be able to avoid trespassing on those kind of areas.[2]

Starved of hard information, newspapers and the electronic media outdid each other with elaborate and often highly detailed depictions of anticipated events. Instead of a controlled flow of information in a single direction, McDonald's policy ensured a flood of speculation, guaranteeing a far freer treatment of potentially sensitive security issues. Three weeks before troops waded ashore at San Carlos, the beachhead had been located and announced in a major British daily newspaper. On 28 April, in an article discussing possible sites for the main landing published in the *Guardian*, David Fairhall observed that 'the most likely choice, from simply looking at the map, would seem to be somewhere round Port San Carlos, at the northern end of the Falkland Sound which divides the two main islands'.[3] Luckily for the Task Force the junta, no doubt, preferred *Newsweek*.

To the consternation of politicians and the military, so-called expert commentators, usually retired officers of senior rank, appeared on television, radio and in the press to authenticate such speculation. Bernard Ingham, the Prime Minister's press secretary, feared that the commentators' knowledge and discussion of strategy might betray the sort of thinking that the Argentines would soon be up against on the battlefield. In order to neutralise any inadvertant leaks, the First Sea Lord, Admiral Sir Henry Leach, proposed that a select team of retired senior service personnel be assembled. Briefed for the relevant task and made available to the military, they would then be 'on their guard accordingly to stop the indiscriminate speculation'.[4]

Many broadcasters dismissed Leach's proposal as a ploy to feed official misinformation through the mass media, and disputed whether the commentators posed a security threat at all. David Lloyd, editor of the BBC's 'Newsnight', attacked 'the idea that old General Menendez wouldn't have known to stay tight at Port Stanley until some former general had said so 'as "absolute nonsense"'.[5] Peter Snow, 'Newsnight's' presenter suggests that the military opposed the employment of expert commentators because it misunderstood the use to which the media would put them. More often than not the experts merely authenticated studio debate: 'we found them useful' claimed Snow 'just to give one a flavour of the sort of attitudes and language and temperament of the people involved in this exercise. Very rarely did we expect any one of them to come out with prophetic information about what they would do.... It was atmospheric'.[6]

Experts were rarely invited to speculate about possibly sensitive manoeuvres: when encouraged to do so most quite reasonably refused. Questioned about the Task Force's options after the sinking of HMS *Sheffield*, Group Captain David Bolton, Director of the Royal United Services Institute for Defence Studies, told the presenter of BBC Radio's 'Today:' 'it would be irresponsible to speculate on detailed consequences or the courses of action that [the Task Force commander] might have in mind'.[7] Transcripts confirm that 'the military commentators appearing on current affairs programmes rarely added much to the factual information being imparted'.[8]

The 'experts' were used not to open up new areas for discussion, but to put the final, legitimating seal on debates whose parameters, like their conclusions, were set. The structure of interviews, in which the presenter invited the commentator to qualify or endorse statements offered in the guise of questions, implies that opinions and the right to express them were rigidly controlled. The curtailment of open and genuine debate was the natural upshot of the ministry's information policy. This not only empowered the ministry to identify the issues at stake in the conflict and set the agenda for discussion, but also enabled it to shape the debate and predetermine its conclusions.

The culture of suppression fostered by the MoD and the military received a resounding political endorsement during the Emergency Parliamentary Debate at the House of Commons on 3 April 1982. The 'debate' was more of a rousing patriotic chorus, counterpointing condemnation of Argentina's 'foul and brutal aggression', with a sabre-rattling anthem to Britain's long and proud tradition of military reprisal.[9] On a day when bellicosity and bombast predominated there was little room and less tolerance for dissent. When Ray Whitney, Conservative MP for Wycombe, cautioned against the misuse of armed force and proposed a negotiated settlement, (which the Task Force was ostensibly dispatched to encourage), he was howled down. Indeed, his very right to express his opposition was challenged: 'If defeatism of this kind is to be spoken', asked John Biggs-Davison, 'should it not be done in secret session?'[10]

The MoD and the Navy were no subtler in their endeavours to fashion and sustain a climate of unanimity. In the first instance they refused to allow *any* media correspondents to travel with the Task Force. Subsequently, 10 were grudgingly allocated places. It was only what Michael Cockerell called 'the most violent media lobbying of No. 10 [Downing Street] in recent history' that assured places for 29 reporters, photographers, technicians and film crew. In a further move to stifle dissent, on at least one occasion the MoD was ready to recruit a reporter whom it felt it could rely upon for positive copy. Brigadier Ramsbotham, the Army's Director of Public Relations (DPR) at the MoD, noted that had Max Hastings not put himself forward he 'would certainly have contacted him anyway'[11].

Hastings did not disappoint the confidence placed in him. Though purportedly in the Falklands as an impartial observer writing for the London *Evening Standard* and the *Daily Express*, he was an unflagging advocate of the MoD's official line on the conflict. His reports promoted the abandonment of neutrality and a committed, patriotic coverage (and reading) of the campaign. In a front-page article for the *Express*, headlined 'WHY NONE OF US CAN BE NEUTRAL IN THIS WAR' Hastings outlined how he saw his job in the Falklands: 'simply to report as sympathetically as possible what the British forces are doing here today'. He quoted his father, Robin Hastings, the *Picture Post*'s 1944 correspondent in Normandy, as personal and professional guarantor for his position on the Falklands: 'When one's nation is at war, reporting becomes an extension of the war effort'.[12] His dispatches rarely ran foul of the censors, and on one occasion he was even allowed to use the SAS's own mobile satellite. link to transmit a laudatory account of their actions back to his newspapers, through SAS HQ at Hereford. Hastings' committed (or compromised) professionalism represented both the ministry and the military's ideal of how the war *could* be reported.

Those who, in the ministry's or the military's opinion, posed a threat to the war effort were simply denied a place with the Task Force. Donald McCullin, the British photo-journalist renowned for his graphic portrayal of the conflicts in Biafra and Vietnam, was consistently refused a passage. A senior civil servant denied that McCullin had been excluded because the ministry feared the consequences of his kind of war photography. He claimed that the two official photographers sent with the task force would be sufficient. They were not. There are no pictures of the battles for Darwin and Goose Green or many other of the conflict's most significant events. The shortage of photographers ensured a sanitised visual record of the war.

The refusal to grant McCullin a passage can be further explained as a symptom of the Vietnam neurosis which haunted the military and the MoD and was one of the crucial reference points for its own information policy. If Vietnam was 'invoked privately by the military as an object lesson in how not to deal with the media' then the Falklands provided the ideal opportunity to redraft the rules for military/media relations in wartime.[13] The first article of the new code stated that the media were no longer free to roam and report at will. As long ago as 1970, Air Vice-Marshal Sir Stewart Menaul claimed that television had 'a lot to answer for [in] the collapse of American morale in relation to the Vietnam War'. In the event of future conflict involving British forces: 'we would have to start saying to ourselves, are we going to let the television cameras loose on the battlefield?' pondered a director of defence operations at the MoD.[14]

Evidently this was a rhetorical question. The military's strict control over access to the battlefield not only dictated what the media could see but also decisively determined how they wrote about it. As men (and woman), unaccustomed to harsh physical conditions and attack from hostile forces, they relied upon the military to advise, equip and look after them. As reporters they were entirely dependant on the military's satellite facilities and ships for the transmission and transportation of their copy. As such, the media owed their lives and livelihoods to the men they were employed to observe and write about with detachment.

These professional and personal imperatives inevitably conflicted. The reporters identified with the units whose risks and hardships they shared at the cost of their professional disinterest. As David Norris of the *Daily Mail* recalled: 'I couldn't help but think of myself as part of the operation. I suppose people might say that that's a bad thing, you should still maintain some impartiality. It's very difficult. On shore I dressed like a soldier. I ate like them, I lived with them. I just began to feel a part of the whole things'.[15] So close were they to the military that the reporters were loathe to portray them unfavourably, thereby vetoing any critical analysis of the broader issues raised by the conflict. The combination of fear, personal loyalties and political proscription made Task Force correspondents, in the words of Gareth Parry of the *Guardian*, manageable, and even malleable to some extent'.[16]

One can hardly blame the journalists for identifying so closely with the forces or portraying them so sympathetically: nor can one condemn the military for making the most of the resulting good press. What one can take issue with, however, is the MoD's assertion that their dispatches represented 'the facts' or 'the truth' about the Falklands conflict. The 'facts' offered to the public as objective truths were premissed on a set of shifting, and yet narrowly defined political imperatives and descriptive determinants. Events or reports which flouted this orthodoxy were denied the status of 'facts', excised, discredited or downplayed. The journalists themselves were under no illusions about the impartiality of their reports. They recognised that reliance upon the military had compromised their independence. 'The situation' claimed Patrick Bishop of the *Observer*, 'was that you were a propagandist; that's how it turned out'.[17]

The MoD, of course, rejects the suggestion that it exercised a restrictive censorship policy or dealt in propaganda during the Falklands War. To some extent this results from its fastidiousness about the terms and the associations they have accrued over the past 60 years. Because of its iconic association with Dr Josef Goebbels, propaganda has been defined, since the early 1930s, as both a symbol and a tool of political repression.[18] In Britain, according to Peter Beck, 'propaganda has been viewed as a rather dubious, disreputable and un-British activity, clearly something of which no British government could be guilty. . . . Consequently, British people have been accustomed to regard "propaganda" as a dirty word'.[19] They have given equally short shrift to propaganda's faithful minion, censorship. Yet there is no natural connection between censorship, propaganda and political repression. This connection depends on the kind of expression silenced by the censorship or promoted by the propaganda.

The MoD claimed that its information policy for the Falklands Conflict, such as it was, was based on 'the overriding dictates of national and operational security and the protection of the lives of our servicemen and servicewomen'.[20] Few would seek to subvert these considerations, least of all the Task Force journalists for whom questions of 'operational security' assumed a new and frightening immediacy locked below decks in an aircraft carrier or crouching in a muddy trench. The evidence, however, shows that both the ministry and the military, exceded this brief. Their censorship strayed beyond questions of security into issues of taste and tone. On 8 June Argentine jets bombed the Landing Support Logistic Ships *Sir Galahad* and *Sir Tristram* at Fitzroy Cove, killing 51, (33 of them Welsh Guardsmen). Robert Fox of the BBC recalls that one of the MoD PROs told the journalists 'we could report the disaster but had to mention the "good news" first, that seven planes had been shot down'.[21] Two voice dispatches from Fitzroy arrived simultaneously in London that night. Michael Nicholson's was, in Robert Harris' words, more 'upbeat', describing 'a day of extraordinary heroism'.[22] The report from Brian Hanrahan of the BBC was far more sombre. Its description of survivors from *Sir Galahad* as 'shaken, some hysterical' having had to 'listen to their colleagues trapped below' upset the censors, who refused to release the tape until the offending line had been deleted.[23] Meanwhile, Nicholson's more positive account of the tragedy was released and broadcast by both Independent Television News (ITN) and the BBC.

Not all censorship was quite so selective. Mick Seamark of the *Daily Star* was in a landing craft tied up alongside *Sir Galahad* when the ship was bombed:

> all these people were coming over the side into the landing craft.... There was all this blood and gore and screaming and smoke, and for some reason, which I am almost ashamed of, I took out my notebook and started taking down notes. It was just an automatic reaction ... I think it was just to save me from going round the bend.

Once ashore he jotted down an account of what he had just seen, then 'handed it to the Land Army PR guy, who read it and ticked it and put it into a helicopter and sent it back to Ajax Bay which was where the MoD were manning the satellite link'. More than a week later, after Argentina's surrender, Seamark spoke to his editor from Stanley only to discover that his piece on the *Sir Galahad* had never made it back to London: 'It had been "mislaid" by the Ministry of Defence'.[24]

Back in London the right to dissent itself was under attack. At a meeting of News and Current Affairs (NCA) editors on 6 April, Ian Trethowan, the BBC's Director-General warned his staff that 'the BBC would come under pressure, as it had during the Suez crisis, to conform to the national interest. There was', he felt, 'a legitimate point in this: the difficulty was to define precisely the "national interest" '. Trethowan thought that the national interest could best be served if the BBC was 'careful not to do anything to imperil military operations or diplomatic negotiations, but it should report accurately and faithfully the arguments arising within British society at all levels'.[25]

Honouring this editorial principle the 10 May edition of BBC TV's 'Panorama' focused on opposition to the government's handling of the dispute. Comments made by Peter Snow on 'Newsnight' eight days previously had already made the BBC particularly unpopular with the government's supporters. In a comparative assessment of available information from the South Atlantic, Snow had concluded that 'until the British are demonstrated either to be deceiving us or to be concealing losses from us, we can only tend to give a lot more credence to their version of events'. John Page, Conservative MP for Harrow West, considered Snow's analysis 'unacceptably even handed' and felt his willingness to view British and Argentine reports with equal scepticism was 'totally offensive and almost treasonable'.[26] Snow's scepticism proved well founded. The military and the MoD *had* concealed losses from and deceived the public. In the eyes of the Tory Party faithful, however, accuracy was no vindication of the right to dissent.

The offending edition of 'Panorama' featured an interview with a member of Argentina's delegation to the UN, who outlined the official Argentine position on the islands' sovereignty. Recorded interviews with dissident Conservative Party MPs, Sir Anthony Meyer and David Crouch followed, in which Crouch expressed his fear that by fighting for the Falklands Britain 'may be judged to be standing on our dignity for a colonial ideal'. Two vociferous critics of the government line on the conflict, Labour MPs George Foulkes and Tam Dalyell, also spoke. Dalyell asked the interviewer Michael Cockerell, if the Argentines were the jack-booted fascists that parliament and the popular press had made them out to be, why then had Britain 'traded with them, welcomed many of their most senior people from the junta in this country, and sold them arms all the time?' Following the film, the presenter, Robert Kee, (who later resigned from the BBC in the row about the programme), interviewed Cecil Parkinson, the Chairman of the Conservative Party and a member of the War Cabinet. Parkinson was invited to respond to specific issues raised by the film, and to put forward the official British position on events in Westminster and the South Atlantic.

Reaction to the programme was sudden and extreme. The following day in parliament, Sally Oppenheimer MP attacked the programme as an 'odious, subversive travesty' which 'dishonoured the right to freedom of speech in this country'. The Prime Minister herself expressed the belief that 'the case for our country is not being put with sufficient vigour on certain – I do not say all – BBC programmes'.[27] The next evening, when George Howard and Alasdair Milne, respectively Chairman and Director-General Elect of the BBC addressed a meeting of the Conservative Party's Media Committee, both men and the BBC were subjected to a hailstorm of abuse in what one MP described as 'the ugliest meeting I have ever attended'.[28]

Nothing said in the programme could be construed as particularly offensive. It was not the content but the premiss of the programme which caused such offence. By demonstrating the existence of and providing a platform for dissent, the BBC demolished the carefully cultivated image of parliamentary and national unanimity over the Falklands issue. In exercising its right to speak freely it had dishonoured the duty, which the government felt it owed, to speak in favour of its policies on this issue. And for that it was punished.

Robert Harris' assertion that 'despite all the abuse, the BBC refused to yield' is, sadly, contradicted by the NCA minutes and its coverage of the conflict subsequent to this wave of attacks on it.[29] Having sought out and reported dissent, the BBC was intimidated back into orthodoxy. The morning after the screening of 'Panorama', the Director–General reminded editors and producers at the NCA meeting that 'the BBC was the *British* Broadcasting Corporation. It was now clear that a large section of the public shared this view and he believed it was an unnecessary irritation to stick to the detached style'.[30] On the same day, the Prime Minister informed parliament she had received an assurance from the Chairman of the BBC stating, 'in vigorous terms, that the BBC is not neutral on this point'.[31]

The abandonment of neutrality trickled down through the organisation. The following evening's edition of the 'Nine O'Clock News' ended with a report on 'a display of patriotism in Merseyside, where more than 500 people gathered to sing songs as a sign of their support for the British troops out in the South Atlantic'. The bulletin closed to the strains of 'There'll always be an England'. Intimidated into abandoning its commitment to 'report accurately and faithfully the arguments arising within British society at *all* levels', the BBC was forced to abide by the other mainstay of its editiorial policy. Yet by ensuring that it did 'not to do *anything* to imperil military operations' (my italics) the MoD could invoke security considerations, both real and imagined, to enforce the corporation's orthodoxy, stifle its dissent, and further enhance the ministry's official line.

That there was no centralised body co-ordinating a sophisticated censorship policy did not make the news vetted and passed by the ministry any less propagandist. The policy may not have been sophisticated, but as the continued credence of the official line on the conflict suggests, it was certainly effective.

'Propaganda', claims Michael Balfour in his study of information policies during World War II, 'need not necessarily involve the use of force to prevent the free dissemination of criticism and of alternative interpretations. It can operate by arousing so emotional an atmosphere and investing its favoured interpretations with such prestige that only an insignificant fraction of the public will consider any alternative'.[32] Rupert Murdoch's mass-circulation tabloid, the *Sun*, helped foster a climate of hysteria which was instrumental in shaping and charging an atmosphere hostile to dissent. In its editorial of 7 May *Sun* listed the BBC among the 'traitors in our midst' who were guilty of 'not properly conveying Britain's case over the Falklands, and (are) treating this country as if she and the Argentines had an equal claim to justice'.[33] Britain's case, it felt, could be best put by a total ban on dissent, and an obligatory, bellicose loyalty to the government line, as demonstrated in its own comic-book coverage of the conflict. When the Leader of the Opposition, Michael Foot, invited the Prime Minister to reprove 'the hysterical bloodlust of the *Sun* and the *Daily Mail*, which bring such disgrace on the journalism of this country', she pointedly refused to do so.[34] The *Sun* was a vital tool in the government's propaganda campaign, offering a natural – if extreme – extension of the official line on the conflict. It was Fleet Street's answer to the parliamentary sabre-rattling which had given the Task Force such a rousing send off.

Yet though the military seems to have benefited from its relations with the media during the Falklands War, it may, in the long run, turn out to have lost as much as it gained. As General Moore knows, and has himself shown, the media can be a useful ally in misleading the enemy about projected operations, while the public has shown some willingness to tolerate misinformation when genuine security issues are at stake.[35] Yet the media's effectiveness in such cases depends upon the degree of public confidence which it enjoys. Explicit intimidation of the media, censorship and suppression of its freedom to dissent corrode its integrity, undermine public confidence in it, and diminish its potential usefulness.

The military clearly has a stake in ensuring that the information policy intended to preserve its security and protect its personnel is, as far as is practicable, politically neutered, and restricted to a narrow range of security issues. That the military should have some say in what is *not* written about is quite reasonable. That it should attempt to influence the treatment of what *is* written about is entirely unacceptable. An effective working relationship between the media and the military should be premissed on friction. A committed rivalry and a productive mistrust, after all, suggest a healthy co-existence between two organisations whose aims, as the reporting guidelines for Task Force correspondents observed, are diametrically opposed. If 'the essence of successful warfare is secrecy and the essence of successful journalism is publicity' then a harmonious co-existence between the military and the media implies that one or the other is failing in its professional responsibilities. The failure of either can only mean the loss of vital, common freedoms.

NOTES

1. Robert Harris, *Gotcha!: The Media, the Government and the Falklands Crisis*, (London: Faber, 1983), p.96.
2. Ibid., p.97
3. David Fairhall, 'The Next Round won't be Plain Sailing', *Guardian*, 28 April 1982.
4. House of Commons Defence Committee (HCDC) First Report 1982–3, The *Handling of Press and Public Information During the Falklands Campaign*, 2 vols. (London: HMSO, 1983). Quotation from Vol.2, Q 1425–6.
5. David E. Morrison and Howard Tumber, *Journalists at War: The Dynamics of News Reporting During the Falklands Conflict* (London: Sage, 1988), p.242.
6. Valerie Adams, *The Media and the Falklands Campaign* (London: Macmillan, 1986), p.168.
7. 'Today' programme, BBC Radio 4, 5 May 1982.
8. Adams, p.58.
9. K. S. Morgan (ed.), *The Falklands Campaign – A Digest of Debates in the House of Commons 2 April to 15 June 1982* (London: HMSO, 1982), p.10.
10. *Guardian*, 5 April 1982.
11. Morrison and Tumber, p.6.
12. *Daily Express*, 8 June 1982.
13. Glasgow University Media Group (GUMG), *War and Peace News* (Milton Keynes: Open University Press, 1985).
14. Phillip Knightley, *The First Casualty: From the Crimea to the Falklands: The War*

    Correspondent as Hero, Propagandist and Myth Maker, 2nd ed. (London: Pan, 1989)., p.411.
15. Morrison and Tumber, p.98.
16. Ibid., p.28.
17. Ibid., p.98.
18. The *Oxford English Dictionary*, Vol.12 (Oxford: Clarendon Press, 1989), notes that propaganda refers to 'The systematic propagation of information or ideas by an interested part, esp. in a tendentious way in order to encourage or instil a particular attitude or response' (p.632). The importance of Goebbels in the 'blackening' of the term is illustrated by the following example of its use in 1929: 'The term propaganda has not the sinister meaning in Europe which it has acquired in America ... In European business offices the word means advertising or boosting generally' (G. Seldes; *You Can't Print That*; quoted in *OED*, p.632).
19. Peter Beck, 'The Anglo–Argentine Dispute Over Title to the Falkland Islands: Changing British Perceptions on Sovereignty Since 1910', *Millenium: Journal of International Studies*, Vol. 12 (LSE, 1983).
20. HCDC, Vol.2. ch.1, para 2. On 8 April 1982 the MoD sent a signal to Task Force ships encouraging the correspondents to 'feel free to file their stories and material'. It identified 10 areas which the journalists should avoid in order to guarantee 'responsible reporting', and these were:

   1. operational plans, which would enable a potential enemy to deduce details of intentions.
   2. speculation about possible courses of action.
   3. state of readiness and detailed operational capability of individual units or formations.
   4. location, employment and operational movements of individual units or formations, particularly specialist units.
   5. particulars of current tactics and techniques.
   6. operational capabilities of all types of equipment.
   7. stocks of equipment and other details of logistics.
   8. information about intelligence on Argentinian dispositions or capabilities.
   9. communications.
  10. equipment or other defects

    From Derrik Mercer, Geoff Mungham and Kevin Williams, *The Fog of War: The Media on the Battlefield*, foreword by Sir Tom Hopkinson (London: Heinemann, 1987) p.156.
21. Robert Fox, *Eyewitness Falklands: A Personal Account of the Falklands Campaign* (London: Methuen, 1982), p.242.
22. Harris, p.61.
23. Brian Hanrahan and Robert Fox; *'I Counted Them All Out And I Counted Them All Back': The Battle For The Falklands* (London: BBC, 1982), p.73.
24. Morrison and Tumber, pp.56–57
25. GUMG, p.13.
26. *The Times*, 4 May 1982, p.11
27. Morgan, pp.231–32
28. Harris, p.85
29. Harris, p.83
30. GUMG, p.30
31. Morgan, p.232
32. Michael Balfour, *Propaganda in War 1939–45. Organisations, Policies and Publics in Britain and Germany* (London: Routledge and Kegan Paul, 1979), p.422
33. *Sun*, 7 May 1982.

34. Morgan, p.233
35. For detailed statistics on the public's tolerance for misinformation, see Morrison and Tumber, pp.319–22.

The Press and Grenada, 1983

VICE ADMIRAL J. METCALF III, USN (RETD)

Saddam Hussein declared the conflict over Kuwait to be the 'Mother of Battles'. He may have been right. History may show that his war with the United Nations fundamentally changed the Middle East. History may also show that while Grenada 1983 was a skirmish in terms of warfare it may also have been the information warfare 'mother of battles'. If this is so, it will be because Grenada was a watershed in relations between the media and the military – the age of instant information. It marked a start toward equilibrium in the relationship between the government, the military and the news media.

At the time of the Grenada intervention, relations between press and the US military had been eroded to an appalling state. The root of the problem was the ill-will between the press and the military that came out of Vietnam. A pall of mutual misunderstanding still enveloped these two elements of American society eight years after the last shots were fired. The military brooded over the loss in Vietnam, and many blamed the press. At the same time, the media was deeply suspicious of those in authority within the military and its surrogate, the Pentagon.

It was an unnatural situation. The normal adversarial relationship between the press and the military that had existed for years had given way to ugly confrontation. The defense establishment, particularly those in senior positions, uniformed and civilian, accused the press of projecting increasingly a distorted, negative picture of military affairs. Unfortunately, out in the field where the captains and colonels worked, the situation was not much better. These were the people who actually fought in Vietnam, and to many, animosity toward the press was deeply felt and very personal.

Military spokesmen in an interview usually felt that the press was out 'to get' them. They felt that the press assumed them guilty of hiding something or lying before the fact. Unfortunately this view marked a

168

common ground, the press as an institution did not trust the military. The result was great antipathy for each other. Both sides felt the deck was stacked against them.

This period was the heyday of the ubiquitous anonymous 'informed sources'. A faceless 'authority' could with impunity question the judgment of the Chairman of the Joint Chiefs of Staff. Paranoia roamed the corridors of the Pentagon. Service chiefs and defense officials spent as much effort reacting to the 'Early Bird'[1] as they did attending to the business of the Cold War. The press and the Pentagon played games with each other. The Department of Defense even resorted to releasing bad news on Friday afternoon, too late for the seven o'clock news. They hoped, and the stratagem usually worked, that by Monday the event would have passed below the threshold of network interest.

My own direct involvement with the press prior to Grenada had consisted of cameo appearances on television and interviews with the reporters serving the military press. I had experienced the television equivalent of 'bait and switch', the 30-minute interview, cut to one minute, out of context and unexpectedly controversial. I had participated in and observed close at hand history in the making and marveled at the differences in what I had seen and what appeared in the media. I had little confidence in the press to report accurately events or make balanced interpretations of what had occurred. I shared a common belief that the media was not inclined to play it straight.

This was the military – media environment in which the Grenada operation and the subsequent media reporting of it took place.

The lapse of time between the notification that I was to lead the Grenada operation and the first landing of troops was 39 hours. In this brief period before combat the only consideration that I gave to the media occurred at about six hours into the 39. A lieutenant commander, a CINCLANT[2] public affairs officer (PAO), came to me and said, 'there will be no press, do you have any problems with this?' I said I did not. My answer came more from attention to urgent operational matters rather than a thought out position on the issue of the press. Was this formulation of media policy by acquiescence or did I have an option? I suspect the policy was de facto but the truth is I do not know.

Combat operations in Grenada commenced at 0500, Tuesday morning 25 October 1983, with the simultaneous landings of the Marines and Rangers and the breaking of radio silence that covered the movement of forces. Information warfare commenced at the same instant with a continuous account of the action transmitted through military channels to CINCLANT in Norfolk, Virginia, and the Chairman of the Joint Chiefs of Staff in Washington.

The first on-scene 'media event' occurred in mid-morning of the first day when an enterprising stringer representing the *Washington Post* appeared in the flagship, demanding that we relay his copy to the paper. He was advised that no immediate press coverage of the operation was permitted and that he would have to wait. This caused considerable consternation on his part. It was also clear that he was more interested in his copy than what was going on. My PAO escorted him below.

In due course, the presence of this journalist was reported up the chain of command. The reaction was swift. The Pentagon demanded an explanation for his presence. The 'no press policy' was reaffirmed, and we were unexpectedly admonished for having allowed the reporter on board the ship.

However, the vagaries of information warfare are swift. Within two hours this same Pentagon was demanding to know when we would allow the press to join the war. I asked 'how many?' The answer was 400. (This works out to be roughly one reporter for every 18 combat troops in the operation on Grenada.) My response was that we could not physically handle such a group. No further assistance or guidance was offered. It was then clear to me that the responsibility for press access policy had shifted.

On the second day of the operation we were petitioned again to allow media on the island. Again, I said no. Combat operations continued in and around the airstrip. The capital, St. George's, was not secure. The location and rescue of the American students were still uncertain.[3] The island was without running water and electricity. The fighting continued. I was also mindful of one of the basic tenets of my operation order; minimum casualties. I did agree to allow a press pool of 25 to visit the combat zone the following day, the third day of the operation.

I also had learned that a number of more adventuresome members of the fourth estate, determined to open up their own second front on Grenada, were on the way by speedboat. My response was to quarantine the island. I established an exclusion zone around Grenada enforced by destroyers and aircraft.

The members of the first press pool arrived from Barbados on the afternoon of the third day and remained on the island for about three hours. In the main they were excellent and professional. I briefed them, and they toured the immediate area of the Salines Airport, interviewed American students, and inspected the warehouses full of arms and ammunition that had been found on the island.

The press pool increased to 50 the following day. We repeated the briefing format of the previous day. On the fifth day of the operation the island was secure in the vicinity of Salines Airport and the town of St. George's. At this time we granted free access to the island, to the troops and to the island's population. The number of press who visited the island was limited to the availability of aircraft to ferry them from Barbados.

I also flew to Kingston, Barbados, and conducted a two-hour news conference for those who had not been able to get to Grenada. This was a very contentious session with more interest expressed by the media in attacking the press policy rather in than gathering news.

The final media event occurred on the tenth day, the last day of the operation. By this time Grenada and the Grenadine islands to the north were secure. The United States had designated an ambassador and he had arrived in St. George's with the nucleus of a country team. I felt that a formal ceremony transferring cognizance of US forces from a US military commander to the US ambassador should be accomplished. Working with the ambassador, I decided that a formal re-establishment of a government for Grenada was necessary. Both objectives were accomplished by a ceremony conducted with pomp and circumstance at the official residence of the Governor-General of Grenada, the representative of Queen Elizabeth II. The event was well-attended and recorded by US, print and television news services, as well by a number of foreign journalists. To my knowledge this occasion, an event of historical importance marking the end of the Grenada operation, never appeared on American television. The students had been rescued and peace restored. A regime that threatened the security of Caribbean region had been removed, and a new government installed.

The defining aspect of the Grenada operation was that the media did not have immediate access to the scene of combat. It is still the issue that transcends all others. Looking back, how was the media policy for Operation 'Urgent Fury' formulated in the Joint Chiefs of Staff and Department of Defense? In my opinion it probably 'just happened'. The policy of 'no media' likely became a logical extension of the tight security that covered the early planning and the diversion of the amphibious force and carrier battle group to the Caribbean.

The initial no press policy stood until the question 'when can you take media' in the first hours of combat. Lacking guidance or prior precedence I established the rules for a media presence during the combat phase operation. They were as follows:

- Safety of personnel – soldiers, marines, students and journalists – was the primary consideration. The media must not interfere with it.
- Troops in a combat area should not be burdened with the responsibility for the safety of the media.
- The media should not be exposed to hostile fire.
- Media, if in the area of troops in combat, would be escorted by a PAO.
- Accommodation for the media must be available whether ashore or aboard one of the ships.

Concern for operational security was not a factor in our media guidance.

Setting aside 'media vs. the Pentagon' religious wars and the timing issue of media gaining access to combat, how was the Grenada operation reported? My general impression was that the working journalists in Grenada did more than an adequate job in ferreting out what went on. As a group, they found the stories. The press uncovered the story of the errant bombs that fell on a mental institution before I did. Not fully explained, this could have turned into a so-called military 'cover up', I am sure. Fortunately, the journalists involved dug deeper than a headline and discovered it was the Grenadian people who kept the damage caused by the incident to themselves. The press missed the story of the capture of Austin and Chord, the two hardline thugs of the previous regime.

My impression of the pool correspondents was that they were very professional. They also gave the impression that many were more interested in being there than in finding out what was going on. With the exception of Charlayne Hunter-Gault of the MacNeil-Lehrer Report, the first group was not particularly rigorous in their questioning. She dominated the press conference and her probing was superb. By the time of the second press conference the attitude of reporters had turned confrontational but not antagonistic. The recurring question probed for body counts, à la Vietnam. There was however, more focus on the operation than in the meeting of the previous day, and in particular it zeroed in on the issue of why the press was not present from the start. The situation was personified by the *Washington Post* stringer, who arrived unexpectedly aboard the flagship and demanded that we relay his copy, totally alienating us and thus losing an exclusive opportunity to watch, close hand, history in the making.

During the operation, my perspective on how well the press was reporting was happily unencumbered by what was reported to the public. The support of the public, as opposed to the brouhaha over the exclusion of the press and the arguments about 'First Amendment Rights' was unknown to me at the time. There were no *New York Times*, no Dan Rather, no Cable News Network to sully up my outlook on the correspondents, print and television, who fed the worldwide media machine.

Looking back over seven years I would say the story was not very satisfactorily reported to the public. This is particularly the case if judged by the standard that the media sets for itself, and jealously guards, that of 'informing the public'. As it turned out, the competence of the reporter in the field was not relevant. Whether a journalist's report ended up on television, on the wire services, or in print depended on an editor. In the actual reporting of Grenada to the American public, the media expended more column inches and time defending their prerogatives than in reporting the story. Freedom for the press to gather the news during the Grenada operation is one issue. What was presented to the public is another. Only the former has been rigorously addressed.

A case in point is the account of the Columbia Broadcasting System (CBS) camera crew that surveyed the people of St. George's shortly after the landings. They moved about the town interviewing Grenada citizens with a line of questions that invited disapproval of the intervention and unhappiness with Americans. As told to me by the escorting PAO, the leader of this nefarious crew was heard to say about what they collected, 'this will not play in New York'. And indeed it did not. The outpouring of gratitude by the people of Grenada for the United States and her soldiers is not one of the lasting impressions that the public has of Grenada.

Was the public well served in the reporting of the Grenada operation? Probably not. Actually all the public really cares about in the long term is that we won. Nevertheless, pundits and anchor-men still talk about Grenada in terms of failure. There is an ethos that surrounds 'Urgent Fury' which denies that in both a military and strategic sense all objectives were realised. This was the story of an operation put together in hours, by forces that had never operated together and was successfully controlled by a command structure that was invented on the spot. The people of the United States were deprived of the story of the part that American pride, ingenuity, training in fighting fundamentals, and luck played in the success of the Grenada rescue operation. Most Americans are proud of what happened in Grenada but they do not know why.

Were the military and the press well served by what happened in Grenada? The answer is yes. When the medical student from Grenada stepped off the airplane and kissed the ground, media and military relations that hit bottom, started to improve. The public – customers the media could not ignore – reacted. The military reacted; they had won one. The press pool concept was back.

NOTES

1. Early Bird,' a daily compilation, under a yellow coversheet, of all source media stories covering military subjects. Published by the Department of Defense it is distributed widely within the Pentagon.
2. CINCLANT: Commander in Chief Atlantic, the US component commander in the Atlantic, and area covering the water areas of the Atlantic from above the Arctic Circle to the tip of South America.
3. All students were rescued late in the afternoon of the second day.

Perspectives from the War in the Gulf

GENERAL MICHAEL J. DUGAN, USAF (RETD)

Limited conflict or, perhaps more appropriately, limited peace, is the normal condition of mankind; certainly more normal than total peace or total conflict. The nation-in-arms and concepts of national and total mobilization are relatively recent phenomena in the history of conflict. The potential for conflict in the future is, as always, high and higher yet that it will be limited. On the other hand, for those personally involved in combat, 'limited' is seldom an apt description. It seems to me that limited war is somewhat like minor surgery. When a surgeon slices your neighbor or one of his family members, it's minor surgery; when a surgeon slices you or your family, it's always major. It makes little difference what procedure the surgeon accomplishes or what organ the surgeon repairs. Similarly, limited war is one that typically involves your neighbors; your vital interests are not at stake. One can be much more dispassionate about limits in a war that involves only one's neighbors. This analogy is not scientific; it is not analytical, but it does capture the essence of a useful idea. A nation at war, even a war with limited objectives and limited resources, is going to find almost unlimited commitment of its national media to covering the war effort. War will be the story of the time and media resources will follow accordingly. Limited war is an operative term for the military, it is only a descriptive term for the media.

The military and the media are both principal beneficiaries of what is called the information age and the information age is upon us – all of us. It affects everyone; it affects people in liberal democracies and those in totalitarian regimes as well. It may not have produced discernible change in some aboriginal cultures – yet; but just as sure as we are here today, changes are on the way. I can not tell you specifically when, where or how; but I can tell you with great assurance that all will feel the consequences; and I can tell you that more impacts are on the way – more than you and I have already experienced. Arrival times of the effects will be different; the circumstances to be changed will be different; nevertheless, the flux of change associated with the information age will continue.

175

There are already easily observed, well-known outcomes in remote areas on widely separated individuals and small communities – in Alaska and here in the outback emergency, transportation, education and all kind of commercial services. These services, based on a new generation of communication technology, have changed the quality of life in remote areas, and perhaps they have changed the nature of that life itself. There are a lot of remote areas in the world – geographically remote areas, culturally remote areas and politically remote areas; the information age is changing all of them.

One culturally remote area is inhabited by soldiers (and sailors). It is more or less remote depending on whether you are a soldier and live within the culture or whether you are an outsider, perhaps a member of the fourth estate and live beyond the pale of military culture. And then for the real skeptic there is always the proposition that military culture is an oxymoron. Soldiers do live in a special sub-culture in virtually all societies, especially all liberal democratic societies. That sub-culture has inherent barriers to communications, whether or not one is dealing with military operations. There is a different focus, different words, different use of the same words, intentional and unintentional effects of military socialization of members, different living conditions, different expectations, different self-images and lots more. The differences are neither good nor bad; they are not the fault of soldiers, nor of non-soldiers; they simply exist and they should be recognized and accommodated if defence and the media mean to have an intelligent conversation in peace or war, and especially during a time of limited conflict.

The information age has already had dramatic impact on military cultures and military operations. Instant and worldwide communications – both for the collection and for the dissemination of information – have changed the pace and the rhythm of policy-making, be it foreign, defense, economic or military. No longer can a head of state and any of his or her subordinates have the luxury of days or even hours of advance notice of a significant event in the world. The information age has made the man in the street, perhaps not as well informed as the policy-maker, but in many cases he is as quickly informed that something of importance has occurred. The defence policy-maker and the military implementor of that policy find themselves operating in a demanding new environment.

Beyond the natural differences discussed above, military organizations have a legitimate and essential right and duty to protect certain information bearing on military operations. Planned operations and in some cases the details of completed operations – their implications for future actions – are, unquestionably, the stuff of military secrets. There should be, however, large differences in the relationship between the military and the media and in the access to, and flow of, information within a nation that means to follow a deterrent strategy as opposed to a nation that means to pursue a pre-emptive or offensive strategy.

In democratic societies the public, in whose name the 'right to know' is so frequently claimed, does not want information that will hazard its sons and daughters, friends and neighbors to be available to any and all. Societies inherently understand that there are boundaries. The typical man in the street is a decision-maker, not a voyeur; he or she wants to know what is happening in sufficient detail and in sufficient time to know when he should change his behavior. They want to make choices about their future. They do not insist on instant access to everything; they do want truth, honesty and balance in what information is available.

The man in the street in Baghdad or any other totalitarian society also wants the truth; he, too, wants to make choices about his future or change his behavior, when appropriate. Even despots ultimately must answer to their populations and political choices made by their populations. Saddam Hussein invaded Kuwait for reasons of domestic politics in Iraq. The Iraqi economy was in shambles from eight years of war with Iran. He could not meet the economic development expectations of his nation. He needed resources; Europe turned down additional credits; OPEC denied a significant increase in the price of oil; Kuwait refused his demands. Saddam chose to take from Kuwait what he could not get elsewhere.

One of the cruel lessons of the recent war in the Gulf – and it is not a new lesson, by any means – is that the people of every nation are responsible for the quality of their government. Governments derive their powers from the consent of the governed. People in democratic as well as despotic nations are responsible for and suffer the consequences of the governments they choose either by acts of omission or commission.

Not only has the change in the technology reduced the time for producing and disseminating news, it has also dramatically reduced the cost; and, consequently, has allowed, even prompted a surge in the numbers of media representatives that can be brought to bear on an important story. As the action in the Gulf increased in scope and intensity the number of media represented grew to over 1,500. The number was not unmanageable, but it was a number that begged for management. A number of rules were promulgated. For our purposes here, the specifics are interesting but not essential; suffice it to say that American reporters were not accustomed to externally imposed 'rules'. There was and continues to be great debate and turmoil in the United States over the extent and the impact of the rules. There were Congressional hearings; columnists wrote articles in the major newspapers; newsmen in the Gulf region were interviewing each other over the rules and their significance. Management of the news is a constitutional issue in the USA.

As an aside I might note that on about the eighth day after the start of the coalition offensive action, there was a noteworthy meeting, convened by General H. Norman Schwarzkopf, at the request of the media – largely the print media – to discuss ground rules. The print media wanted – and got – the televised daily briefings reduced in length and scope. They wanted the amount of material presented directly to a broad audience reduced. They wanted access for themselves to fresh military material that had not already been seen worldwide. The media, or at least a segment of the media, wanted General Schwarzkopf to 'manage the news' for their benefit.

As the war in the Gulf approached the 30-day point there was a heightened sense of expectancy on the part of the press. Many of the 1,500-member press contingent accredited to the coalition headquarters were bored; they were tired of daily briefings; they were war correspondents; they wanted stories and images of carnage; they needed personal involvement in combat action. Aerial combat was described by the media as 'antiseptic', perhaps because it is accomplished at somewhat longer range than bayonet work – more likely, because there was no convenient opportunity for direct media involvement. The media needed a 'ground war' to justify itself, whether or not it made sense for the coalition strategy. The idea that there had not been war on the ground was curious. Surely had anyone asked an Iraqi newsman or an Iraqi 'ground' combatant, officer or non-commissioned officer, they would have attested to fighting for their lives – on the ground – for weeks.

The quantity and quality of press access to the war in the Gulf was much discussed in the American media. The discussion got mixed reviews from the American people. Every working man and woman has routine problems dealing with his or her working environment: 'and, I don't need to pay to read about or listen to yours, thank you very much'. I suspect that Americans and Australians share similar biases in this regard. I believe the American press lost some credibility and stature by over-doing its own problems of covering this war and by interviewing one another about news process and reporting it as news product. On the other hand, I believe the press recovered credibility because the Gulf War was a good story, on balance well covered.

The newsmen in the Gulf had more restrictions placed on them than they were used to; individually each of them, with the exception of Bob Simon and his three CBS colleagues, had a narrowed range of movement; each of them had fewer contacts than he or she was accustomed to. From an individual perspective the rules and restrictions were an irritant, a grievance; collectively, the American public had more information than it could stand. Daily, live coverage briefings from the headquarters in the Gulf and from the Pentagon via television and radio, reports from the 1,500 and then echoes – and there were lots of echoes from columnists, correspondents, consultants and assorted pundits in the United States and abroad – all served to keep the American public informed.

How well it was informed is open to question. There are some horror stories of media reports, photographs and videotape being delayed for days, awaiting censor review, or worse, just waiting. Every newsman has a story on how his or her work was compromised by the Department of Defense rules or by the implementation of those rules in the field. These complaints should be addressed; the rules should be adjusted; the 'minders' should be better trained; the censors should be more sensitive, but in the final analysis a larger view must prevail. How did the average American view his access to knowledge of the war? Did the media provide sufficient facts? Was the story covered to meet the needs of the public? Was the story delivered in a timely fashion? Was the man in the street comfortable? In my view, the man in the street left no doubt about his view of the war: he supported the effort with growing confidence as the war progressed. Weekly polls, accomplished independently by various national news organizations, gave the President, his policy and the implementation of the policy consistently high grades – 80 per cent approval ratings.

Does an 80 per cent approval rating say anything about press coverage? I believe it does. In a democratic society the theory holds that the people are always right; certainly they are always responsible.

There is a certain collective sophistication in the body politic. The man in the street knows what he likes, what he needs to make choices and why. Timeliness issues should be considered from the perspective of the consumer, not solely from that of the media.

What does all this mean for the future? In my view, it means that soldiers and sailors will continue to live in a relatively unknown subculture; technology will continue to evolve and present new challenges; leaders must continue to lead; defense policy must pursue military and political objectives that are clearly defined and achievable within the limited resources available. The media must continue to search out and tell the story; defense must generate the facts that support a story they want told, for a story will definitely be told.

In the United States there is a good deal of ill-feeling among military members about the role of the press in the Vietnam War. The media sought out and reported the story that the facts prompted. In many cases there was a bad story to tell. A ten-year war on remote foreign soil will almost always be a bad story in a liberal democracy. The Gulf War, on the other hand, was a good story, not for anything the media did, but for the facts that were generated by the actions of the participants. The easiest way for defense establishments to manage the media is to generate a compelling story.

I am satisfied that societies are sophisticated enough to accept the truth about their defense forces, their successes and their failures. Embellishing success and covering up failure are both bankrupt policies. The utility of propaganda is questionable except in very narrow situations – constrained by time, locale and circumstance – and then focused only on one's enemy. In the long run the truth will out and people who have been duped by their own governments will exact a price. There are additional implications for national leaders resulting from the advance of technology. Leaders must lead more effectively; planners must prepare for more contingencies; steps must be taken to posture military and diplomatic options to anticipate more often and to respond more rapidly than in earlier days. Governments must learn to exploit the new technology, not merely react. The military and the media both need to examine, understand and adapt to modernization.

Military organizations will continue to need support from their nation's people. The most effective channel of communication to the people is the nation's media. Military organizations need support in times of peace and war. Thus, a continuing dialogue among the military and the media will, in my view, be essential for a healthy military. For the media there is not the same continuing need. They march to a different drummer. The soldiers will be obliged, in many cases, to initiate the dialogue and promote its development.

The Gulf Crisis: The Media Point of View

COLONEL DAVID H. HACKWORTH, US ARMY (RETD)

Well here it comes, get ready for it. I think that truth and the freedom of the press took a tragic beating during the Gulf War.

But before we get into the details of that beating let me tell you about generals and the military mind, through a little story. A French officer by the name of Colonel Clemont was severely wounded during one of the final charges at Waterloo and taken to a field hospital where the surgeon was operating. He realized that the extent of the good colonel's wound was such that he would have to remove the top of his head. In those days we are talking about a very very difficult operation with limited medical means, so there was only an ordinary house saw available. The doctor took the top of his head off, not unlike you would a pumpkin, and the surgeon began to repair the bullet wound to the brain. About this time a great white charger came galloping up to the small chateau where Colonel Clemont was being put together, ridden by an aide of the Emperor who shouted: 'Where is General Clemont?' and the surgeon said 'We have no General Clemont but we have a Colonel Clemont on the table,' The colonel started moving on his feet, got on the ground and stood up. He reached down and picked up the top of this pumpkin head and plumped it back on his skull and started moving toward his horse. The surgeon said 'Wait a minute, hold on you've forgotten your brains' Clemont replied 'Now I am a general, who needs brains?'

And that might have been true in 1815 when generals did not need brains and certainly we saw right up to General William C. Westmoreland's time in Vietnam great brain power was not necessary. But I think that since Vietnam we have seen a great improvement in the general officer corps and certainly in the Gulf it was the generals' brains not the politicians which employed such great thinking that brought about such a quick decisive victory with so few casualties.

Tactially the Gulf operation, from beginning to end was a brilliant show, but I think that these same generals with their handling of the press tainted their impressive military laurel, and it will reverberate for a long time among the free nations of the world until this abuse of the freedom of the press is corrected.

In the Gulf, the US military acted not unlike George Orwell's Big Brother in *1984*. Journalists were restricted from free access, fired upon by our own troops, blindfolded, thumped with rifle butts, arrested, duped into playing out the propaganda scheme of the higher military command, interrogated and treated with total arrogance.

Many journalists had their credentials removed or were threatened with having their credentials removed because of petty violations. The US military trampled on the American and the Australian peoples' right to know and I think it is important to realize that in those two countries it was an elected Congress, an elected Parliament, that gave the elected President and the elected Prime Minister, permission to wage the Gulf War. And the people who elected those members of Congress and Parliament damn well deserve to know what the military was doing because it was their permission that sent them there. And I think this is what we lose sight of. The press in the Gulf was totally controlled by the military. It started with a mechanism called the Joint Information Bureau, known as the JIB which I thought was the thought control center of all time. You reported into the JIB, you showed your credentials, if you wanted to go somewhere you submitted a request to visit the 3rd Squadron of the such and such navy or the 1st Battalion of the such and such infantry unit and then that request was processed and in time you would hear whether it was approved or not approved. All press activity was confined to pools, you were normally organised in five-man pools, that were controlled by a minder and if you asked a soldier sailor or airman a question, you could well have the minder say 'No, that won't be answered'. The minders I thought were very much like thought-control police employed by the German Army in World War II. Throughout the battlefield there were roadblocks thrown up to deny press access to the front line units and so on. No press could go forward of a certain line without a military escort, and the military escort would approve everything you saw, every question that you asked and so on. Totally controlled.

The military personnel themselves were ordered not to talk to the press, full stop. Remember in the main it was an all-volunteer force out there and these guys had their jobs at stake and in 99 per cent of the cases they were not about to talk to someone from the press. I had a number of terrible experiences. One day after spending a week with an American Special Forces unit way into Kuwait, far beyond the front, we were coming back, pretty high. We had a great story, and my photographer, who I always travelled with, decided to take a picture (and they can get you into a lot of trouble, photographers) and he put his big zoom camera out of the window and took a picture. Suddenly we were surrounded by a 1st Air Cavalry platoon of infantry, fixed bayonets, weapons chambered, and these guys were really fierce and threatening and trying to take the film and all of that. And this photographer had gotten me in such trouble over the weeks that we had worked together that I said 'Mark, you get yourself out of this one' and the sergeant then said to me 'Get out of the car' and he treated me like a criminal and I just said 'Sergeant, get stuffed and I refuse to obey your orders'. He was starting to threaten me, but the thing I had over him was that I understood the military mind, I understood that he could not do anything because he had to follow the rules of engagement. He could not shoot me even though he theatened to shoot me simply because I had not shot at him first, and he finally let us go. But this happened all the time.

Another time I was with a combat infantry battalion, an old outfit of mine, in 18th Airborne Corps, and had snuck down to the unit, because I had known the commander and I had not gone through the JIB and all of that. This is how I operated and the commander just gave me free access to his battalion. He had nothing to hide, he knew that his unit was straight. And so I was inside the perimeter, it was just getting dark and being one who at my age likes to have a walk, I had a good walk around the perimeter and being an old infantry man, I like to have a look at fields of fire and positions and all of that. So I was checking all that out, which was just a natural bent, when I was assaulted by two young buck sergeants, fixed bayonets, weapons pointed and all the rest, challenging me with 'Was I a Third World indigenous individual that has penetrated their perimeter'. I said 'Look I'm from *Newsweek* Magazine your colonel knows I'm here' and so on, and he's pointing the weapon at me and being very fierce and I finally told him, again knowing the rules of engagement, what he could do with that weapon. We had a fierce discussion. But if that was the attitude of the military throughout the regular units, it was not true of the National Guard or Reserve units that were brought in. If you have seen the movie *Dances With Wolves*, there is a bit at the end which shows how the regular army horse cavalry treated the Indians and that attitude just grabbed me in the cinema that very attitude, the military mind frightened me so I thought 'My God, that's exactly what I saw in the Gulf'.

So the military treated the press corps like animals in a zoo. The press corps was caged up in five-star hotels and was thrown scraps of meat, mostly from a staged theatre-like briefings which were an incredible joke because nothing of value came from them. The old hands, the old pro reporters that I knew, simply did not go to those briefings because those things were of no value. You could ask 'Where was that bridge you've just shown us this wonderful smart bomb destroying?' And the briefer would say 'We can't tell you' but you knew damn well that Saddam Hussein knew where that bridge was and so it went on. The press became like vultures, few got out in the field. The ones that did get out in the field, mainly French or British, really knew how to operate on a battlefield from years of doing it in Africa and the Middle East whereas the Yanks were new to this kind of game. They were used to going to Fort Bragg and getting permission and going with the public relations officer and all that junk.

I took my lead from how the French and British operated. They wore uniforms, they spray painted their four-wheel drive vehicles in desert colors, put military markings on them and pretended they were in the military and got through. This heavy duty restriction of press activity really affected those of us in the press corps who had been around and covered other wars, for example, Simon of CBS and his film crew were captured. He was very chafed by the heavy-handed military treatment and thus, like a lot of us in the press, he took great chances. He went up to far beyond the front lines and was captured. A reporter friend of mine was in Baghdad and came from Baghdad down to Saudi Arabia to cover that aspect of the war. Once he was exposed to the JIB and the Allied press control, he told me 'There's more freedom of the press over there' talking about Iraq than there was in Saudi Arabia, which for me was a very very scary comment. Because the press were treated not unlike spies, spies for Saddam Hussein. Those personnel that I talked to, and I tried to stay away from them as much as I could (which I'll discuss in a minute), wanted to report the soldiers' story, the grit, the sacrifice of combat, they wanted to get the human side of the story.

I think that history shows that when a press is not free, freedom suffers and the consequences are dreadful. Let me give a recent example of this, only 45 years ago after the end of World War II we saw a great number of German citizens denying that there were such things as Nazi concentration camps. This claim just does not wash when you stop and think how little they objected when Hitler closed down the newspapers and put a clamp on freedom of the press. Certainly today we cannot compare our leaders in America or Australia with Hitler, but, because of the way that the press was treated in the Gulf, I think Americans and Australians were not permitted to see and hear the full story of what their forces did and one day possibly one day like Nazi Germany there could not be a free press in our countries.

I think this happened simply because of the Pentagon myth (and it was a myth) that Vietnam was lost because of uncensored press coverage. In the Gulf I found that the ghost of Vietnam lived on and fuelled all of the paranoia. Many of the generals of the Gulf era were captains and majors during the Vietnam period and they had read all of Westmoreland's comments. And I think General Dugan telling it like it was really created heavy-duty paranoia out in the Gulf because people were just reluctant to say anything. This was especially true after the deputy commander Lieutenant General Waller, reported on 18 December 1990 that the forces were not ready and he reported that to the press. These instances of people who bravely stood up and told the truth created incredible division and paranoia between the military and the press. The military worked overtime to prevent the press reporting the true story. There were 1,000 reporters in the Gulf, most marooned in five-star hotels, few got to the field. Most fed off of each other. They were like vultures sitting up on a fence post and when a little young rabbit ran by they really jumped on him. So if you came back from the field and you had a bit of dust on your boots you could go into the JIB to discover out what was happening and find yourself attacked by sixty vultures all trying to glean a story from you.

And it got to the point where luckily in my case I lived far away from the International Hotel, where most of the press were housed, just by the good fortune that there were no billets available. I did not have to deal with the American press corps, instead mainly with the French and the British and that is where I learned all those tips which I mentioned earlier. I could have spent my whole time just providing stories to the press because they had no one else to feed off. And they certainly did not get anything from the military. So there is little wonder that few reporters and so-called military experts got it right about the war. Since the American and the Australian people did not know what was going on there, little wonder that fear, hysteria and anxiety reigned here in Australia and America. It existed because no one knew what the hell was going on and it was little wonder that so little of the reporting that came out of the Gulf dealt with human beings. Instead most dealt with high technology and thus the Gulf War became a very antiseptic war. All of this is good for security, good for the policymakers but bad for freedom and bad for democracy, and it is also bad for those young soldiers, sailors and airmen who were out there fighting for freedom which included the muzzled press corps' right to tell their story.

A free press reveals when bad leadership exists, when bad equipment exists, when there is violation of state and international rules (e.g., many times during the Vietnam War), bad training, inadequacies of supply and materiel, troop safety and the status of troop morale. A free press can discover friendly fire casualties, safety issues, for example, the strike on a nuclear reactor in Iraq and the attendant fallout from that, or the after effects of the oil well fires. If the press is not looking for and reporting those matters at the time, the truth has a way of being buried on a battlefield never to be dug up again. The public in America still does not know the truth of the 1989 Panama operation, which is tragic, the known deaths are over a thousand innocent civilians and thousands of innocent civilians wounded. All of this was because the military clamp on the press in Panama did not reveal the truth to the American people. It proved a very good dry run for the Gulf.

Now to look at the press themselves, when I was in the States I found an article which said it all, written by some guy from Arizona and he said 'Editor, this war has made one thing very clear, intelligence is not a requirement to be a member of the news media' which I thought was very accurate. I very seldom watched those 'five o'clock follies' with Generals Tom Kelly and Neale, but I did on a couple of occasions witness press people asking really stupid questions and I just wanted to bury my head in the sand. The press corps in the Gulf had very few veteran reporters, probably of the thousand out there only 50 to 75 people were of the quality of Peter Harvey. Most were young kids trying to make a name for themselves – many were irresponsible, most were unqualified, all were frustated, few tried to learn about tanks and planes before they got there. Most did not know a tank from a turd. There were a thousand reporters out there, one in seven ended up in one of these pools that I mentioned to you so about 130 people were out in the field in five-man pools tightly controlled by the military and you had 870 in the hotels feeding off one another.

Another fault of the press is they simply refused to raise hell; as a consequence few got it right and their employers were at fault. It was not just the reporter on the ground who was to blame but also the reporter back at CNN in Atlanta or wherever. The major US media made big bucks out of the war and got soaring ratings and great public approval. Many large news media networks were openly pro-the war and very harsh on reporters who told the truth. I can give many examples of friends of mine who were veteran reporters who filed stories that were just killers that never hit the press. The JIB greatly exploited the press corps, and divided them, and gave special press opportunities to those who were the military apologists, those who were not boat rockers, to those people who'd write a favourable story and whereas they kept tabs on the people they knew who were bashers.

I was considered an Army basher for many reasons including my publications in the *Washington Post* and my book. I put 21 requests into the JIB on day one when I got there. It took about three hours as I filed these and that was from General Schwarzkopf down to Lieutenant General Waller because I wanted to know why General Waller said we were not ready to fight when in the White House the President's press secretary said that General Waller did not mean what he said. None of these 21 requests were approved. Such refusals resulted in a lot of fabrication as a lot of reporters made up stories or filed shallow stories. For example, I was getting ready to go into the field and I always brought a bunch of goodies to take to the troops. It is called bribery. A big stack of newspapers, fruit cocktail and things that soldiers in the field like. I was loading my four-wheel drive and there was a woman reporter interviewing two mess sergeant looking guys – they were huge like this – with their camouflage gear, US Air Force, way back at Dhahran. I could not help but overhear the conversation and she was saying 'Now what if your buddy got blown away next to you, how would you handle this?' And the guy said 'We're fighting for freedom here. We're fighting to stop aggression. It would be my loss that my good mate had died but it would be for the country and what is right' and so on. I thought 'This is a mess sergeant' but back home when someone was reading that copy they would not know that he was a mess sergeant.

Now a bit about my reportage, I fell into a rare bird category as an

ex-military man who was also a journalist at his eighth war and I
thought probably my final war. I wanted to report it correctly so I took
on many disguises, the oil man, I had ID from Aramco, Sergeant
Hackworth an old reserve sergeant who was called back on active duty,
Colonel Hackworth and Cameraman Hackworth for an Army team
and this allowed me to get to many places that the average press guy
could not. I had many friends there who were my lieutenants back in
the 1960s that were now generals and colonels. One commander
assembled his staff of 29 senior officers and said to them 'This is my
former battalion commander from Vietnam. He is a straight shooter,
tell him whatever he wants to know' and all I could think of was 'Oh if
Colonel Malvey of the JIB could see me now'. These officers told me
what was happening. And they were straight and they were good and
they were honest and they were soldiers who wanted to protect their
men. They wanted to make sure their men were well led, well trained,
well equipped and if there was a shortage they wanted to tell the press,
to tell me because they knew I would do something about it. Very
judiciously, in many cases, I found information, I knew exactly when
the ground attack day was. By staying with a unit for a week they forgot
I was there which was an advantage. Suddenly I'm a member of the
unit and suddenly at the briefings they are telling me everything that
there is and I worked out that if the LD, here, and they are going to be
here on this day, and what day the attack date was going to be as it was,
but I did not go to *Newsweek* and tell them and nor did I go to anyone
else and tell them. I censored myself.

So I painted my four-wheel drive camouflage color as the French
and the British had done, put the V invasion marker on it, wore a
uniform, dressed up my photographer, who was an old Rhodesian
Special Forces Scout anyway, in uniform and we just penetrated the
lines with no problem. I found that how to get through a roadblocks
was simply to sit there and I'd have Mark, the photographer at
attention and I would salute and the guy with his machine-gun would
not know what to do and he'd salute. So we would salute like this and
we would drive through. I had more guns pointed at me in those two
months in the Gulf than I had in eight years of combat. I was arrested
dozens of times. My photographer, Mark, a very brave and exceptional photographer, was butt stroked when he took a picture of a dead
Iraqi soldier because there were not going to be any pictures of dead
Iraqi soldiers at that point in the war in the press. It was a tough war to
cover, it was a huge front, we had to drive 1,200 kilometers over really

tough roads to get to the battlefront to get to the story. There was virtually no front, the Americans were back about 20 kilometers and up on the front lines were Saudis, Kuwaitis, the Multi-National Arab Allied camp who were easy to penetrate, I just travelled in the desert in a four-wheel drive vehicle pretending I was Rommel with a compass and I made damn sure I did not go too far north. I wandered into Kuwait several times. For example, the Battle of Khafji, I was there five days before the Iraqi attack and during the attack. Throughout the time I was there the old soldier's sense came back and I could smell that something was going to happen.

After the Battle of Khafji I spoke to the prisoners and their teeth were falling out, they had not eaten in days, they were living for months on a handful of rice, they had no fighting spirit, so I realized 'Hey these guys are not nine feet tall, these guys are just amateurs in the soldiering game and they are going to have the snot slapped out of them once the big boys get into the arena'. I climbed up on the tanks and the APCs and saw the oil levels and the condition of the maintenance, the tracks sagging, all these things which say to a soldier 'Not a very good outfit here'. These guys were not supermen, they were not these great tough guys that had been reported by the Army War College, by the Pentagon, by the staff and by the media. These guys are lightweights and they are going to have the hell kicked out of them. I realized that the Iraqi Army was myth, not mean, not ten feet tall and would be quickly whipped, because I was in the field. I saw, I felt, I smelled, I listened and got the true information through my own eyes and not through somebody else. In my *Newsweek* columns I wrote the war was going to be 30 to 40 days, I was kind of like the good general, and that the ground war would be no more than 7 days because I knew that they were whipped by air and there was simply no way that they would be able to fight.

But I did get a lot of indications that our air, our A-10 Thunderbolt 'tankbusters' were doing a magnificent job and I went down to an A-10 squadron and interviewed four pilots and all told me that they had knocked out 20 armoured vehicles each, tanks and APCs. Then I talked to one pilot who was an old pro who had been flying A-10s for years and who had flown 260 missions in Vietnam and he said 'Don't accept that as absolute truth'. That told me maybe something was wrong with the A-10, maybe it is not that dynamite machine I believed it was, so I went to the field with the specific thought of finding out something about the A-10s. And I joined an Egyptian commando battalion that was out in no man's land and they were having a bunch of strikes that day with A-10s. And about 2 kilometers from us was an Iraqi position, an Iraqi flag and antennae, visible personnel and army trucks. This A-10 rolled in and as I was talking to this Special Forces team it dropped two 500lb bombs in our concern because we had a bunker that was identical to the bunker that the Iraqis had. We had an antenna that was exactly the same.

I watched four sets of A-10s – eight aircraft – put their ordnance in on the Iraqi targets and the only thing that hit the targets was the 30mm gun on the nose, the bombs missed, the Maverick missiles missed, so I turned to the Ground Controller and said 'What's the deal?' And he said to me 'Look the A-10 is a brilliant weapon, it's designed for that 30mm, the rest are secondary weapons and its like throwing rocks at a pond.' I saw the 30mm drill holes in the Iraqi positions but not the bombs, not the Mavericks which led me as a reporter to say 'Hey, maybe all of these armoured vehicles we are supposedly destroying are not being knocked out'. And I think I will end it with that.

PART III
THE AUSTRALIAN EXPERIENCE

Changing Australian Opinion on Defence: Trends, Patterns, and Explanations

IAN McALLISTER and TONI MAKKAI

Public opinion in Australia is now less favourably disposed towards defence than at any time since the end of the Second World War. In particular, the past decade has witnessed a noticeable decline in support for increased defence spending, always an important measure of the standing of defence in the popular mind, and in perceptions of a long-term threat to Australia's security. But there have also been significant changes in more peripheral indicators in recent years, such as support for acquiring nuclear weapons, conscription, and visits by nuclear-powered warships.

In part, this important and significant change in public opinion is the result of the collapse of communism in Eastern Europe, more favourable relations with China and other Asian countries, and moves towards democracy in the Soviet Union. But they also stem from more fundamental changes in social and political values in Western democracies, and from the different experiences and life-chances of their populations. There is now considerable evidence that these two trends – the improving international climate and value change – are converging to radically transform popular attitudes towards the military in many societies.[1]

Despite the potential significance of these changes, the characteristics of contemporary attitudes towards defence are not well-documented, nor has there been much systematic comparison between contemporary attitudes and those of previous periods[2]. There has also been little appreciation of the direction in which attitudes have changed and the political implications of these changes, and insufficient attention has been devoted to understanding how these attitudes vary between different sections of the population. In this paper we seek to fill these gaps, using opinion poll data collected by a variety of organisations and groups in Australia since the late 1940s.

I. Public Opinion on Defence: A Model

The range of potential influences on public opinion towards defence can be separated into three categories. First, there is the individual's primary socialisation and their experiences while growing up, all of which will have an impact on the values that they hold. Second, there is the individual's socio-economic status, which will help to determine their level of interest in national and international events. This knowledge will have consequences for their perceptions of the external threat faced by their country and, we would hypothesise, for their general level of support for defence.[3] Third, there is the individual's political partisanship, which will help to mould their views about

FIGURE 1

A HYPOTHETICAL MODEL OF THE FACTORS WHICH INFLUENCE
ATTITUDES TOWARDS DEFENCE

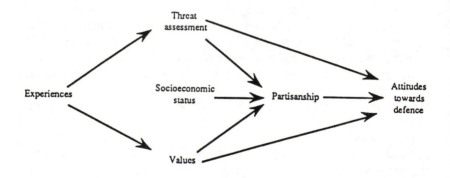

defence and other issues which fall into the realm of party politics. The interaction between these influences and their relationship to attitudes towards defence are shown in the hypothetical model in Figure 1.

The link between childhood and adolescent experiences and the social values held by individuals is explained in what has become known as the theory of postmaterial values.[4] The intellectual origins of the theory lie in the work of A.H. Maslow[5] who argued that individuals act to fulfil a variety of basic needs which are then pursued in a hierarchical order. The position of any single need in the overall hierarchy is determined by the importance of that need to the individual's survival. In Maslow's hierarchy, material needs such as food and shelter are a primary concern, but once these are satisfied, non-material needs such as pleasure and personal fulfilment replace them and become the primary objectives. Maslow's hierarchy of needs theory has been adapted to explain cultural change in Western advanced industrial societies. It is argued that the unprecedented affluence and physical safety of Western societies in the postwar years has satisfied the material needs of these populations. Those who have grown up in this period have therefore been concerned less with material issues such as economic and physical security than with non-material or postmaterial concerns such as social equality and the quality of life.

There is now considerable evidence that the materialist-postmaterialist division within Western societies has become politically important, as these new social goals within the population have been translated into party political debate.[6] From the perspective of the current analysis, it follows that those holding postmaterialist values will be less supportive of defence than their materialist counterparts, whose social values derive from their experiences of the Second World War and the immediate postwar years. For postmaterialists, the physical and economic security provided by their society means that defence has a lower priority when compared with social and environmental concerns.

A variety of studies have examined the role of socio-economic status in formulating attitudes towards defence and foreign policy. Since surveys have shown that those with lower socio-economic status tend to have less political interest and knowledge about national and international events,[7] it might be hypothesised that those most favourable to defence would have lower socio-economic status. However, American research conducted during the Vietnam War indicated that the reverse was the case and that those most in favour of American military efforts had higher socio-economic status, largely because of their internationalist and interventionist outlook.[8] Indeed, it appeared that attitudes towards the use of military force were linked in a complex way to other foreign policy attitudes, with socio-economic status occupying a central position.[9]

The third potential influence on attitudes towards defence, partisanship, acts as a filter through which individuals interpret the political world. Just as individuals become socialised into expressing loyalty towards certain primary groups such as the family or religion, theories of partisanship suggest that they also become socialised into loyalties towards particular political parties.[10] Parties therefore provide a framework within which voters place themselves on contemporary political issues. Since issues such as defence spending, foreign intervention and military alliances are frequently matters of party political debate, we would expect partisanship to influence attitudes towards defence.

These influences represent a potential model of how public opinion towards defence attitudes is formed, and how and why it varies across the population. The model hypothesises that opinion on defence is based primarily on a combination of three elements: social values, threat assessment, and partisanship, with these factors in turn being predicated on experiences and socioeconomic status. In section V we test this model using national survey data collected in Australia during 1984, but before moving to that analysis, we outline broad trends and patterns in public opinion on external relations and defence since the 1940s.

II. Popular Perceptions of External Threats

Since the Second World War Australia has committed personnel to five military operations overseas: the Korean War (1950–53), the Malaya Emergency (1950–60), the Indonesian Confrontation (1963–66), the Vietnam War (1962–72), and the Gulf War (1990–91). With the exception of Vietnam, relatively small numbers of military personnel were involved and in each of the five cases there was no direct threat to Australia's security.[11] The Australian population has, therefore, not been faced with a direct challenge to the country's territorial integrity since 1942. In addition, since its implementation in 1951, Australia has tended to rely on the ANZUS alliance with the United States as a basis for ensuring regional security. In this section we analyse public opinion on three elements of Australia's external relations: perceptions of an external threat; the source of the threat; and trust in the United States to defend Australia.

Popular perceptions of an external threat to Australia's security in the medium term (5 to 10 years) and long term (15 years) have fluctuated as international circumstances have changed (Figure 2). Popular perceptions of a medium term threat declined after the end of the Vietnam War in 1975, but increased in the late 1970s, peaking at 64 per cent in 1981, the year after the Soviet Union's invasion of Afghanistan. Thereafter, the trend has followed an overall downward path, although it is notable that almost the same proportion in 1989 as 1967 thought that there was a medium-term threat.

Perceptions of a long-term threat follow the same general pattern, with a peak in the early 1980s, but show considerably larger variations. However, the decline in perceptions of a threat have also been more consistent over the past decade; in 1988, 30 per cent considered that there would be a threat to Australia's border in the next 15 years, compared with 64 per cent in 1980. The reduction in international tensions (*pace* the Gulf War) has therefore created a climate in which popular opinion has become more positive towards Australia's long-term future, while doubts remain about the potential threats which may arise in the medium term.

The proportions identifying particular countries as a threat to Australia are shown in Table 1 (p.201). Until the mid-1970s, China was considered to be the greatest threat, but the normalisation of relations between Australia and China in 1973 and the end of the Vietnam War in 1975 have reduced this substantially; by 1987 only 2 per cent still considered China a threat, compared with 31 per cent in 1967, although the Tiananmen Square massacre in 1989 resulted in an increase to 15 per cent. Russia was increasingly perceived as a threat in the 1970s, being mentioned by 40 per cent in 1980, but declined thereafter. Until the late 1970s fewer than one in ten Australians considered Indonesia a threat, but events in Timor and Irian Jaya and Indonesia's increasing military capacity have made it seem a more potent military threat. As a result, for the past decade around one in five have considered Indonesia a threat to Australia's security. From the mid-1960s until the late 1980s Japan was not perceived as a threat by the vast majority of Australians. However, in 1989 there was an increase to 22 per cent, dropping to 13 per cent in the last poll in the series. The reasons for this change are unclear, but may have been attributable to the death of Emperor Hirohito, perhaps resurrecting memories of the

FIGURE 2
PERCEPTIONS OF A THREAT TO AUSTRALIA, 1978–68

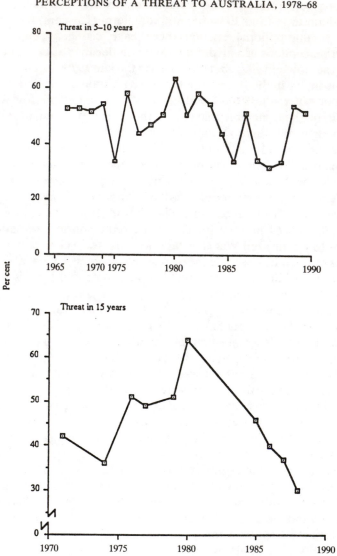

Sources: Matthew and Ravenhill (1987), Morgan Gallup, Age Poll, USIS, Frank
Small.

Second World War. If this was the cause of the increase, opinion polls conducted in the future should show an equally dramatic decline in the proportions who see Japan as a threat to Australia's borders.

In conjunction with the decline in popular perceptions of an external threat, there has been a change over the past two decades in the proportions who think that the United States would come to

TABLE 1

COUNTRIES CONSIDERED A THREAT TO AUSTRALIA, 1967–89

	China	Indonesia	(%) Japan	Vietnam	Russia
1967	31	7	4	9	13
1968	32	6	5	14	11
1969	30	8	7	9	16
1970	27	10	8	7	15
1975 (Sept.)					
	25	0	3	0	11
1975	21	7	6	13	12
1976	17	10	7	2	20
1978	14	14	9	8	16
1980	14	12	6	5	40
1982	7	18	5	2	24
1983	14	17	6	7	36
1984 (May)	7	19	2	1	13
1984 (Sept.)	7	24	3	3	19
1986 (Oct.)	2	21	2	1	16
1987 (May)	4	17	3	2	17
1987 (Sept.)	2	7	2	1	8
1988 (Oct.)	2	12	2	1	6
1989 (May)	6	23	22	3	8
1989 (June)	15	22	13	1	6
Change, 1967–89 (%)	−16	+15	+9	−8	−7

Source: As for Figure 2.

Australia's defence in the event of an attack (figure 3). Since 1975, those expressing 'considerable' trust have consistently stood at about 45 per cent of the population. However, those expressing 'little' or 'no' trust have increased in numbers since 1972, largely at the expense of those who had 'very great' trust in the United States. By 1985, however, they still numbered only one in four of the population.[12] The overall trend though, appears to be one of declining trust in the United States to come to the aid of Australia if the subcontinent's borders

were threatened by an external force. This gradual decline may have
been halted by the events of the Gulf War.

Australia's physical isolation from the rest of Asia, her sometimes
difficult relations with her Asian neighbours, the country's sparse
population, and her defence alliance with the United States, have all
combined to influence public opinion on external relations in a variety
of ways. The changing climate of international relations has resulted in

FIGURE 3
TRUST THAT THE UNITED STATES WILL COME TO AUSTRALIA'S
DEFENCE, 1972–89

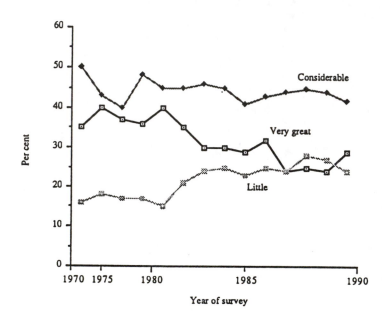

Source: USIS.

a much reduced public perception of a long-term threat, while at the
same time bringing into sharper relief fears of a potential medium term
threat to Australia. Although there is no consensus on where this
threat will materialise from, a plurality consider Indonesia to be the
most likely origin. Perhaps because of these differing perceptions, and
notwithstanding New Zealand's removal from the ANZUS alliance,
popular opinion maintains a high level of trust in the United States to
defend Australia's security.

III. Public Opinion on Defence Since 1945

There are a variety of problems inherent in tracing changes in public opinion over any extended period of time and these problems are compounded when the topic is one such as defence, in which interest has waxed and waned according to the prevailing political and international climate. First, the questions asked in opinion surveys frequently change; a change observed in popular attitudes may therefore be less a real change in opinion than an artifact of alterations in the survey instrument. A second, related, problem is that the sampling method often changes, particularly in a large country such as Australia where rural sampling (at least in the era before mail and telephone surveys) is expensive. Third, the available data often make consistent breakdowns of the data by even basic demographic variables such as age difficult. These inconsistencies, which are documented more fully in the Appendix, should be borne in mind when evaluating the results that follow.

In disaggregating the results by demographic group, we have relied solely on gender and age. As have already hypothesized, age – or, more properly, the period in which the individual was socialised and entered the active electorate – is a major potential influence on attitudes towards defence. For the purposes of the analysis, we dichotomise age into those aged under 30 years, and those aged 30 years or over. Gender has been shown to be an important variable, with women being less likely to support military expansion or aggressive foreign policies which could ultimately involve the application of military overseas.[13]

Conscription

The most complete trend opinion poll data are available for conscription. Conscription has been part of Australian defence policy for several periods in the twentieth century. Compulsory military training ceased in 1929, but was reintroduced with the start of the Second World War in 1939, lasting until 1946. Australia's involvement in the Korean War again resulted in compulsory military training being used from 1951 until 1959. With the introduction of a military commitment, Vietnam in 1962, conscription was reintroduced in 1964, lasting until 1973, one year after Australia withdrew her remaining forces.

Figure 4 shows attitudes for and against conscription from 1943 until

1989, the last date for which survey data are available. Two patterns are apparent. First, throughout the 46-year period, more individuals have consistently favoured conscription than have opposed it, although in 1985 only eight percentage points separated the opposing views. Second, despite the consistent majority which has favoured conscription, support for it is in long-term decline, notwithstanding two peaks of support after the end of the Korean War and towards the end of Australia's Vietnam involvement, respectively. Throughout the late 1980s, more opposed conscription than at almost any time since the 1940s. Third, there seems to be relatively little correlation between support for conscription and periods when conscription was in operation. To the extent that attitudes towards conscription are influenced by contemporary events and policies, government policy on compulsory military training would appear to have little effect.

The results disaggregated by gender and age are shown in Figure 5.

FIGURE 4

ATTITUDES TOWARDS CONSCRIPTION IN AUSTRALIA, 1943–89

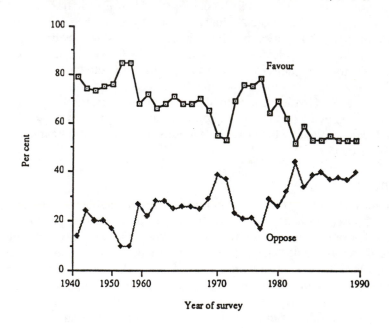

Sources: Morgan Gallup, Frank Small.

There are comparatively few gender differences, with the partial exception of the mid-1960s when men were more likely to favour conscription than women, and in the early 1970s when this pattern was reversed. Overall, however, the gender differences are minor. The most notable difference is the emergence of the generational gap in the 1970s. Since 1977, the difference in support for conscription among those aged 30 years or over and those aged under 30 years has never been less than 21 percentage points; in 1985, for example, the last year in which age breakdowns are available, 66 per cent of those aged 30 years or over were in favour of conscription, compared with 39 per cent of those aged under 30 years.

Nuclear weapons

The introduction of nuclear weapons is linked to the whole question of the development of nuclear power in Australia. There was little serious discussion of using nuclear power as an energy source until 1969, when the then prime minister, John Gorton, proposed the construction of a nuclear power station at Jervis Bay. Gorton's successor, William McMahon, was unconvinced about the economics of the project and it was halted. In contrast to the peaceful use of nuclear energy, calls for the acquisition of nuclear weapons by the Australian defence forces have never been endorsed by the major parties, although neither did they formally rule out such a policy.[14] As a result of persistent fears about China's nuclear capacity and Indonesian intentions of developing a nuclear capability, it was not until 1973 that Australia signed the Nuclear Non-Proliferation Treaty.

Public opinion has shifted considerably in the past decade on the issue of nuclear weapons (Figure 6). Until 1974 opinion was in favour of Australia acquiring nuclear weapons, although only narrowly so in the mid-1960s. Since 1974, with the exception of one poll in 1980, those opposing the move have outnumbered those opposing it. Indeed, in the most recent poll, conducted in 1988, those opposing the acquisition of nuclear weapons outnumbered those favouring it by more than three to one. Until 1975, the gender differences on the issue were significant, ranging from 15 to 22 percentage points; thereafter, the differences are negligible (Figure 7). As is the case with conscription, it appears that gender is today not an important factor in explaining attitudes toward nuclear weapons. Although those aged under 30 years have been slightly more opposed to nuclear weapons than those

FIGURE 5
GENDER AND AGE DIFFERENCES IN SUPPORT FOR CONSCRIPTION

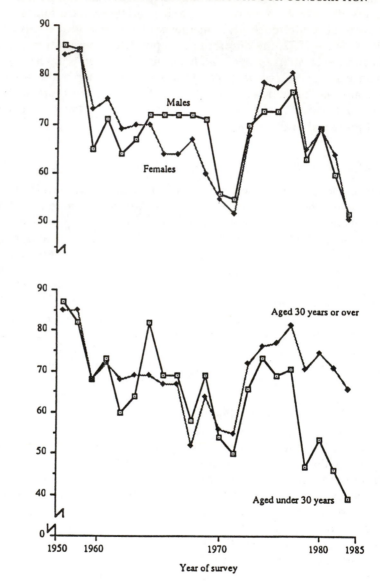

Sources: As for Figure 4.

aged over 30, the differences were slight until the 1970s. Like attitudes to conscription, there has been an emerging age gap on the issue during the past decade with younger adults less in favour of nuclear weapons.

FIGURE 6

ATTITUDES TOWARDS AUSTRALIA'S ACQUISITION OF NUCLEAR
WEAPONS, 1957–88

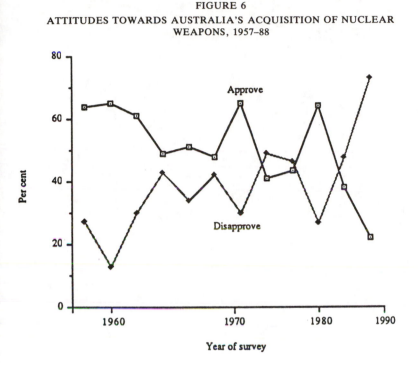

Source: AGP, Morgan Gallup, Frank Small.

Visiting nuclear warships

An issue which is related to nuclear energy is the question of nuclear-powered ships visiting Australian ports. Between 1971 and 1976 there was a moratorium on the visit of nuclear-powered warships but since 1976 nuclear-powered ships have been subject to the normal maritime rules governing Australian ports. The issue was central to New Zealand's decision to terminate the ANZUS alliance with the United States, and largely as a result of this, it surfaced periodically in Australian political debate during the 1980s.

FIGURE 7
GENDER AND AGE DIFFERENCES IN SUPPORT FOR NUCLEAR WEAPONS

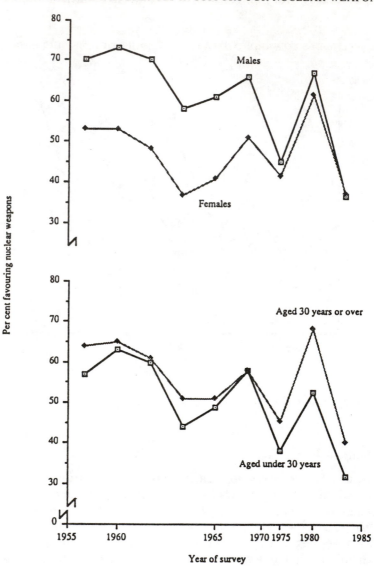

Sources: As for Figure 6.

In 1976, when the moratorium was lifted, those in favour of the presence of nuclear-powered ships outnumbered those opposed by three to one (Figure 8). Since then, however, support has declined consistently, to less than half of the 1976 level. In particular, since 1987 the polls have shown that those opposing visits have outnumbered those favouring visits by an average of 15 percentage points. There are significant gender and age variations in these patterns, as we would expect. Women have consistently outnumbered men in their opposition to visits by these ships, as have those aged under 30 years (Figure 9). Indeed, the extent of the gender differences in attitudes are such that it is hardly an exaggeration to say that most of the opposition to these warship visits comes from women.

These results provide impressionistic evidence about changing public opinions towards defence. None of the three issues – conscrip-

FIGURE 8

ATTITUDES TOWARDS NUCLEAR-POWERED WARSHIPS VISITING
AUSTRALIAN PORTS, 1976–89

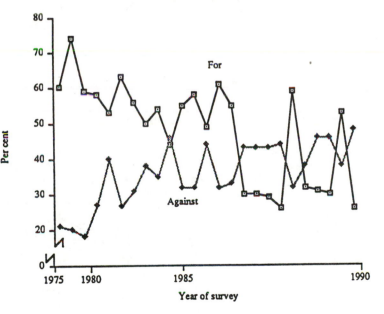

Sources: Morgan Gallup, APOP, USIS, Frank Small.

FIGURE 9
GENDER AND AGE DIFFERENCES IN SUPPORT FOR NUCLEAR POWERED
WARSHIPS VISITING AUSTRALIAN PORTS

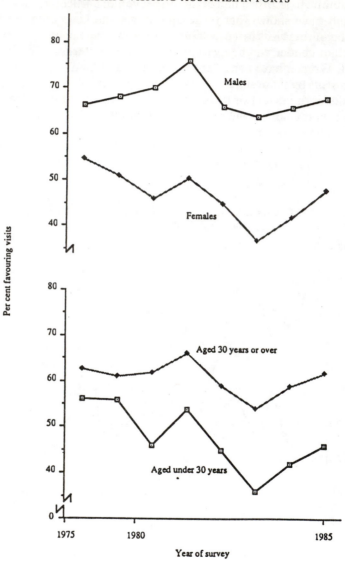

Sources: As for Figure 8.

tion, the acquisition of nuclear weapons or nuclear-powered ships visiting Australian ports – measure any aspect of current or likely defence policy in Australia. They do, however, provide indirect estimates of how the population regards defence-related issues. The common theme which runs through the data indicates that a major change took place in the mid-1980s: conscription became less popular, a large majority emerged to oppose the acquisition of nuclear weapons; and those opposed to permitting nuclear-powered ships into Australian ports outnumbered those in favour for the first time since 1976. Clearly, the last decade, and more precisely the last five years, are pivotal for understanding changes in Australian attitudes towards defence in Australian. In the next two sections, we test some explanations for these changes.

Attitudes to Defence Spending

Attitudes towards public expenditure on defence are a sensitive barometer of public opinion towards defence as a whole. In times of war or international crisis, public opinion favours increased defence spending, since that provides a means of allaying the potential threat to the country's security. When there is no discernible threat, however, public opinion finds it more difficult to justify defence spending, particularly given demands from competing areas such as welfare and health. Opinions favouring cuts in military expenditure typically correlate most strongly with opinions about aid to minority groups, cooperation with the Soviet Union, and support for increased standards of living.[15]

Placed in international perspective, albeit more than five years ago, Australian attitudes towards defence spending are in line with those found in the United States and Italy (Figure 10): in all three countries, nearly two-thirds of the population favour an increase in government spending. Britain heads the list, with three-quarters of the population in favour of an increase, a finding which is at least partly explained by the repercussions of the 1982 Falklands War. Denmark and Austria show the least support for an increase, although it is notable that in each case the majority favour the status quo rather than a reduction in spending.

Placed in longitudinal perspective across a variety of countries, popular support for defence spending has declined considerably. In the United States, Stanley and Niemi (1988) analysed survey data from

1960 to 1987 measuring attitudes towards public spending for 'national defence and military purposes'.[16] From 1974 to 1981 the polls indicated that support for military spending grew; from 1982 until 1987, however, the trend reversed and those who thought that spending was 'too much' greatly outnumbered those who said 'too little'. In 1987, 44 per cent said that 'too much' was being spent, compared with only 14 per

FIGURE 10

ATTITUDES TOWARDS PUBLIC EXPENDITURE ON DEFENCE IN SIX COUNTRIES, 1985

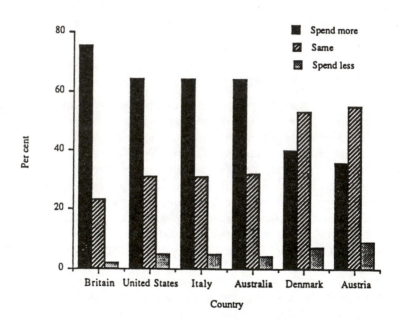

Source: 1985 ISSP.

cent who said 'too little'. The net result is that more Americans now believe that defence should be cut than at any time since opinion polls began to monitor the subject in the 1930s.[17]

Australian opinion on defence spending has generally followed the American pattern, with the exception that the rapid decline in support for defence expenditure has come within the last four years. Although the figures should be treated with caution because of changes in question wording, Figure 11 indicates that support for more expenditure followed an upward trend during the late 1970s, peaking at 77 per cent in 1981, a year after the Soviet invasion of Afghanistan. In line with public opinion in the United States, there has been a consistent decline in support since 1981, with the partial exception of 1985. By 1987 the proposition was supported by a minority of the population (49 per cent) and by 1990 more people actually favoured a reduction in

FIGURE 11

ATTITUDES TO EXPENDITURE ON DEFENCE, 1975–90

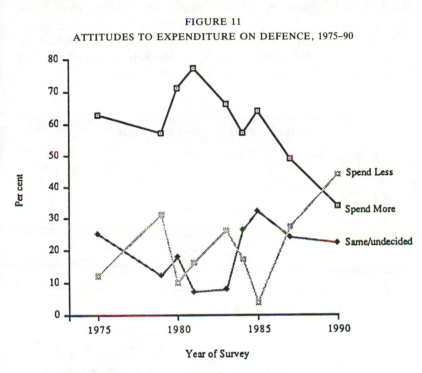

Year of Survey

Sources: Morgan Research Centre, ANPAS, AES, NSSS.

spending than more spending (44 per cent, as against 34 per cent). In the relatively short space of a decade – judged by the normally glacial changes in public opinion – support for defence spending in Australia has been reduced by more than half.

How do we account for this large and significant change in public opinion? The shifting international climate and the declining threat from the Soviet Union and the former Eastern Bloc countries are specific, one-off events which have affected popular attitudes. Another explanation suggests that value change may be an important, continuing influence on public opinion. As we explained in section 1, value-change theories argue that shifts in attitudes have been the result of differing experiences in childhood and adolescence. In this view, those most in favour of defence spending would have grown up during the war years or before, while those most opposed would be the young who have grown up in the 1970s and 1980s. Moreover, this pattern should hold for whatever survey is examined, since the explanation rests on generational change within the population, rather than age *per se*. In other words, since it is the political experiences of the period that have moulded attitudes towards defence, this will be the same regardless of the year in which the survey was conducted.

FIGURE 12

SUPPORT FOR DEFENCE SPENDING BY THE PERIOD IN WHICH THE
VOTER ENTERED THE ELECTORATE

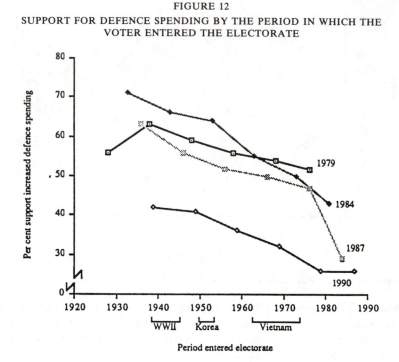

Period entered electorate

Sources: as for Figure 11.

We can test this hypothesis by plotting support for defence spending across the 1979, 1984, 1987 and 1990 surveys by the period in which the individual entered the electorate, estimated roughly at 18 to 22 years.[18]

Figure 12 suggests that there are two influences at work in determining attitudes to defence spending. On the one hand, there is a clear generational effect, with those who came of age during the Second World War showing the strongest support for increased defence spending, those who came of age in the post-Vietnam War years showing least support. To that extent, there is support for the values explanation of attitudes towards defence spending. On the other hand, however, the 1990 survey suggests that there has been a secular change in support for defence spending, which is unrelated to generation; for each generation, support for spending is about 15 percentage points down on the same figure in the 1987 survey. The only exception to this pattern is the most recent generation, which produces a similar figure in both the 1987 and 1990 surveys.

There is, then, partial support for the values hypothesis, as reflected by political generation, to explain attitudes towards defence spending in Australia. The most dramatic change appears to have taken place among those who began to enter the electorate during the 1980s. Among this group, support for defence spending is at an all-time low. In addition to this generational change, there would appear to have been a more widespread change in attitudes affecting all of the generational groups. To that extent, the changes in the international political climate which have taken place between 1987 and 1990 have had a profound impact on popular attitudes towards defence spending.

V. Attitudes to Defence: Evaluating the Influences

It is evident from the results presented so far that attitudes towards defence in Australia have undergone substantial change in recent years. Moreover, there is only partial support for the hypothesis that this change is related directly to value change within Western societies. Indeed, the most recent data collected in 1990 suggest a significant secular change in attitudes across the electorate. In this section we test the importance of the various potential influences on popular attitudes towards defence. For this purpose, we use data collected in 1984, the most recent data which include the variables required to test the model.[19] Since we have shown that there were substantial changes in attitudes since 1984, the time at which these data were collected should be borne in mind when interpreting the results.

The model outlined in section 1 contains four elements: the experiences of individuals as they entered the electorate; an assessment of the threat to Australia from overseas; socio-economic status; values; and partisanship (see Figure 1 above). To measure their relative impact in shaping attitudes towards defence, these effects are operationalised as follows. Experience is measured by four dummy variables which correspond to the prevailing political atmosphere when the individual entered the electorate, with the youngest group, those who grew up in the post-Vietnam period, acting as the excluded category. The international threat posed to Australia is measured by perceptions of the threat coming from four countries: the Soviet Union, China, Indonesia, and Japan.[20] Socio-economic status is measured by education, scored in years, and by whether or not the individual is a non-manual worker.[21] Values are measured by two multiple-item scales measuring materialist and postmaterialist values, respectively.[22] Finally, partisanship is measured by Labour partisanship or Liberal-National partisanship, with those giving a minor party loyalty or saying that they had no partisanship forming the excluded category.

The 1984 survey included a measure of attitudes towards defence spending, in addition to a measure asking the respondent to rate confidence in the military, as well as confidence in a variety of other groups and institutions. The survey found that the average level of popular confidence in the military placed it sixth in rank order out of 12 institutions, following (in order) banks, the police, universities, small business, and state schools. At the other end of the scale, the press was ranked 11th and trade unions 12th.

The factors influencing attitudes to defence spending and confidence in the military are shown in table 2, grouped under the headings of experiences, threat, socio-economic status, values and partisanship. In addition, three control variables are included in the equations for gender, residence, and birthplace, respectively. The figures are standardised regression coefficients, which show the relative effect of a variable measured against the others in the equation. For example, in the defence spending equation being a member of the Vietnam War generation (standardised coefficient of .04) is about half as important as being from the Second World War generation (coefficient of .08) in predicting support for increased defence spending.

The results indicate that by far the predominant influence on defence spending is values: those who hold materialist values are significantly more likely to support greater spending, while those with postmaterialist values are significantly less likely to support an increase, net of other things. Indeed, around half of all of the variance in defence spending explained by the model is attributable to the influence of values. Perceptions of threat are next in importance, and those who perceive Indonesia as a potential threat are those most likely to favour an increase in spending. There are more modest,

TABLE 2
FACTORS AFFECTING DEFENCE SPENDING AND CONFIDENCE IN THE MILITARY, 1984

	(Standardised regression coefficients)	
	Defence spending	Confidence in military
Experiences (post Vietnam War)		
Vietnam	.04	.07**
Cold War	.05	.03
Postwar, Korea	.03	.04*
Second World War	.08**	.12**
Threat		
Soviet Union	.08**	.03
China	.05*	.03
Indonesia	.12**	−.05*
Japan	−.04	−.01
Socio-economic status		
Education	−.09**	−.11**
Non-manual worker	.01	−.03
Values		
Materialist	.35**	.21**
Postmaterialist	−.24**	−.11**
Partisanship (Other, none)		
Labor	−.03	−.01
Liberal-National	.12**	.04
Control variables		
Male	.08**	−.05
Urban resident	.07**	.10**
Overseas born	−.03	−.07**
R-squared (adjusted)	.23	.10

** p<.01, * p<.05, two-tailed.

a OLS regression analyses showing standardised regression coefficients predicting the probability of support for more defence spending and confidence in the military. Where dummy variables are used, the excluded category is shown in parentheses.
Source: 1984 NSSS.

though still statistically significant, effects for the Soviet Union and China (bearing in mind this survey was conducted in 1984), and no significant effect for Japan, as we would predict. By contrast, all of the other influences are more minor. Only the Second World War generation shows an increased likelihood to support an increase in spending, as do those with less education and who are Liberal-National partisans.

Values also dominate the equation predicting confidence in the military, although less of the variance is explained.[23] In this case, experiences exert more influence, with those growing up in a period when a war was in progress (either the Vietnam War or the Second World War) expressing greater confidence in the military than those who grew up in either the postwar or Cold War generations, or the post-Vietnam War generation. In contrast to spending, perceptions of external threat have little impact; the sole effect is that those who perceive Indonesia as a potential threat have less confidence in the Australian military.

Although the data on which these results are based were collected in 1984 and, as we have already indicated, there have been significant changes since then, they provide strong support for the values explanation for changes in public opinion towards defence. As we have already argued, values are formed during socialisation and are normally stable and relatively enduring; they do not change as a consequence of particular events or of short or medium-term changes in the individual's life or in the circumstances of the society as a whole. This suggests, therefore, that the long-term decline in support for defence will continue, as the values of the society gradually change, barring major international crises, direct military threats to Australia, or catastrophic domestic instability.

VI. Discussion

So far, our analysis has assumed a policy environment in which public opinion plays a central, even a predominant, role. While public opinion is undoubtedly important in policy formulation, public policies are determined by political elites, and they themselves play an important role in shaping mass attitudes towards foreign policy and military issues[24]. Since the general population is usually regarded as less informed and generally unconcerned about military and foreign policy problems, elites have considerable freedom to develop and implement policies in this area.[25] In the United States, for example, it is argued that presidents have more leeway to initiate policy in the foreign sphere than in domestic politics, where they encounter more opposition and engender more conflict.[26]

Bearing in mind the discrepancy between the knowledge and interest of voters in foreign policy and military issues compared with the political elite, a model of defence policy-making in Australia might place less weight on the direction and intensity of public opinion, than on the attitudes and perceptions of the elite. It is this latter group, it might be argued, who have the information to assess the current situation, identify the appropriate policy options, and ensure that the policies arrived at and their implications are accurately communicated

TABLE 3

FEDERAL PARLIAMENTARY CANDIDATE ATTITUDES TO DEFENCE
SPENDING, 1987

	Labour	Liberal-National	Democrat	All[1]
Spend more	12	78	30	46
Doesn't matter	57	8	55	36
Spend less	31	14	15	18
Total (%)	100	100	100	100
(N)	(120)	(182)	(101)	(541)

Note 1. Includes major as well as non-major party candidates.
Source: 1987 AES.

to the mass public. The views of political elites towards the issue of defence can be gauged by the attitudes of federal parliamentary candidates in 1987 and 1990. In each election, candidates were asked their views about defence spending, although the question differed between the two surveys.

In 1987, there were major partisan divisions between the candidates, which were a sharper reflection of the partisan divisions to be found within the electorate as a whole (Table 3). More than three of four Liberal-National candidates proposed that more money should be spent on defence, compared with about one in eight of the Labour candidates. Indeed, most Labour candidates (57 per cent) regarded the level of defence spending as an issue of minor importance, as did the majority of Democrat candidates. If 1987 is taken as a benchmark for the direction of spending on defence, then elite opinion was moderately in favour of increasing expenditure, albeit divided on a strongly partisan basis.

By 1990, however, elite opinion on defence spending would appear to have changed. Although direct comparisons with 1987 are difficult because of the different format of the questions, it would appear that there was considerably less support for increased defence spending among Liberal-National candidates. When asked to rank nine areas of government spending in terms of their priorities for increased or reduced spending, candidates of all parties singled out defence as a top priority for a reduction, and almost the lowest priority for an increase.[27] Overall, 47 per cent of the sample saw defence as the top priority for reduced expenditure, with unemployment benefit being the next most frequently mentioned area (19 per cent), and help for industry (8 per cent) ranking third. As Table 4 indicates, there were comparatively few partisan variations in this pattern, with 46 per cent of Liberal-National candidates agreeing that defence should be a top priority for cuts. At the other end of the spectrum, hardly any candidates viewed defence as a top priority for increased spending; defence ranked third from the bottom, just ahead of unemployment benefit (mentioned by 1 per cent) and the police (0.3 per cent). The two areas to gain most support for increased spending were education (38 per cent) and protection of the environment (26 per cent).

Like voters, then, elite opinion would appear to have changed its

TABLE 4

FEDERAL PARLIAMENTARY CANDIDATE ATTITUDES TO DEFENCE
SPENDING, 1990

	Labour	Liberal-National	Democrat	All[1]
First priority for increase	0	3	1	2
Second priority for increase	1	2	0	1
(Total increase)	(1)	(5)	(1)	(3)
First priority for cut	55	46	66	47
Second priority for cut	11	9	9	10
(Total Cut)	(66)	(55)	(75)	(57)
Neither cut nor increase	33	40	24	40
Total (%)	100	100	100	100
(N)	(114)	(149)	(139)	(426)

Note 1. Includes major as well as non-major party cnadidates.
Source: 1990 AES

views about defence spending within the last five years. Although caution is needed in drawing firm conclusions from these data because of the altered question formats between the two surveys, the results do suggest that elite opinion – at least measured by the views of federal parliamentary candidates – has undergone considerable change. Clearly, these results do not imply that there will be a rapid change in policy on defence expenditure. But the results do suggest that the climate of elite opinion in which defence could count on at least a stable level of funding in the medium term is becoming increasingly unfavourable to the military and to defence in general. Political elites may be becoming exposed to the same value changes that would appear to have altered Australian voters' opinions in the past decade.

VII. Conclusion

In this paper, we have used a range of public opinion poll data to examine attitudes towards defence in Australia. Our major conclusions are as follows:

1. There has been a significant decline in the proportions seeing a long-term threat to Australia, though there are fluctuations in the numbers mentioning a medium-term threat.

2. There is no consensus on the source of the threat, although the largest single group see Indonesia as more likely to pose a threat than any other country in the region.

3. Trust in the United States to come to Australia's defence remains at a high level, although there appears to be a gradual decline over the last two decades.

4. On the defence-related indicators of conscription, nuclear weapons and nuclear-powered warships, significant shifts of opinion against them have taken place in the last decade.

5. Opinions on defence spending have experienced very substantial changes in the past five years, with a majority in favour of an increase in spending being transformed into a majority in favour of a reduction.

6. The multivariate analysis reveals that the major influence on attitudes towards defence spending is values, with threat perceptions playing a more minor role.

7. Elite opinion also appears to have changed in the past five years, with federal parliamentary candidates becoming con-

siderably less favourable to defence spending in 1990 than
they were in 1987.

NOTES

A paper prepared for the First International Conference on Defence and the Media in
Time of Limited Conflict, Queensland University of Technology, Brisbane, 3–5 April
1991. The 1967 and 1979 Australian National Political Attitudes surveys were collected
by Don Aitkin, the 1987 Australian Election Study by Ian McAllister, Anthony Mughan
and Roger Jones, the 1990 Australian Election Study by Ian McAllister, Elim Papa-
dakis, David Gow and Roger Jones, and the 1984 National Social Science Survey by
Bruce Headey, Robert Cushing and Jonathan Kelley. All are available from the Social
Science Data Archives at the Australian National University, as are the Morgan Gallup
data; neither the original collectors of the data nor the disseminating agency bear any
responsibility for the analyses or interpretations presented herein. Our thanks to
Anthony Bergin for helpful comments and suggestions, Dan Scheer for supplying data
commissioned by USIS, Gina Roach and Gillian Evans for assistance with accessing the
Morgan Gallup data, and to Pramod Adhikari and Miriam Landau for research
assistance. The usual disclaimer applies.

1. Russell J. Dalton and Manfred Kuechler (eds.), *Challenging the Political Order*
   (Cambridge, UK: Polity, 1990).
2. Cf. David Campbell, *Australian Public Opinion on National Security Issues* (Canberra: Peace Research Centre Working Paper No.1, 1986 and Alistair Marshall,
   Australian Public Opinion and Defence: Towards a New Perspective (Canberra:
   Peace Research Centre Working Paper No.92, 1990).
3. There are, of course, a range of influences which determine attitudes towards
   defence between different countries. These include the political culture of the
   countries concerned, the character of their civil-military relations, and the type of
   political systems involved.
4. Ronald Inglehart, *The Silent Revolution: Changing Values and Styles Among
   Western Publics* (Princeton, NJ: Princeton University Press, 1977). Idem, *Culture
   Shift in Advanced Industrial Society* (Princeton, NJ: Princeton University Press,
   1990).
5. A. H. Maslow, *Motivation and Personality* (New York: Harper and Row, 1954).
6. Inglehart, *Silent Revolution* and *Culture Shift*. The literature on postmaterialism is
   voluminous, but useful reviews can be found in Inglehart's work, and for their
   applicability in Australia, in Brian Graetz and Ian McAllister, *Dimensions of
   Australian Society* (Melbourne: Macmillan, p.248ff, 1988), and Ian McAllister and
   Clive Bean, 'Explaining Labor's Victory' in Clive Bean, Ian McAllister and John
   Warhurst (eds.), *The Greening of Australian Politics* (Melbourne: Longman
   Cheshire, 1990).
7. James Rosenau, *Public Opinion and Foreign Policy* (New York: Random House,
   1961). Robert W. Oldendick and Barbara Ann Bardes, 'Mass and Elite Foreign
   Policy Opinions', *Public Opinion Quarterly* Vol.46 (1982), pp.368–92.
8. Richard F. Hamilton, 'A Research Note on Mass Support for Military Initiatives',
   American Sociological Review, Vol.33 (1968), pp.439–45. Andre Modigliani,

'Hawks, Doves, Isolationism and Political Distrust: An Analysis of Public Opinion on Military Policy', *American Political Science RReview*, Vol.66 (1972), pp.960–78.

9. Sidney Verba *et al.*, 'Public Opinion and the War in Vietnam', *American Political Science Review*, Vol.62 (1967), pp.317–33.

10. Angus Campbell *et al.*, *The Voter Decides* (Evanston, IL: Row, Petersen, 1954).

11. Some 14,000 Australians served in Korea, 7,000 in Malaya, 3,500 during the Indonesian confrontation, and 50,000 in Vietnam (McAllister *et al*, 1990, p.142).

12. In turn, there is strong support in the United States to come to the aid of countries such as Australia. See John M. Benson, 'The Polls: US Military Intervention', *Public Opinion Quarterly*, Vol.46 (1982), pp.592–98; and Bruce Russett and Miroslav Nincic, 'American Opinion and the Use of Military Force Abroad' in Franklin D. Margiotta (ed.), *The Changing World of the American Military* (Boulder, CO: Westview, 1978).

13. Robert Y. Shapiro and Harpreet Mahajan, 'Gender Differences in Policy Preferences: A Summary of Trends from the 1960s to the 1980s', *Public Opinion Quarterly*, Vol.50 (1986), pp.42–61. Harold W. Stanley and Richard G. Niemi, *Vital Statistics on American Politics* (Washington, DC: Congressional Quarterly Press, 1988).

14. David Campbell, *Australian Public Opinion*. The only political party formally to advocate the acquisition of nuclear weapons was the Democratic Labour Party.

15. Robert S. Erikson, Norman Luttbeg and Kent L. Tedin, *American Public Opinion* (New York: Macmillan, 1988), p.87.

16. Stanley and Niemi, *Vital Statistics*.

17. James Clotfelter, *The Military in American Politics* (New York: Harper and Row, 1973); p.128. Other research, however, has suggested that opinion on military spending is volatile, cf. Michael Corbett, *American Public Opinion* (New York: Longman, 1991), p.182.

18. These were the four surveys which were easiest to analyse by age group. The period of entry to the electorate obviously varies according to the particular timing of elections, and in 1973 the voting age was reduced from 21 to 18 years. However, since we are interested in socialisation rather than first vote, the error introduced by these uncertainties should be minimal.

19. The 1987 and 1990 Australian Election studies lack variables on threat assessment. A 1990 National Social Science Survey was collected at the Australian National University in late 1990 which included many of the necessary variables, but it has not been made available for academic research.

20. In preliminary analyses, we combined these items (which correlate, on average, at .40), but disaggregated them for the final analysis. Data were also collected on the United States; in all of the surveys, few mentioned the US as a potential threat and it has been excluded.

21. In preliminary analyses, we also included variables for university education and occupational status. These added little to the substantive results and for parsimony we have excluded them here.

22. These values are more normally measured by a single, unidimensional scale, scoring materialists at one extreme, postmaterialists at the other. For the reasons outlined in Graetz and McAllister, pp.250–51, we use two separate scales; the correlation between the two scales is .51.

23. The variance explained by the model in the confidence in defence equation (measure by the R-squared statistic) is about half the variance explained in the defence spending equation.

24. Oldendich and Bardes (n.7).

25. Voters in Australia are also less concerned about domestic issues, mainly socio-economic in nature [(an McAllister, 'Party Adaptation and Factionalism Within the

Australian Party System', *American Journal of Political Science*, Vol.35 (1991), pp.206–27; and idem, 'Party Elites, Voters and Political Attitudes: Testing Three Explanations for Mass-Elite Differences', *Canadian Journal of Political Science* (1991)], but the mass-elite gap in knowledge and information in generally considered to be larger on international policies (Oldendick and Bardes, 1981).
26. Cronin, 1980.
27. This question was also asked of voters in the 1990 federal election, but unfortunately about one-third answered the question incorrectly. To the extent that mass-elite comparisons are possible (and the mass sample is obviously biased in favour of the better-educated), they suggest that voters are equally as likely to favour cuts in defence spending as their parliamentary candidates.

Other Sources

Campbell, Angus *et al*, *The American Voter* (New York: Wiley, 1960).
Gilens, Martin, 'Gender and Support for Reagan: A Comprehensive Model', *American Journal of Political Science*, Vol.32 (1988), pp.19–49.
McAllister, Ian *et al*, *Australian Political Facts* (Melbourne: Longman Cheshire, 1990)
Matthews, Trevor and John Ravenhill, 'ANZUS: The American Alliance and External Threats', *Australian Outlook*, Vol.41 (1988), pp.161–72.

APPENDIX TABLE: SURVEY DETAILS

Survey title/date	Principal investigator	N	Question wording	Age groupings
Figure 2				
Morgan Gallup Poll 194, Nov. 1967		1,928[b]	In your opinion, are there any countries which are a threat to Australia's security? Yes, no, can't say. Which countries are a threat to Australia's security? America, China, Indonesia, Japan, North Vietnam, Germany, Russia	21–29 yrs
Morgan Gallup Poll 198, June 1968		2,071[b]	In your opinion, are there any countries which are a threat to Australia's security? Yes, no, can't say. Which countries are a threat to Australia's security? America, China, Indonesia, Japan, North Vietnam, Germany, Russia	21–29 yrs
Morgan Gallup Poll 203, April 1969		2,092[b]	In your opinion, are there any countries which are a threat to Australia's security? Yes, no, can't say. Which countries are a threat to Australia's security? America, China, Indonesia, Japan, North Vietnam, Germany, Russia	21–29 yrs
Morgan Gallup Poll 209, Feb. 1970		2,121[b]	In your opinion, are there any countries which are a threat to Australia's security? Yes, no, can't say. Which countries are a threat to Australia's security? America, China, Indonesia, Japan, North Vietnam, Germany, Russia	21–29 yrs
Foreign Trade, Foreign Investment and ANZUS, Australian Attitudes, Sept. 1975	USICA	933[a]	In your opinion, are there any countries which are a threat to Australia's security? Yes, no, can't say. Which countries? Japan, China, Vietnam, Soviet Union, United States, Indonesia, others.	
Morgan Gallup Poll, 1975 (Source: Campbell, 1989)		1,905	In your opinion, are there any countries which are a threat to Australia's security?	
Morgan Gallup Poll, 1976 (Source: Campbell, 1989)		na	In your opinion, are there any countries which are a threat to Australia's security?	
Morgan Gallup Poll, 1978 (Source: Campbell, 1989)		na	In your opinion, are there any countries which are a threat to Australia's security?	
Foreign Trade, Foreign Investment and ANZUS, Australian Attitudes, March 1978	USICA	1,135[a]	In your opinion, are there any countries which are a threat to Australia's security? Yes, no, can't say. Which countries? Japan, China, Vietnam, Soviet Union, United States, Indonesia, others.	20–29 yrs
Age Poll, April 1980	Irving Saulwick and Associates	2,013[d]	In your opinion are there any countries which are a threat to Australia's security? Yes, no, don't know. Which countries? China, Russia, Vietnam, North Vietnam, Indonesia, Japan, America, other, Don't know.	21–34 yrs

APPENDIX TABLE: SURVEY DETAILS CONTD

Survey title/date	Principal investigator	N	Question wording	Age groupings
ANZUS and Australia's security: Australian Attitudes, July 1982	USIS	1,093[a]	In your opinion are there any countries which are a threat to Australia's security? Yes, no, can't say. Which countries? America, China, Indonesia, Japan, East Germany, West Germany, Russia, Vietnam, other.	20–29 yrs
Morgan Gallup Poll 512, April 1983		1,976[a]	In your opinion, are there any countries which are a threat to Australia's security? Yes, no, can't say. Which countries are a threat to Australia's security? America, China, Indonesia, Japan, North Vietnam, Germany, Russia	20–29 yrs
ANZUS and Australia's security: Australian Attitudes, May 1984	USIS	1,127[a]	In your opinion are there any countries which are a threat to Australia's security? Yes, no, can't say. Which countries? America, China, Indonesia, Japan, East Germany, West Germany, Libya, Russia, Vietnam, other.	20–29 yrs
ANZUS and Australia's security: Australian Attitudes, Sept. 1984	USIS	1,141[a]	In your opinion are there any countries which are a threat to Australia's security? Yes, no, can't say. Which countries? Japan, China, Vietnam, Soviet Union, United States, Indonesia, others	20–29 yrs
ANZUS and Australia's security: Australian Attitudes, Oct. 1986	USIS	1,117[a]	Thinking about 10 years from now. In your opinion, do any countries pose a military threat to the security of Australia, over next ten years? Yes, no, can't say. Which countries will pose a military threat to the security of Australia in the next five years? If yes, which country or countries? China, Indonesia, Japan, Russia, Vietnam, any others, no none, don't know	
Morgan Gallup Poll 825, May 1987		1,295[a]	In your opinion, are there any countries which are a threat to Australia's security? Yes, no, can't say. Which countries are a threat to Australia's security?	20–34 yrs
ANZUS and Australia's security: Australian Attitudes, Sept. 1987	USIS	1,110[a]	Thinking about 5 years from now. In your opinion, do any countries pose a military threat to the security of Australia, over the next five years? Yes, no can't say. Which countries will pose a military threat to the security of Australia in the next five years? If yes, which country or countries? China, Indonesia, Japan, Russia, Vietnam, any others, no none, don't know	

APPENDIX TABLE: SURVEY DETAILS CONTD

Survey title/date	Principal investigator	N	Question wording	Age groupings
Frank Small and Associates, July 1988		1,300[c]	In your opinion, is Australia likely or unlikely to face a military threat from another country in the next 10 years, or is it just too difficult to tell? Likely, unlikely, too difficult to tell, don't know. Which country or countries are likely to threaten Australia? Indonesia, Soviet Union, Japan, Indonesia, United States, Libya, South East Asia, any others.	
ANZUS and Australia's security: Australian Attitudes, Oct. 1988	USIS	11,067[a]	Thinking about 5 years from now. In your opinion, do any countries pose a military threat to the security of Australia, over the next five years? Yes, no can't say. Which countries will pose a military threat to the security of Australia in the next five years? If yes, which country or countries? China, Indonesia, Japan, Russia, Vietnam, Any others. No none, don't know	
Morgan Gallup Poll 965, May 1989		1,187[a]	In your opinion, are there any countries which are a threat to Australia's security?	20–34 yrs
Morgan Gallup Poll No. 969, June 1989		956[a]	In your opinion, are there any countries which are a threat to Australia's security?	20–34 yrs
Figure 3				
International Political Economic Issues, Australia, May 1975	USICA	999[a]	If Australia's security is threatened by some other country, how much trust do you feel Australia can have in the United States, to come to Australia's defence – a great deal, a fair amount, not very much or none at all?	20–29 yrs
International Political Economic Issues, Australia, Sept. 1975	USICA	933[a]	If Australia's security is threatened by some other country, how much trust do you feel Australia can have in the United States, to come to Australia's defence – a great deal, a fair amount, not very much or none at all?	
Foreign Trade, Security Investment and ANZUS, Australia Attitudes, March/April 1978	USICA	1,135[a]	If Australia's security is threatened by some other country, how much trust do you feel Australia can have in the United States, to come to Australia's defence – a great deal, a fair amount, not very much or none at all?	20–19 yrs
ANZUS and Australia's Security: Australian Attitudes, Oct. 1982	USIS	1,070[a]	If Australia's security is threatened by some other country, how much trust do you feel Australia can have in the United States, to come to Australia's defence – a great deal, a fair amount, not very much or none at all?	20–29 yrs

APPENDIX TABLE: SURVEY DETAILS CONTD

Survey title/date	Principal investigator	N	Question wording	Age groupings
ANZUS and Australia's Security: Australian Attitudes, Oct. 1983	USIS	1,117[a]	If Australia's security is threatened by some other country, how much trust do you feel Australia can have in the United States, to come to Australia's defence – a great deal, a fair amount, not very much or none at all?	20–29 yrs
ANZUS and Australia's Security: Australian Attitudes, May 1984	USIS	1,127[a]	If Australia's security is threatened by some other country, how much trust do you feel Australia can have in the United States, to come to Australia's defence – a great deal, a fair amount, not very much or none at all?	
ANZUS and Australia's Security: Autralian Attitudes, May 1984	USIS	1,141[a]	If Australia's security is threatened by some other country, how much trust do you feel Australia can have in the United States, to come to Australia's defence – a great deal, a fair amount, not very much or none at all?	20–19 yrs
Foreign Affairs Issues, Australia, June 1985	USICA	1,041[a]	If Australia's security is threatened by some other country, how much trust do you feel Australia can have in the United States, to come to Australia's defence – a great deal, a fair amount, not very much or none at all?	
Foreign Affairs Issues, Australia, Dec. 1985	USICA	1,198[a]	If Australia's security is threatened by some other country, how much trust do you feel Australia can have in the United States, to come to Australia's defence – a great deal, a fair amount, not very much or none at all?	20–29 yrs
Foreign Affairs Issues, Australia, Oct. 1986	USICA	1,117[a]	If Australia's security is threatened by some other country, how much trust do you feel Australia can have in the United States, to come to Australia's defence – a great deal, a fair amount, not very much or none at all?	
Foreign Affairs Issues, Australia, Sept. 1987	USICA	1,110[a]	If Australia's security is threatened by some other country, how much trust do you feel Australia can have in the United States, to come to Australia's defence – a great deal, a fair amount, not very much or none at all?	
Foreign Affairs Issues, Australia, Oct. 1988	USICA	1,067[a]	If Australia's security is threatened by some other country, how much trust do you feel Australia can have in the United States, to come to Australia's defence – a great deal, a fair amount, not very much or none at all?	
Foreign Affairs Issues, Australia, Aug. 1989	USICA	1,001[a]	If Australia's security is threatened by some other country, how much trust do you feel Australia can have in the United States, to come to Australia's defence – a great deal, a fair amount, not very much or none at all?	

APPENDIX TABLE: SURVEY DETAILS CONTD

Survey title/date	Principal investigator	N	Question wording	Age groupings
Figures 4 and 5				
Australian Gallup Polls, 1943 (*Source:* Campbell, 1989)		2,000	Do you favour or oppose compulsory military training for young men?	
Australian Gallup Polls, 1945 (*Source:* Campbell, 1989)		2,000	Do you favour or oppose compulsory military training for young men?	
Australian Gallup Polls, 1946 (*Source:* Campbell, 1989)		2,000	Do you favour or oppose compulsory military training for young men?	
Australian Gallup Polls, 1948 (*Source:* Campbell, 1989)		2,000	Do you favour or oppose compulsory military training for young men?	
Australian Gallup Polls, 1949 (*Source:* Campbell, 1989)		na	Do you favour or oppose compulsory military training for young men?	
Australian Gallup Polls, Survey 94, April 1953	APOP	1,782[b]	At present all young men of 18 must go to military camp for 3 months. Are you for, or against, that?	21–29 yrs
Australian Gallup Polls, Survey 133, Sept. 1958	APOP	1,736[b]	The first question is about the call-up of 15,000 young men each year for military training. What do you think we should do – continue to call up 15,000 a year – or give ALL young men military training – OR – abolish military training altogether?	21–29 yrs
Australian Gallup Polls, Survey 141, Dec. 1959	APOP	1,965[b]	The next question is about the Government's plan to end compulsory military training. What do you think we should do – give ALL young men military training – OR – continue to call up 15,000 young men a year or – abolish military training altogether?	21–29 yrs
Australian Gallup Polls, Survey 150, June 1961	APOP	1,746[b]	Next about compulsory military training, for ALL young men 17–21. Would you FAVOR or OPPOSE, again having compulsory military training?	21–29 yrs
Australian Gallup Polls, Survey 157, June 1962	APOP	2,088[b]	And a question about military training. In America every young man must spend two years in the armed forces. Would you be for – or against – having two years military training here?	21–29 yrs
Australian Gallup Polls, Survey 164, Aug. 1963	APOP	1,866[b]	Next a different question, on military training. Would you be for – or against – two years' full-time military training for all young men who are fit?	21–29 yrs

APPENDIX TABLE: SURVEY DETAILS CONTD

Survey title/date	Principal investigator	N	Question wording	Age groupings
Australian Gallup Polls, Survey 173, Nov. 1964	APOP	1,697[b]	And now on military training. The Government plans to register all young men of 20, and to call up about 7,000 a year for two years full-time service – overseas if necessary. Do you favour – or oppose – that?	21–29 yrs
Australian Gallup Polls, Survey 179, Sept. 1965	APOP	1,952[b]	Next about the Government's plan to increase the call-up of 20-year-olds for military training, by 1,500 a year – from 6,900 to 8,400. Are you for or against that increase?	21–29 yrs
Morgan Gallup No. 184, July 1966		2,071[b]	Next, about military training. Each year about 8,000 20-year-olds are called up for two years' military training, with possible overseas services. Are you for – or against – that call up?	21–29 yrs
Morgan Gallup No. 184, Nov. 1966		2,071[b]	Next, about military training. Each year about 8,000 20-year-olds are called up for two years' military training, with possible overseas services. Are you for – or against – that call up?	21–29 yrs
Morgan Gallup No. 184, Nov. 1967		2,071[b]	Next, about military training. Each year about 8,000 20-year-olds are called up for two years' military training, with possible overseas services. Are you for – or against – that call up?	21–29 yrs
Morgan Gallup No. 201, Dec. 1968		2,071[b]	Next, about military training. Each year about 8,000 20-year-olds are called up for two years' military training, with possible overseas services. Are you for – or against – that call up?	21–29 yrs
Morgan Gallup No. 210, April 1970		1,762[b]	Now one on military training. Of all young men aged 20, 1-in-12 is now called up by ballot for 2 years military training, with possible overseas service. Do you think that should be continued, or ended?	21–29 yrs
Morgan Gallup No. 220, June 1971		2,076[b]	Now one on military training. Of all young men aged 20, 1-in-12 is now called up by ballot for 2 years military training, with possible overseas service. Do you think that should be continued, or ended?	21–29 yrs
Morgan Gallup No. 223, Sept. 1971		2,420[b]	Next, about compulsory military training, which is being reduced from 2 years to 18 months. In your opinion, should compulsory military training continue, or be ended?	21–29 yrs
Morgan Gallup No. 230, April 1972		2,391[c]	Next, about compulsory military training. Would you say the number at the end of the line which comes closest to your ideas about compulsory military training? No military training, full-time volunteers, all for three months, all for six months, 1-in-12 for 18 months, no opinion.	21–29 yrs

APPENDIX TABLE: SURVEY DETAILS CONTD

Survey title/date	Principal investigator	N	Question wording	Age groupings
Morgan Gallup No. 235, Oct. 1972		2,189[c]	Now one on military training. Of all young men aged 20, 1-in-12 is now called up by ballot for 2 years military training, with possible overseas service. Do you think that should be continued, or ended?	21–29 yrs
Morgan Gallup No. 240, March 1973		2,270[c]	And one on military training. Would you favour – or oppose – all young men going to military camp for several months?	20–29 yrs
Morgan Gallup No. 154, Feb. 1977		2,307[a]	Next a different question, on military training. Would you be for – or against – two years' full-time military training for all young men who are fit?	20–29 yrs
Morgan Gallup No. 307, Feb. 1980		2,234[a]	Next a different question, on military training. Would you be for – or against – two years' full-time military training for all young men who are fit?	20–29 yrs
Frank Small and Associates, Aug. 1987		1,300[c]	Would you support or oppose the introduction of compulsory military training for young adults in the military service?	
Frank Small and Associates, March 1988		1,300[c]	Would you support or oppose the introduction of compulsory military training for young adults in the military service?	
Frank Small and Associates, Sept. 1988		1,300[c]	Would you support or oppose the introduction of compulsory military training for young adults in the military service?	
Frank Small and Associates, Nov. 1988		1,300[c]	Would you support or oppose the introduction of compulsory military training for young adults in the military service?	
Frank Small and Associates, March 1989		1,300[c]	Would you support or oppose the introduction of compulsory military training for young adults in the military service?	
Frank Small and Associates, May 1989		1,300[c]	Would you support or oppose the introduction of compulsory military training for young adults in the military service?	
Frank Small and Associates, Dec. 1989		1,300[c]	Would you support or oppose the introduction of compulsory military training for young adults in the military service?	

Figures 6 and 7

Survey title/date	Principal investigator	N	Question wording	Age groupings
Australian Gallup Polls, Survey 126, July 1957	APOP	1,958[b]	And now a really big subject – atom bombs – which Britain may offer to Australia, Canada and New Zealand. Are you for, or against, equipping our air force with atom bombs?	21–29 yrs

APPENDIX TABLE: SURVEY DETAILS CONTD

Survey title/date	Principal investigator	N	Question wording	Age groupings
Australian Gallup Polls, Survey 143, April 1960	APOP	1,517[b]	And finally, a question about nuclear missile bases, and early warning radar bases – like those America has been allowed to set up in England. If America wanted to set up similar bases in Northern Australia, should we allow them or not?	21–29 yrs
Australian Gallup Polls, Survey 157, June 1962	APOP	2,088[b]	And now a very important question, about having American bases for NUCLEAR weapons in Australia. How would you feel about that? Would you be for it – or against it?	21–29 yrs
Australian Gallup Polls, Survey 160, Dec. 1962	APOP	1,615[b]	Do you approve or disapprove of a defence system for Australia which includes nuclear weapons.	21–29 yrs
Australian Gallup Polls, Survey 179, Sept. 1965	APOP	1,975[b]	About atomic weapons. If America asks us for naval bases in northern Australia for its atomic-armed submarines – do you think we should allow America those bases – or should we keep atomic weapons out of this part of the world?	21–29 yrs
Morgan Gallup No. 186, Nov. 1966		2,052[b]	About atomic weapons. If America asks us for naval bases in northern Australia for its atomic-armed submarines – do you think we should allow America those bases – or should we keep atomic weapons out of this part of the world?	21–29 yrs
Australian National Opinion Polls, 1971 (Source: Campbell, 1989)		na	Do you approve or disapprove of building a defence system for Australia which includes atomic weapons?	
Morgan Gallup No. 80 July 1975		1,801[a]	In your opinion should nuclear weapons be kept out of Australia – or should we ask America and England to base nuclear weapons here?	20–29 yrs
Morgan Gallup No. 327 May 1980		2,048[d]	In your opinion should nuclear weapons be kept out of Australia – or should we ask America and England to base nuclear weapons here?	20–29 yrs
Frank Small and Associates, April 1988		1,300[c]	Do you think Australia should consider developing nuclear weapons as part of our defence system?	20–29 yrs

APPENDIX TABLE: SURVEY DETAILS CONTD

Survey title/date	Principal investigator	N	Question wording	Age groupings
Figures 8 and 9				
Australian National Opinion Polls, 1976 (*Source*: Campbell, 1989)		1,961	Do you agree with American nuclear-powered ships coming into Australian ports?	
Morgan Gallup No. 137, Sept. 1976		2,073[a]	First about an American submarine with nuclear-powered engines visiting Melbourne. Are you for – or against – visits by American warships with nuclear-powered engines?	20–29 yrs
Morgan Gallup No. 203, Feb. 1978		1,745[a]	First about an American submarine with nuclear-powered engines visiting Melbourne. Are you for – or against – visits by American warships with nuclear-powered engines?	14–29 yrs
Australian National Opinion Polls, 1982 (*Source*: Campbell, 1989)		2,000	Do you agree with nuclear-powered ships coming into Australian ports?	
ANZUS and Australia's Security: Australian Attitudes, July 1982 (same survey as Morgan Gallup No. 446, June 1982)	USIS	1,093[a]	ANZUS is a treaty among Australia, New Zealand and the United States. The treaty allows the United States' warships and submarines with nuclear-powered engines to visit Australian ports. Are you for – or against – visits by American warships with nuclear-powered engines?	20–29 yrs
ANZUS and Australia's Security: Australian Attitudes, Oct. 1982	USIS	1,070[a]	Next, about visits by American nuclear-powered warships to Australia's ports. Do you favour or oppose visits by American nuclear-powered warships? Favour strongly, favour somewhat, oppose somewhat, oppose strongly, don't know.	20–29 yrs
ANZUS and Australia's Security: Australian Attitudes, Oct. 1983	USIS	1,117[a]	Next, about visits by American nuclear-powered warships to Australia's ports. Do you favour or oppose visits by American nuclear-powered warships? Favour strongly, favour somewhat, oppose somewhat, oppose strongly, don't know.	20–29 yrs
ANZUS and Australia's Security: Australian Attitudes, May 1984	USIS	1,127[a]	Next, about visits by American nuclear-powered warships to Australia's ports. Do you favour or oppose visits by American nuclear-powered warships? Favour strongly, favour somewhat, oppose somewhat, oppose strongly, don't know.	20–29 yrs
ANZUS and Australia's Security: Australian Attitudes, Sept. 1984	USIS	1,141[a]	Next, about visits by American nuclear-powered warships to Australia's ports. Do you favour or oppose visits by American nuclear-powered warships? Favour strongly, favour somewhat, oppose somewhat, oppose strongly, don't know.	20–29 yrs

APPENDIX TABLE: SURVEY DETAILS CONTD

Survey title/date	Principal investigator	N	Question wording	Age groupings
Australian National Opinion Polls, 1985 (Source: David Campbell, 1989)		2,079	Do you agree with nuclear-powered ships coming into Australian ports?	
Foreign Affairs Issues, Australia, June 1985	USICA	1,041[a]	Next, about visits by American nuclear-powered warships to Australia's ports. Do you favour or oppose visits by American nuclear-powered warships? Favour strongly, favour somewhat, oppose somewhat, oppose strongly, don' know.	
Foreign Affairs Issues, Australia, Dec. 1985	USICA	1,198[a]	Next, about visits by American nuclear-powered warships to Australia's ports. Do you favour or oppose visits by American nuclear-powered warships? Favour strongly, favour somewhat, oppose somewhat, oppose strongly, don' know.	20–29 yrs
Foreign Affairs Issues, Australia, Oct. 1986	USICA	1,117[a]	Next, about visits by American nuclear-powered warships to Australia's ports. Do you favour or oppose visits by American nuclear-powered warships? Favour strongly, favour somewhat, oppose somewhat, oppose strongly, don' know.	
Foreign Affairs Issues, Australia, Sept. 1987	USICA	1,110[a]	Next, about visits by American nuclear-powered warships to Australia's ports. Do you favour or oppose visits by American nuclear-powered warships? Favour strongly, favour somewhat, oppose somewhat, oppose strongly, don' know.	
Frank Small and Associates, Dec. 1987		1,300[c]	I'd like you to tell me how you feel about visits to Australian ports by nuclear-powered warships. Favour, don't care, oppose.	
Frank Small and Associates, March 1988			I'd like you to tell me how you feel about visits to Australian ports by nuclear-powered warships. Favour, don't care, oppose.	
Frank Small and Associates, Sept. 1988		1,300[c]	I'd like you to tell me how you feel about visits to Australian ports by nuclear-powered warships. Favour, don't care, oppose.	
Foreign Affairs Issues, Australia, Oct. 1988	USICA	1,067[a]	Next, about visits by American nuclear-powered warships to Australia's ports. Do you favour or oppose visits by American nuclear-powered warships? Favour strongly, favour somewhat, oppose somewhat, oppose strongly, don't know.	

APPENDIX TABLE: SURVEY DETAILS CONTD

Survey title/date	Principal investigator	N	Question wording	Age groupings
Frank Small and Associates, Nov. 1988		1,300[c]	I'd like you to tell me how you feel about visits to Australian ports by nuclear-powered warships? Favour, don't care, oppose.	
Frank Small and Associates, March 1989		1,300[c]	I'd like you to tell me how you feel about visits to Australian ports by nuclear-powered warships? Favour, don't care, oppose.	
Frank Small and Associates, May 1989		1,300[c]	I'd like you to tell me how you feel about visits to Australian ports by nuclear-powered warships? Favour, don't care, oppose.	
Foreign Affairs Issues, Australia, Aug. 1989	USICA	1,001[a]	Next, about visits by American nuclear-powered warships to Australia's ports. Do you favour or oppose visits by American nuclear-powered warships? Favour strongly, favour somewhat, oppose somewhat, oppose strongly, don't know.	
Frank Small and Associates, Dec. 1989		1,300[c]	I'd like you to tell me how you feel about visits to Australian ports by nuclear-powered warships? Favour, don't care, oppose.	

Notes

a Persons aged 14 and over throughout Australia/area cluster sample with sex quota.
b Persons aged 21 years and over throughout Australia/Area cluster sample with sex quota.
c Persons aged 16 and over in Brisbane, Sydney, Melbourne, Adelaide and Perth/multistage random probability with sex and age quota.
d Persons aged 18 years and over and enrolled to vote/Area cluster sample excluding the NT.

Abbreviations

APOP – Australian Public Opinion Polls
USICA – United States International Communications Agency
USIS – United States Information Service
MGP – Morgan Gallup Poll
na – not available

Terrorism, Violence Against the Public and the Media: The Australian Approach

ALLAN J. BEHM

Public officials and members of the media share a healthy mutual scepticism. Myths and stereotypes abound, but they are no less powerful for that. Many journalists, whether they are members of the electronic or print media, seem to think that the key aim of public officials (and here we should include police and military officers) is to veil incompetence in the cloak of secrecy. The public official is fair game: break through the wall of anonymity, and there will almost certainly be a scoop between the filing cabinets and the unwashed tea cups!

Public officials, on the other hand, have often had unfortunate experiences with the media and, in consequence, do not trust journalists. Nor do they hold them in high esteem. Contact with the media is to be avoided: the public interest is always distorted by sensationalism, or the public official made to look foolish with no right of reply. Adlai Stevenson spoke for many a public official when he said: 'Newspaper editors are men who separate the wheat from the chaff, and then print the chaff'. The same view was put in different, if no less compelling, terms by another statesman who is particularly well known to Queenslanders – Sir Joh Bjelke-Petersen. 'The greatest thing that could happen in the State and the nation is when we get rid of the media. Then we could live in peace and tranquillity and no one would know anything.'

For politicians and public officials alike, documents such as the Australian Journalists' Association 'Code of Ethics' are regarded with the same sort of wry amusement that greets the public official's 'frank and fearless advice'. The public official will say that the journalist's only aim is to make a name for himself and money for the proprietor. And the journalist will claim that the public official's only aim is to hide the truth.

While it is evident that the attitudes depicted above are overdrawn and distorted, they unfortunately do represent something of the tension which is inherent in the relationship between government and the media. In the field of counter-terrorism and the protection of the public against violence, this tension has a real potential to cause loss of life. Just as the public official may feel that an inquisitive and free-wheeling press will compromise operational objectives, so too may the journalist feel that obsessive secrecy fundamentally erodes the public's right to know.

This paper, then, seeks to examine the balance between the apparently competing objectives of government and the media in the general area of violence against the public. In Australia, we have a strategy for handling the issues associated with terrorism and the media. We do not pretend that our approach is the only solution to the problem, nor do we suggest that a solution developed for the specific demands of a terrorist incident offers normative guidance on the relationship between the media and defence in time of limited conflict. But the solution developed under the auspices of the Standing Advisory Committee on Commonwealth/State Cooperation for Prevention Against Violence (SAC-PAV) – Australia's most authoritative body in this field – may serve as a useful model.

It may seem odd that a conference dealing with defence and the media in time of limited conflict should give any consideration at all to the role of the media in the management of terrorist incidents. Yet limited conflict, or, to use the language of the 1987 *Defence of Australia* White Paper, low level and escalated low-level conflict, is by its nature unpredictable. Incidents tend to be sporadic and targets dispersed. The adversary's 'operations' would seek to impose a disproportionately heavy burden on the defender's response capabilities by employing apparently random acts of violence rather than a more clearly defined 'campaign'. Terrorism, that is the indiscriminate use of violence against the public, may well be a favoured option. In such circumstances, media management issues would be especially difficult, reflecting the disaggregated nature of the circumstances: in low level and escalated low-level conflict, the first point of contact for the media may well be the state police operations centre or the Protective Services Co-ordination Centre in Canberra, rather than the Australian Defence Force media liaison unit.

The Changing Face of Terrorism

Who, even five years ago, would have imagined the extraordinary changes which have occurred on the world stage during the last three years, or would have projected the direction of strategic change. The political geography of Europe has been, and continues to be, fundamentally reshaped. The strategic geography of Asia is also undergoing change as Asian nations adjust to global economic developments. With these fundamental changes has come a new way of doing political business. Indeed, not only have the international political agenda changed, but the ways in which they are implemented have changed too.

Change, of course, may bring with it various benefits. But it almost always brings with it uncertainty. While the recent developments at the level of global security may have engendered a safer world, our nation and our region become no more secure for that. Change in the familiar global order will mean greater strategic uncertainty elsewhere, including in Australia's region: a generally safer world does not necessarily mean a more tranquil region.

What all of this might mean in practice has yet to be seen: but with respect to conflict, including conflict within our own region, a number of possibilities suggest themselves:

- major powers which might have either exported terrorism or supported surrogate terrorist groups in the past may be less inclined to do so in the future – we are already seeing a withdrawal of financial and materiel support by most of the former sponsors;
- but, as we shall see below, weak states may well continue to find the use of terror a low-cost means of punishing other powers;
- conflicts between states will probably not enjoy any clear legal status, in that states will probably avoid any formal declaration of war;
- in periods of strategic fluidity at both the regional and global levels, we may see the rise of new, and possibly more ambiguous, forms of violence perpetrated on the public;
- ambiguity and unpredictability may become the principal characteristics of armed conflict at the regional and sub-regional levels (Iraq's attack on Kuwait notwithstanding);
- to achieve ambiguity and unpredictability, the adversary's

> preference will probably be for civilian rather than military
> targets; and,
>
> - disavowability may also be an attractive objective in the
>   prosecution of low-level conflict, thereby creating uncer-
>   tainty in the mind of the defender as to who the adversary
>   might be and whether violent incidents are domestic criminal
>   acts, externally-inspired terrorist acts, or acts of war.

In brief, these possibilities (which are indicative rather than definitive) suggest that terrorism may well be an attractive option to an adversary in the conduct of low-level conflict.

The face of terrorism as an international phenomenon is also changing. The use of terror by a state, usually described as state-sponsored terrorism, is almost always a clear sign of political weakness. States whose legitimacy is under challenge, or states which lack the political, economic or military power to transact business according to the more traditional forms of diplomacy, may use terror as the least expensive and most dramatic means of achieving specific ends.[1] Interestingly, as this century demonstrates with ample instances, the use of such terror is usually a losing strategy. The fact is that states which enjoy a measure of legitimacy and international standing eschew the use of terror. Terror undermines the international order, stability and the status quo.

State-sponsored terrorism, then, may be expected to continue as a form of limited conflict, though principally employed by weak states rather than strong ones. There are four other forms of terrorism, however, which may provide more testing challenges during the next decade. These are: faction-sponsored terrorism, crime-related terrorism, narco-terrorism and issue-motivated terrorism.

Faction-sponsored terrorism remains the principal international manifestation of the use of terror for political ends. Unfortunately, as events in the United Kingdom all too eloquently testify, the use of terror by political groups is alive and well. While, as with the use of terror by states, terrorism conducted by political groups is often a reflection of their inability to achieve political objectives by legitimate means, its real impact on the lives of the population can be very much more profound. It is to be hoped that the decline in the availability of funds and materiel from the less responsible states (such as the late but unlamented German Democratic Republic) will have an impact on the activities of such groups. But the fact remains that, for the foreseeable future, we will continue to see political groups which retain random violence in their political armouries.

Crime-related terrorism is a traditional form of violence against the public, whether it takes the form of gang warfare, piracy or hooliganism. It is something of a commonplace that the next century will be the century of economic strength rather than political or military power. And, if that is so, the emergence of money, rather than politics, as a prime motivation for violence against the public needs to be considered. In Australia, we have already seen criminals resort to the indiscriminate use of bombs in public places as a means of furthering criminal interests and of settling old scores with the law enforcement agencies. The Russell Street bombing in 1986 provided a salutary reminder of the reality of criminal terrorism. The expansion of criminal activity into so many aspects of the national economy has the capacity to bring with it novel forms of public pressure.

Narco-terrorism is a relatively new term in the terror lexicon. While, for most purposes, it is a sub-element of crime-related terrorism, it is significant enough to be considered in its own right. Some political scientists regard narco-terrorism as the syndication, as it were, of narcotics trafficking to terrorist groups in return for the funds with which to conduct terror. But, in the Asia/Pacific region, narco-terrorism is more likely to describe the use of force by drug traffickers (and particularly the cartel bosses) to force changes in the law, as has already been seen in countries such as Colombia. In its various forms, narco-terrorism has been a fact of life in Burma since the late 1940s, and has come to notice in Thailand and Indo-China from time to time. It certainly does share some of the characteristics of low-level conflict.

Issue-motivated terrorism is a new form of random violence against the public, and one which is particularly difficult to handle. Groups which coalesce around various social issues (such as racial equality, pro- and anti-abortion, animal liberation, and nuclear issues), environmental concerns, land and other economic rights, or other matters impinging on the public conscience generally operate within the bounds of legitimate democratic dissent. But there are instances where such groups have exceeded the bounds of legitimate protest.

Each of these five forms of terrorism raise substantial problems in managing the relationship between the relevant government agencies and the media.

Australia's Counter-Terrorism Strategy

Strategy is inevitably dynamic, and the process for developing strategies is iterative. But what is 'strategy'? At the very least, strategy comprehends both *ends* and *means*. It concerns equally *what* needs to be done and *how* the task should be achieved. Moreover, to be effective, a strategy cannot be simply reactive, since, if it is so, it is fundamentally flawed in that the so-called strategy assumes its own defeat before it can be activated. In other words, a reactive counter-terrorism strategy must assume that a terrorist event has actually occurred *before* the strategy can be implemented.

Consequently, an essential aspect of an effective strategy is that it be *pro-active*, to employ a much over-worked term. An effective strategy for protecting the public against violence must focus as much on *prevention* as it does on the handling of actual incidents. Moreover, an effective strategy for protecting the public against violence must comprehend the enhancement of the security environment within which they live. So, the 'ends' towards which a strategy is directed must be comprehensive. The same consideration applies to the 'means'. The means cannot afford to be narrowly focused on the modalities of response: they must also be directed to preventive measures.

Australia's counter-terrorism strategy is, then, holistic. It goes beyond the simple idea of response to attacks on the public to include the promotion of public security through maximising the benefits that can be obtained from the cooperative arrangements already in place, *including liaison arrangements with the media*. Australia's broad-based strategy towards protection against violence means that the net effect is synergistic. In other words, the whole is greater than the sum of the parts.

What, then, are the principal features of our national counter-terrorism strategy for the 1990s? Because 'international' terrorism is such a disaggregated phenomenon, Australia's counter-terrorism strategy is directed towards those forms of random violence against the public which could credibly occur *here*. The three fundamental elements of that strategy are:

- integrated and co-ordinated *preventive measures* designed to minimise the scope for any incident to occur;
- a comprehensive capability for *response* to any incident which might occur – a capability which is, in fact, already in place; and,
- a positive *enhancement* of the national security environment, which is to suggest that *all* elements in our society regard security as a cooperative endeavour in which *each* element has a particular contribution to make.

These elements merit a little more discussion.

In 1979 the then Prime Minister, Malcolm Fraser, proposed to his state counterparts that national arrangements should be developed to foster co-operation and to encourage co-ordination among the various agencies responsible for the management of responses to politically-motivated violence. As a result of that initiative, the SAC-PAV was established. Since then, the agencies which come together under the auspices of SAC-PAV have devoted considerable energy and resources to the development of comprehensive *response* capabilities. The Commonwealth and the states work together to ensure that there are police and military response units which are properly equipped, trained and exercised. Australian capabilities in this area are second to none, and significant effort is directed towards ensuring that high standards are maintained. Emphasis is given to reinforcing the essential features of our national response policies. Three aspects continue to be of special importance:

- the maintenance of a firm policy of *no concessions* on substantive demands which terrorists might make;
- operational and negotiating practices which *maximise uncertainty* for the perpetrators of public violence; and,
- *media liaison and management techniques* which limit as far as possible the opportunities for media exploitation by perpetrators of public violence.

Since one of the principal aims of any terrorist is to obtain the maximum media exposure, co-operation between the response agencies and the media is of paramount importance.

It is clear that a comprehensive capacity for response exerts a *deterrent* effect on would-be perpetrators of violent actions affecting the public. This is a significant benefit. A policy of deterrence, however, which rests solely on response capabilities would be a limited and ultimately ineffectual strategy. Deterrence is always a consequence of well-planned action, not its primary objective. Indeed, were *deterrence* to become the primary focus of our counter-terrorism strategy, then our strategy would be purely reactive. And, as noted above, a reactive strategy is a losing strategy.

In recent years, the Australian government has placed much greater emphasis on *preventive* capabilities, more narrowly defined, especially in the areas of intelligence collection, assessment and transmission and, of course, barrier controls. Much innovative work has been done by the state police forces and the federal authorities such as Immigration, Customs, the Department of Transport and Communications, the Federal Airports Corporation, and the Department of Foreign Affairs and Trade – to name but a few – to establish effective preventive regimes. Government is pressing ahead with these efforts, combining technological advances with appropriate administrative and regulatory reforms. One more recent feature of Australia's preventive regime is the work that has been done to develop improved *regional* cooperative mechanisms. Consistent with the principles enunciated in the parliamentary statement *Australia's Regional Security*[2] delivered by the Minister for Foreign Affairs and Trade, Senator Gareth Evans, in December 1989, Australia is expanding its cooperative arrangements with the countries of ASEAN and the South Pacific Forum, albeit coincidentally or in forums outside SAC-PAV.

Finally, Australia's counter-terrorism strategy provides for the *enhancement* of the national security environment. It is probably fair to say that, during the past 12 or so years, Australia's counter-terrorism co-ordinating mechanisms have been developed along the lines of the structures progressively erected in Europe. While we clearly have much to learn from Europe's experience of terrorism, it is important that Australia's national approach is directed towards *Australian* problems. It is with this in mind that the Australian government has given added impetus to deriving maximum benefit from the various counter-terrorism activities and programmes, and to ensuring that the programs and activities are able to contribute to and support endeavours in other law enforcement areas. This has become increasingly the case as government financial management programmes focus on getting the maximum benefit from public sector expenditure programmes. Australian government policies are directed towards demolishing any barriers between discreet areas of Government activity where such barriers might impede the attainment of shared objectives. This is not to suggest a need for any change to existing institutional arrangements as they bear on operational or co-ordinating arrangements. But it most definitely is to suggest that agencies avail themselves of every opportunity both to learn from the experience of other agencies and to contribute their experience to an improved security environment for all Australians.

It should go without saying that any counter-terrorism strategy can only operate within a legal environment. The Australian legal environment is one in which acts of terrorism are, generally speaking, treated as crimes, while those aspects of terrorism which have been the subject of international conventions, such as aircraft hijacking and attacks on heads of state, diplomats, etc. are the subject of special legislation. There is, however, no special legislation of the kind in force in the United Kingdom – the Prevention of Terrorism (Temporary Provisions) Act 1989 – with its emphasis on measures such as detention and exclusion orders.

Typically, legislation implementing international conventions provides that an alleged offender who is present in Australia is liable to prosecution irrespective of the place of the offence. Such a person is also liable to be extradited to a requesting state if the offence was committed in that state's jurisdiction. The basis for such 'universal jurisdiction' is Australia's acceptance of the proposition that the crime is international in character. One practical effect of universal jurisdiction is to deny a safe haven to terrorists in any country which is a party to the particular convention. In the event that international agreement is ever reached on a convention against terrorism, Australia could implement it by applying the ordinary criminal law of the Australian states, and providing for universal jurisdiction in relation to any alleged offender apprehended in Australia.

An equally important aspect of the legal environment in a democratic state is that the intelligence and security services should be subject to the rule of law. The powers and functions of the Australian Security Intelligence Organisation (ASIO) are established in legislation for all to see. And the fact that the Australian Secret Intelligence Service (ASIS) is also subject to the law of the land was demonstrated very clearly in the litigation which followed the 'Sheraton Hotel Incident' and by Mr Justice Hope's separate Royal Commission report on that incident.

Some Facts of Life

One might well ask how all of this relates to the media. As was suggested earlier, terrorism relies for its effect on the manipulation of various political or social symbols in order to set or change the political agenda. The media play a crucial role in this process, a fact which terrorist groups understand well. The notorious terrorist 'Carlos' gave clear expression to this strategy when he wrote:

> The co-ordination of urban guerrilla action ... is the principal way of making armed propaganda.

> These actions, carried out with specific and determined objectives, inevitably become propaganda material for the mass communications system....

> The war of nerves or psychological war is an aggressive technique, based on the direct or indirect use of mass means of communication and news transmitted orally in order to demoralise the government.

> In psychological warfare, the government is always at a disadvantage since it imposes censorship on the mass media and winds up in a defensive position by not allowing anything to filter through.[3]

Indeed, access to the media becomes, typically, a terrorist negotiating ploy.

There is a substantial body of evidence to suggest that terrorist groups have developed effective media strategies to maximise the impact of terrorist acts. These strategies embrace at least five key objectives:

- to demonstrate the ability of the terrorist organisation to act at random in order to hold political, economic or social institutions to ransom;
- to derive maximum political exposure from a relatively small operational investment;
- to recruit support for the cause;
- to demonstrate the inability of government organs to prevent violent acts from occurring; and/or,
- to bring home to the population at large a sense of vulnerability, leading either to the adoption of a 'soft line' policy or the imposition of more restrictive 'law and order' measures.

Whatever the terrorists' basic media strategy might be, its net effect is to undermine the democratic institutions on which the media depend for their existence in a free society. In his 1978 report on the future of broadcasting in the United Kingdom, Lord Annan wrote:

> Terrorism feeds off publicity: publicity is its main hope of intimidating government and the public: publicity gives it a further chance for recruitment. The acts terrorists commit are each minor incidents in their general campaign to attract attention to their cause. No democracy can tolerate terrorism because it is a denial of the democratic assumption that injustice can, in time, be put right through discussion, peaceful persuasion and compromise. By killing and destroying, the terrorists are bound to extort publicity – and hence one of their ends – because such news will be reported[4]

In short, terrorists need the media to achieve their ends.[5]

For their part, the media bring events to the people. G. K. Chesterton may have had a point when he wrote, 'Journalism largely consists in saying "Lord Jones is dead" to people who never knew that Lord Jones was alive'. Yet the media are certainly the most important source of information for the population at large, and play a crucial role in the maintenance of a free society. For the media not only provide information: they also ventilate opinion and give expression to views of all complexions. More importantly, the media place the use and abuse of power on the record equally. When managed responsibly, investigative journalism helps substantially to preserve civil liberties and democratic freedoms. And, clearly, the media depend on 'events' to exercise this role.

Yet the media is also driven by other, more immediate, imperatives. There is the pressure to be 'first with the news'. There is the pressure to capture the attention of the public. There is the pressure to maintain profitability for the proprietor and the shareholders. And, as a number of senior Australian journalists noted in a recent edition of the *Bulletin*[6], there is the pressure on many senior journalists in both the print and the electronic media to exercise influence and power. Basically, the media need 'event' if they are to accommodate these pressures, too.

All of which places the media on the horns of a dilemma: how are the media to meet their basic political and social roles responsibly, and at the same time to beat the competition and earn a profit? Paul Johnson has a rather mordant view: 'Most journalists are scoundrels. They can't tell the difference between hard news and scandal, except that they like scandal because it makes money. They should all be locked up.'

It is this dilemma which comes to the fore in a terrorist incident. If the terrorist needs the media, then, in a peculiar sense, the media need the terrorist. This is not to suggest any measure of symbiosis. Rather, it is to suggest, as 'Carlos' understood only too well, that the media are exploitable by the terrorist simply because the media survive, in a democratic society, only to the extent that they report and comment on events: the greater the drama, the greater the impact! Fundamentally, this is where the media are most vulnerable, a vulnerability which is central to the 'media management' issue in the counter-terrorism field.

The third of the 'facts of life' concerning terrorism and the media relates to the role of the media in combating terrorism. If the terrorist needs the media in order to achieve his ends, so does government in preventing the terrorist from so doing. Much of the contumely which characterised government/media relations in the past (and which led to the proliferation of 'media relations consultants') reflected the stereo-types described at the beginning of this paper. It was, unfortunately, the practice in decades past that those responsible for counter-terrorism positively sought to exclude the media from both the actual scene of an incident and from any of the command centres. With the benefit of hindsight, this was a mistake. For the media can play a constructive role both in the management of particular incidents and in the more important task of denying to the terrorist the credibility and public acceptability which are central to the terrorist strategy. At one level, the media are going to be there anyway (if CNN's coverage of the Gulf War is to be any guide). But, at a more fundamental level, government shares with the media a common interest in defending the democratic values upon which our society rests. It is *this* community of interest which underlies the Australian government's media strategy in protecting the public against indiscriminate violence.[7]

Towards Shared Objectives

It is not surprising that government, including both the political and administrative institutions, share a common dependence on the demo-cratic institutions which form the basis of our society. After all, the rule of law and freedom of speech are among the strongest defences of liberty – and they are mutually supporting. However, in circumstances where violence is used to express political or social dissent, and where lives are at risk, more immediate demands may cloud these common interests. Government is focused on containing and defeating the violence and protecting lives, while the media are intent upon reporting *all* the facts: both sides of the issue are canvassed. The harsh light of criticism falls equally on the criminal and the upholder of the law. In the heat of the moment, it is always difficult to keep fundamental objectives clearly in view. Individual terrorist incidents are always fast-moving, and it is this intrinsic fluidity which causes problems between those responsible for crisis management and the media.

International experience suggests that there are no easy answers. Problems will always arise, and there will always be differences of opinion and approach. No matter how much consultation and training is undertaken by individuals on both sides of the government/media divide, the fact that no actual incident is ever like the training exercise and the fact that different individuals are always involved means that the risk of a co-ordination breakdown cannot be eliminated. But it can be very much reduced. Those responsible for developing liaison procedures between government and the media in terrorist situations are becoming increasingly aware that there are key shared objectives. These include:

- the safety of those who might be directly at risk, whether they are hostages, members of the public, police or military officers responsible for resolving the situation, or members of the media responsible for reporting the incident;
- an effective and speedy resolution of the incident;
- post-incident analysis and evaluation which are open to public scrutiny and comment.

These three elements seem to be constant in all situations where the public may need to be protected against violence. Considerations such as these have formed the basis of the Australian government's media strategy in the management of terrorist incidents.

Australia's Counter-Terrorism Media Strategy

Since its inception in 1979, the SAC-PAV has devoted considerable energy to developing a coordinated anti-terrorist plan. This plan, which is called *The National Anti-Terrorist Plan (NATP)*, has been endorsed by the Commonwealth and state governments, and forms the basis of Australia's counter-terrorism program. The fourth edition of the NATP, as amended in October 1988, contains an unequivocal statement on the role of the media in any terrorist incident.

MEDIA LIAISON

31. Effective media liaison is essential to the successful management of an incident of terrorism or politically motivated violence. The agencies responsible for media liaison, the preparation of media releases and arrangements for media briefings are detailed in Annex H.

32. *ADF Media Liaison Arrangements*. Until 'Call Out' has been initiated, all media liaison is the responsibility of the civil authorities. After 'Call Out' Australian Defence Force (ADF) public relations personnel will be deployed to major command and control centres. Only ADF public relations personnel will provide information relating to ADF involvement to the media through liaison officers located at the CPC [Crisis Policy Centre], SCC [State Crisis Centre] and PSCC [Protective Services Coordination Centre].

Annex H, which is referred to in paragraph 31 of the NATP, is set out in full in the Annex to this paper.

During the past couple of years, the SAC-PAV has been developing a basic strategic guidance document to provide an agreed structure for its many activities. SAC-PAV has agreed that the implementation of the NATP requires a fourfold strategy for dealing with the media. The elements of this strategy are:

- public communication policies and guidelines;
- the incorporation of media response and incident management strategies;
- media skills and techniques; and,
- physical control.

They merit more detailed consideration.

Public Communication Policies and Guidelines: In addressing the media role in reporting on terrorist incidents, the fundamental starting point is the recognition that the media has a legitimate role in obtaining and reporting to the public as much information as possible. This is not to say that individual journalists will not exceed agreed boundaries. There is a tendency, particularly during ongoing incidents, to impinge on the balance between the public's right to know and the need for operational secrecy in resolving the incident. An effective media strategy will reduce, but not eliminate, this difficulty through physical controls on media access and comprehensive, regular and properly timed media briefings.

Under current NATP arrangements, the considerations attaching to media control and access place the primary emphasis on preventing the terrorists and their supporters from gaining information through the media which might disadvantage response operations. Too little attention is given to the need for a comprehensive media strategy aimed at winning and maintaining public support for the government's handling of the incident. One of the chief objectives of government in managing a terrorist incident is to ensure that it is the government and not the terrorists that are in charge. Clearly, this cannot be achieved if the media are excluded. Rather, it requires a positive public communications strategy and a facility to brief comprehensively and well.

Public Communication and Incident Management: To complement the media arrangements set out in Annex H to the NATP, SAC-PAV has accepted the following guidelines.

- A spokesman should inform the media that resolution of the incident will be a complex and sensitive matter requiring the co-operation of the media in refraining from doing or reporting anything which could jeopardise the response operation, and, in particular, endanger the lives of the hostages or their rescuers. This request should be made publicly so that it becomes a stated element of the response strategy. It can also be made privately to media representatives and repeated throughout the incident.
- For major incidents, consideration should be given to the Police Commissioner's or the Duty Minister's contacting media representatives at editor level and requesting media cooperation.
- The quid pro quo for cooperation will be full and regular media briefings at the operation and policy levels at specified

locations, including one near the scene of the incident. These briefings should be timed so as to allow important media deadlines to be met, and every effort should be made to adhere to the briefing timetable.

- Spokespersons should explain the complexity and sensitivity of the situation and help develop an understanding that a quick resolution of the incident may not be possible. Expectations to the contrary should be handled patiently.

- Spokespersons should avoid adopting an uncompromising position, or painting the government into a corner regarding terrorist demands. The line to adopt is that the Australian government has stated its opposition to acts of violence and such acts will be dealt with firmly.

- Spokespersons should concentrate on the 'what', the 'where' and the 'when' of an incident, and place less emphasis on the 'who' and the 'why'.

- Media reporting of an incident should be analysed for its effect on operations and policy. Responses to media reporting should become an integral part of incident management. For example, where reporting is unfavourable to government or police handling of an incident, it will be necessary to address those criticisms. Where criticism is misconceived, efforts must be made to remove the misconceptions and to re-establish favourable reporting. Where the criticisms reveal a genuine problem, the problem should be fixed where possible, and public told that it has been fixed. Where media reporting is favourable, steps should be taken to maintain it.

Media Training: During the last four years, SAC-PAV has introduced a Media Liaison Officers' seminar within its training program. In view of the critical role which the Media Liaison Officers play at all levels, it is essential that they have regular opportunities to familiarise themselves with counter-terrorism prevention and response arrangements at the policy and operational levels. Moreover, considerable attention has been paid in the national counter-terrorism exercise program to injecting a higher level of media content and realism. It has been recognised that further work needs to be done to ensure that the Police Forward Commanders' course and the State Crisis Centre and Crisis Policy Centre training courses contain appropriate media elements.

Physical Controls: Traditionally, physical access to incident sites has been controlled by putting in place outer and inner cordons. This is an established and proven practice. This serves not only to contain the incident, but also to keep innocent bystanders, including the media, away from operational areas. However, it is well recognised that most sites chosen by terrorists will not prove to be inaccessible to long-range photography and TV recording. There is, for the response teams, the ever-present danger that long-range cameras will reveal operational details which may jeopardise the safety or the outcome of the operation. This is particularly so where an incident is subject to live coverage, as was the case with the Iranian Embassy siege in London in 1980. The SAC-PAV plans recognise that there is no certain means of preventing this, though Media Liaison Officers monitor broadcasts carefully so that the Operational Commander can at least be alerted to the possibility, and take appropriate 'damage control' measures.

Crisis Management Policy: Since 1978 successive Australian governments, in consultation with state and territory governments, have adopted a firm 'no concessions' policy in response to possible terrorist demands. This is fundamental to any consistent or coherent counterterrorism program, and similar approaches have been adopted by most Western countries.

This strategy has, in fact, been formulated into a set of guidelines for the media to apply when covering a terrorist incident. In April 1990, these guidelines were forwarded to the Australian Journalists' Association (AJA) for its consideration, and in the hope that the Association would be able to recommend the guidelines to its members. As it turned out, the AJA replied in September 1990 to say that the Executive had resolved not to endorse the guidelines since it considered that the AJA's 'Code of Ethics' provided adequate guidance to AJA members in such circumstances. To judge from overseas experience, the AJA is incorrect in this assumption: clearer and more specific guidelines *are* necessary. The SAC-PAV endorsed guidelines read as follows:

GUIDELINES FOR MEDIA COVERING A TERRORIST INCIDENT

Responsible media coverage of terrorist incidents not only provides the public with information it has a right to expect, it can also aid in the successful resolution of such an incident and minimise risks to innocent hostages or potential victims.

In view of the important role played by the media in any crisis situation the Standing Advisory Committee on Common-wealth/State Co-Operation [*sic*] for Protection Against Violence (SAC PAV) has developed a set of guidelines which, if followed, would assist those trying to resolve the crisis but not hinder the media in its coverage of the event.

The guidelines are:

- Media representatives should not take independent or unauthorised action which could further endanger the lives of hostages.
- Media representatives should ensure they do not become part of the story – this could endanger their lives and add to the complexity of the situation, thereby further en-dangering the lives of the hostages.
- To avoid giving terrorists an unedited propaganda plat-form, live television or radio interviews with the terrorists should not be broadcast.
- No direct contact should be made with the terrorists, as this could prejudice the work of trained negotiators and thereby further endanger the lives of hostages.
- Reporting of terrorist demands should be free of rhetoric and propaganda: ideally such demands should be para-phrased in media reports, however, it is noted that the demands are an essential element of the story.

At the very least, these guidelines set out in clear terms what crisis managers and the counter-terrorism response organisations expect of the media.

To give practical effect to its media strategy and the consequent guidelines, the Commonwealth and state governments attach con-siderable importance to ensuring that media issues and concerns are an integral part of the SAC-PAV program. There are three main avenues through which this is implemented: consultations with the media; media skills training for both policy and operational personnel; and an identifiable media element in the majority of counter-terrorism exerc-ises. It is through the practical implementation of the annual SAC-PAV programs that Australia maintains an effective govern-ment/media liaison policy in the field of counter-terrorism.

Conclusion

As was noted earlier in this paper, the approach to government/media relations developed for counter-terrorism offers at least one answer to a problem which has beset many operational commanders in circumstances where indiscriminate violence may be used against the public. In the view of the Commonwealth and state and territory goverments, it is a workable approach because it is pragmatic. It offers practical guidance to media representatives as well as those responsible for counter-terrorist operations. Not long after he helped to draft the US Declaration of Independence, Thomas Jefferson wrote: 'Were it left to me to decide whether we should have a government without newspapers, or newspapers without a government, I should not hesitate a moment to prefer the latter'. Australia's approach to the role of the media in the more specific circumstances of a terrorist incident basically reflects this view. The media are central to the effective working of our democratic institutions, including our law enforcement agencies. And, for their part, the law enforcement agencies are integral to the security of our society. To the extent that there is any antinomy here, Australia's approach is to resolve it pragmatically.

NOTES

1. For a brief but interesting treatment of state-sponsored terrorism, see the US Government publication *Terrorist Group Profiles* (Washington: US Government Printing Office, 1988), p.1.
2. Senator the Hon. Gareth Evans QC, *Australia's Regional Security* (Ministerial Statement) (Canberra: Department of Foreign Affairs and Trade, 1989).
3. Carlos Marighella, *Minimanual of the Urban Guerilla* (Havana: Tricontinental, n.d.), p.103. For a more elaborate discussion of this point, see Yonah Alexander, 'Terrorism, the Media and the Police', *Journal of International Affairs*, Vol.32, No.1 (Spring/Summer 1978), pp.101–13.
4. *Report of the Committee on the Future of Broadcasting*, Cmnd 6753. (Annan) (London: HMSO, 1977), p.270.
5. This idea has been well developed by Michael J. Kelly in 'The Seizure of the Turkish Embassy in Ottawa: Managing Terrorism and the Media', in Charles Rosenthal and 't Hart (eds.), *Coping with Crises: The Management of Disasters, Riots and Terrorism* (Springfield, IL: Charles C. Thomas, 1989), pp.117–38.
6. *The Bulletin*, 26 March 1991, pp.26–40.
7. For an excellent treatment of the place of the media in a democratic society, see Richard Clutterbuck, *The Media and Political Violence* (London: Macmillan, 1981), *passim*. Sir Robin Day's foreword and the introduction are particularly relevant.

ANNEX

MEDIA LIAISON ARRANGEMENTS
(Annex H to NATP dated August 1990)

Introduction

1. These arrangements have been developed following discussions with all governments in Australia and are designed to achieve an efficient and rapid flow of cleared information to the media during a terrorist incident so as to defuse speculation, inform and reassure the general public and assist the work of authorities in handling the incident.

2. Successful handling of the public relations aspects of a terrorist incident, consistent with security requirements, requires close and effective co-operation with the media. A Police Commander may also need to seek the co-operation of the media in the execution of his operational plan.

3. The arrangements give emphasis to the need to coordinate information released to the media at all management levels and locations throughout the incident, namely:

    a. Scene of incident;
    b. Police Operations Centre (POC);
    c. State Crisis Centre (SCC); and
    d. Crisis Policy Centre (CPC) in Canberra.

4. *Any release of operational information must be cleared with the Police Commander.*

Appointment and Responsibilities of Media Liaison Officers

5. Police media relations should be handled either by a journalist trained in police affairs or a police officer experienced in media liaison. The Media Liaison Officer (MLO) in the SCC and the Co-ordinator of the CPC Media Liaison Group should be senior journalists.

6. At each level of response under the NATP the MLOs have specific duties and responsibilities with which officers designated to assist the media should be thoroughly familiar. Each MLO should have access to, and become thoroughly acquainted with, the NATP and State

counter-terrorism contingency plans and procedures supporting the NATP.

7. *Police*. Arrangements for media liaison on police operational matters will be under the control of the Police Commander who will appoint MLOs to function at the scene of incident and the Police Operations Centre, and issue policy guidelines for the release of, and level of approval of, media information on such operational matters.

    a.   *Scene of Incident*. The MLO at the scene of incident is responsible for ensuring that media representatives do not disrupt police officers involved in the operation and that the safety of any hostages is not jeopardised by media activity. He will act as the focal point between the media representatives at the scene and the MLO in the POC. Information cleared by the Police Commander in the POC should be made available to the MLO at the scene of incident for issue to media representatives. The Police Commander should provide guidelines delegating those media relations responsibilities appropriate to the MLO. The MLO may be required to organise media briefings by senior police officers. He should have a voice-protected communication link to the POC. He may also be a source of information/intelligence to the Police Intelligence Group because of his location and interaction with the media.

    b.   *Police Operations Centre*. The MLO appointed at the Police Operations Centre is responsible for the preparation of information on operational matters, to issue those items delegated by the Police Commander and to clear other releases with the Police Commander. He is to maintain close liaison and consult with MLOs at the scene of incident, the SCC and the CPC and advise the Police Commander on the clearing of operational information contained in media releases from these centres.

8. *State Crisis Centre*. A MLO will be appointed by the Premier's Department at the SCC with responsibility to the State Duty Minister for liaison with the media on State government matters. This officer is responsible for monitoring local media coverage and providing summaries to the SCC, the CPC and the Police Commander. The MLO may be delegated authority to issue media statements within guidelines provided by the State Duty Minister.

9. *Crisis Policy Centre.* The co-ordinator of the Media Liaison Group in the CPC in Canberra will be responsible to the Duty Minister for the preparation, clearance and dissemination to the media of information concerning Commonwealth government involvement in the incident. All media releases must be cleared with the Commonwealth Duty Minister. The Media Co-ordinator will arrange monitoring of the media and provide the CPC with summaries of media coverage and reaction. The Media Co-ordinator will maintain close liaison and consult with the MLOs in the SCC and the POC. The Media Co-ordinator will advise the Minister's Executive Committee on handling sensitive media issues. The Media Co-ordinator may be delegated authority to release information to the media within guidelines issued by the Commonwealth Duty Minister.

Provision of Information

10. From the outset of an incident, MLOs are likely to be an important source of information to police and governments.

11. Every effort should be made to provide the media with sufficient information to enable them to meet their requirements. Official media releases should be made only through media liaison arrangements outlined in this Plan and not through departmental or other channels; conflicting statements from various sources could be detrimental. A constant flow of information to the media should be maintained. Refusal to release information would only encourage the media to speculate or seek information from alternative and less reliable sources. Active and regular briefings are therefore considered essential.

12. The release of information at each of the four levels of media liaison should be based on the following principles:

   a. *Crisis Policy Centre (CPC)* – Information related directly to Commonwealth Government policy, responsibilities and initiatives, and as approved by the Commonwealth Duty Minister or his delegate.

   b. *State Crisis Centre (SCC)* – Information related to the State Government policies, responsibilities and initiatives, and as approved by the State Duty Minister or his delegate.

   c. *Police Operations Centre (POC)* – Operational information approved by the Police Commander or his delegate.

   d. *Police Forward Command Post (PFCP)* – Operational information including verbal briefing of the media at the scene, approved by the Police Forward Commander or his delegate, in consultation with the POC MLO where appropriate.

e. MLOs at all levels must maintain a timed log of media requests, responses and press releases and briefings.

Consultation and Co-ordination

13. To avoid potential conflict where the media could play one source of information against another it is essential to maintain a continual exchange of information between media liaison officers at each level. The two-way flow of information should include:

a. details of operational information released;
b. matters covered at briefings and press conferences;
c. draft media releases for clearance;
d. the text of authorised media statements; and
e. advance warning to all levels when major initiatives, either operational or in the release of information, are about to be implemented.

14. Direct links must be maintained between all MLOs to ensure effective and timely consultation.

15. All statements on Commonwealth responsibilities and interests to be released to the media in Canberra will be passed to the relevant SCC MLO and be available for release through the State Media Centres. The Coordinator CPC Media Liaison Group will advise his State counterpart of the content of any proposed statement prior to its release to ensure there is no conflict with State government policy or detriment to police operational management of the incident.

16. The SCC MLO will be responsible for advising his police counterpart of any Commonwealth media release. Questions asked about a Commonwealth statement released through a SCC Media Centre, or about other Commonwealth matters, should be referred to the Coordinator CPC Media Liaison Group. The reverse applies in respect to State matters.

17. If it is decided to make a joint Commonwealth/State Government statement, the MLOs at each centre will consult each other on the preparation of the release. After approval, the statement will be issued simultaneously in Canberra and the State in which the incident has occurred.

18. Any queries received by a MLO which relate to matters not the responsibility of the organisation he represents should be referred to the appropriate MLO.

Media Queries to Government Departments and Authorities

19. Queries from the media directed to government departments and authorities must be referred to the appropriate MLO at the crisis centres. No statement is to be made without prior consultation with the appropriate officer. MLOs at the crisis centres are responsible for providing all involved departments and authorities with guidelines on media releases at an early stage of an incident.

Communication Arrangements

20. Dedicated and voice-protected communication links should be established between the Co-ordinator CPC Media Liaison Group and the MLOs at the SCC, POC and the scene of the incident.

Media Centres

21. The Crisis Policy Centre and the State Crisis Centre will establish Media Centres. Approved media releases should be made available at these centres.
22. Media Centres should be used for media briefings and press conferences. Transcripts of briefings and press conferences should be made available, as quickly as possible, to all MLOs. These officers will be responsible for organising briefings and press conferences and for advising the media as to where and when they will be held (see also paragraphs 10–12 above).

ADF Media Liaison Arrangements

23. When releasing information to the media relating to possible or actual Australian Defence Force (ADF) assistance with the termination of a terrorist incident, the ADF Public Relations Officer (PRO) located at the POC, SCC or CPC must be consulted to clear information so as to ensure that the security of current or intended ADF assistance is not compromised.
24. ADF PROs located at the various command/crisis centres are to clear all ADF input, before release to the media, through the Public Relations Watch Desk located at the ADF Command Centre (ADFCC).
25. When the decision is made that the ADF is to terminate a terrorist

incident, the ADF PRO located at the SCC will move to the POC or PFCP to provide direct media liaison assistance to the military commander tasked to terminate the incident.

26. On termination of the incident by the ADF, and if a news conference is arranged at either the POC, SCC or CPC, it is essential that an ADF PRO be present to provide specific information relating to ADF involvement.

Personal Experiences of Australia's Public Information in Time of War

TERRY O'CONNOR

When United States aircraft began using Turkey's Incirlik airbase to launch raids against Iraq, the BBC reported the fact thus: 'we can tell you that 36 aircraft took off from the base laden with bombs and later returned without them'. The assumption of course was that the aircraft were raiding Iraq, but because the BBC reporter standing outside the gates of Incirlik had not seen the aircraft actually drop the bombs, nor had there been any official statement to that effect, the BBC felt constrained to report only the bare facts. If Incirlik had been the Australian airbase at Darwin, and I had been the BBC reporter, I could also have reported such an event, but if I had been an accredited correspondent given full access to the base, it is doubtful whether I could report how many aircraft took off, or at what time.

The Australian Defence Force (ADF) now has an official policy for dealing with the media during war. It is the Joint Services Policy (AS)41, 'Defence Public Information Policy During Periods of Tension and Conflict', and has been officially promulgated by the Chief of Defence Force. JSP(AS)41 was extensively tested during individual and joint service exercises before being accepted. It was also used during the ADF's deployment of a naval task force to the Gulf of Oman and Persian Gulf for the war with Iraq. On face value JSP(AS)41 marks the military's acceptance of the media's 'right to report', and the policy's acceptance by media organisations marks their recognition there are some things better left unreported.

In essence, journalists become accredited correspondents (AC-COR) given an introduction to basic military training, kitted out, accommodated, transported, briefed, escorted, and if needs be, evacuated by the military. Non-accredited journalists would not be given such assistance, and would be actively hindered in reporting. In exchange for this assistance, an ACCOR and his or her organisation, agree that copy, pictures or actuality will be reviewed by a Media Review Officer (MRO) before being released. The MRO, who would be an operational officer with no training in public relations or the media and thus, in practice, likely to have little understanding of the difference between propaganda and truth, is supposed to object to stories only if they contain 'operationally sensitive' material and not object on grounds of taste, accuracy or style.

The term 'operationally sensitive' covers a wide variety of information, a list of which is supposed to be handed to the ACCOR at the very beginning of the deployment. The security guidelines contained in JSP(AS)41 list examples of what an ACCOR can and cannot report: creating exactly the mindset among the military which the policy is supposed to avoid. By listing what *can* be reported, the military mind automatically assumes that nothing else may be. But even if the MRO is an enlightened sort, the list of what *cannot* be reported without prior consultation may be all-encompassing. An ACCOR *can* report on enemy actions provided such information is not gathered by intelligence means, but *cannot* report on the results of such actions which may reveal friendly locations, intentions, force levels, units or plans – presumably the only types of enemy actions not gathered by intelligence means. You could say they attacked but that would be it unless, of course, the enemy are shatteringly defeated and in full retreat (the MRO would prefer the term routed of course). I accept there is a real need for some check on reportage that may endanger lives but I believe the Australian system is still open to abuse by the military.

I have seen JSP(AS)41 in action during air force and combined services exercises in Australia and during the Gulf War. I was one of two ACCOR (the other being a *Sydney Morning Herald* photographer) embarked with the Australian task force when it left Fremantle for the Gulf in late August 1990. The policy worked, in that we were embarked on a warship heading to a potential war, assured of full navy co-operation in doing our jobs. The reality of the experience, that Australia's first contingent were only involved in enforcing the trade embargo, lessened the opportunities to test in full the policy's weaknesses. But my experiences then reinforced attitudes I held from covering several exercises.

The ACCOR are effectively at the whim of the person reviewing their copy – matters of taste, style and accuracy (supposedly out of bounds for an MRO) were routinely raised. This was in part because the copy was reviewed not only by an MRO but by the ship's captain who had to clear all signals off his vessel, and eventually by the task force commander as well. The stories were also routinely passed around the ships after transmission (to which I had no objection) so the sailors could read what was being written about them. In a small and confined community peer group pressure becomes intense, so when I wrote an article stating that the Australian's presence was not required on military grounds, making the obvious point that Australia was involved for political reasons only, the article became the subject of much angst among the officers. One even warned that such 'negative' articles could sway opinion aboard against me, and others tried by persuasion to ensure I did not write any more articles in a similar vein. There was also constant criticism of the 'tone' of my stories, or of the perceived 'political' ramifications of them, from Maritime Head-quarters and ADF command in Canberra. This was sent as rebukes to the commanding officers of the ships for 'allowing' the stories to be sent. It was obvious the bureaucracy either did not understand the ACCOR system or chose to ignore it. This led me to question the military's enthusiasm for the entire concept, which subsequent events reinforced, although I must stress I have never encountered any significant problems with the sailors, soldiers or airmen in the field who correctly see that the journalist is providing publicity for them, while obviously not trying to endanger his own life.

But surprisingly, the biggest 'problem' during that first deployment aboard the task force arose because the military chose not to interfere with the system. As I was the only journalist aboard I agreed to provide actuality for radio and television, and to help operate the television camera aboard. The videotapes were to be mailed back to Canberra for review and subsequent release. This invariably took several weeks, so when it was decided by my organisation to bring me home in mid-October I decided to bring the latest tape with me. I informed by the telephone the officer in Canberra responsible for reviewing the tapes that I would be back in Australia on the Wednesday carrying a tape showing various bridge scenes, an intercept of a merchant vessel and other footage. On the Tuesday, the day before I arrived in Sydney, a different tape sent several weeks earlier arrived on the desk of the relevant officer, Commander Paddy Hodgeman of naval public relations.

He assumed, incorrectly, that the tape was also from me. It contained footage of sailors aboard the supply ship *Success* dressed as Arabs for a boarding exercise. They were showing off for the camera in their flowing sheets and headdresses, and during the boarding exercise conducted a mock prayer meeting – all to try to make the boarding party's job as difficult as possible. Commander Hodgeman said he wanted to remove the material because he believed it would be offensive to Australia's Arab community, but could not as he believed it was material collected by an ACCOR which did not compromise the 'operationally sensitive' guidelines. It was released the next day, was shown by SBS television to several Arab Australians who objected to its release (but largely accepted the sailors were simply letting off steam), and aired that Wednesday night. The footage created a controversy, and the navy was eventually forced to apologise to the Arab community. But the footage was not taken by me, nor at my request, nor by the other ACCOR aboard. It was shot by a navy photographer on a tape I did not know existed, when I was embarked in a different vessel heading towards the first real boarding carried out by Australian sailors in the Gulf! Commander Hodgeman insists that had he known those facts the footage would never have been released because of its impact on the navy's public image – a public relations, and not public information issue.

But the problems created by that footage, the fact the Australian ships spent several months patrolling to intercept non-existent Iraqi tankers, and a general dislike of the media by the Defence Minister, all combined to highlight another problem with JSP(AS)41. ACCOR can only go with Australian Forces if the politicians agree – for all the military's beating of hearts and pronouncements of belief in the public's right to know, it is still up to a politician acting if he chooses on military advice. On 10 August it was officially announced the ships were going, and the media informed unofficially that there would be space aboard for two. But it was not until the night of the 15th that Defence Minister Robert Ray gave his approval and even then only because the Chief of Defence Force recommended he did so. After I left the ships in October, no other ACCOR were sent. In fact no Australian journalists, ACCOR or not, visited the second group until 10 January when they were in the Persian Gulf itself waiting for the deadline for war to expire.

I believe senior navy officers, smarting from the Arab video incident, decided they did not want any more prying eyes aboard, and told Senator Ray there was no space. His personal dislike of the media ensured that advice was not questioned. It was not until after a meeting of media representatives with the ADF Director General of Public Information in early December that Senator Ray addressed the issue again, and probably only because the media representatives had promised to make an issue of the lack of access to the Australian ships. Suddenly the media were told there was space available for limited visits, but it was not until 10 January that such a visit took place, and then only for three days. The *Sydney Morning Herald*, whose journalist was among the small group visiting the task force on that occasion, then published a series of articles claiming the decision to not allow the group to stay aboard was an attempt to censor news about the task force. Senator Ray did seek non-military opinion on whether the navy's objections were valid, and in a subsequent interview with me stressed the government was more than happy to have journalists aboard provided the navy gave its approval. A wonderful example of the bureaucratic muddling likely in any future use of the ACCOR system in a real conflict. The navy did not want ACCOR, and could claim it was all a political decision while the politicians were saying it was all up to the navy.

I did not visit the second group for nearly two weeks towards the end of the war, when they were escorting US carriers in the middle Gulf. Once again I had no problems in talking to the individuals or gaining material for stories (although the amount of 'hard news' was limited). This was a real war, even though the Australian ships were in no immediate danger other than from floating mines. I was privy to much information about upcoming events, and to some information gathered through intelligence means. But delays in transmission of my stories (I hasten to add these were due to technical problems not censorship) meant news of the events would have been made public ashore through the daily televised briefings well before my humble contributions could have hit the wires. There were still some occasions however, when the MRO did object to some information being included in my stories – mainly because he was unaware the information had already been publicly released in Riyadh, Washington or London, such as the names of specific ships in the area. If I had spent as much time aboard as he, however, rather than watching four weeks of CNN, I doubt I would have been able to convince him to leave the material in.

My experiences have identified several problems in the operation of the JSP(AS)41 which I am sure would be exacerbated in the case of a conflict on continental Australia or in the south Pacific when media access could not be as easily controlled by the military and where they would not have a monopoly over communication access, but I would caution those who believe the policy's negative aspects out-weigh any positive. It does still allow a great deal of open access to the military during exercises and even if it would not work in war, such access in peace can only help educate the military and the media about each other's needs and aspirations. Although flawed, this is a good first attempt and beats the hell out of the Grenada-style exclusion.

Returning again to what I see as the major issue facing all media in Western democracies when trying to deal with the military-political control. I doubt anyone of us here would seriously consider removing all political controls over the defence force which I have always understood to be a servant of the government. But whether it should directly serve government's interests to fulfill purely political motivations is quite a different issue. When defence public relations press releases dealing with non-controversial purely defence matters have to be cleared by the minister's offices, as is the case here in Australia, the government has gone too far in exerting direct control.

In the case of the Gulf, even the public information plan of the defence forces included political considerations. Its aim was, and here I paraphrase as unfortunately I no longer have a copy of the plan, to present government policy and the ADF's implementation of it, in as favourable a light as possible. Actively to seek to make the politicians look good, as I believe that plan was intended to do, is surely going too far for the military. I listened with interest to General Moore's speech yesterday when he outlined his three objectives for his public information plan and was interested to note he did not mention politics.

Political sensitivities are always going to be an issue for commanders and by extension for any journalist's covering their actions either in peace or war. But I do believe that in Australia's case during the Gulf War the military commanders in Australia were overly politically sensitive and their refusal to allow media access to the Australian ships did affect the crews' morale. The crew of the frigate *Sydney* took to referring to themselves as the super stealth frigate as they felt invisible in the media – no coverage. That was felt particularly strongly by the crews of the second task force and I believe it did affect their families.

I know that while I was there trying to do my job, and by extension getting my name and my organisation spread around, I was also being used in a way to meet public relations requirements. All publicity is good publicity as the maxim goes and in the case of the Gulf War, my stories did play their part in maintaining morale of the families at home – something General Moore again quoted as one of his public infor mation aims. That's the secret of a healthy relationship between 'us' and 'you' – a recognition that we are both trying to use the other. I see nothing wrong with it provided there are acceptable controls.

In Australia's case, and from personal experience, I believe the military and the media have those controls about right, although, as I have said, there are some modifications required. I look forward not only to reading those new guidelines in the near future but seeing the politicians' reaction to them as well.

The Australian Experience

BRIGADIER ADRIAN D'HAGÉ

One of the few advantages of writing a speech on the run, and then addressing a conference such as this well down the batting order, is that you can cheat. But since we in the military are always scrupulously honest with the media, I will 'fess up' to making some adjustments to my paper – particularly after I listened to Peter Young yesterday. Admiral Metcalf described his approach to the media as having a set of 'rules of engagement'. I *could* describe my approach as including flexibility as a principle of war – but I won't. Because, as I hope to make clear today, I want to get away from suggestions of confrontationalism. So I will describe my cheating as a 'pragmatic approach' – with an eye perhaps to a future political career.

Before I take a look at what is titled the 'Australian Experience', on behalf of defence I would like to congratulate Peter Young and his hard-working team for giving us the opportunity to put our point of view. Having said that, as a background to this presentation I will use my own experience during the 1987 Fiji Crisis and, more recently, the Gulf Crisis. During the Fiji and Vanuatu crises I was General Gration's Director of Joint Operations and my team and I actually drafted the *military* options for government, should there have been a need to evacuate Australian nationals from those areas of the South Pacific.

Those of my colleagues who know me well maintain that it is simply a case of my many past sins catching up with me, – but more recently and a few days before the Tomahawk missiles 'map read' their way across the Arabian peninsula and turned left at the traffic lights for Baghdad – I took over as the Director General of Defence Public Information. It is amazing how quickly you can learn when you have to – but I suppose with that sort of background I am as qualified as many to put the Australian Defence Force (ADF) view on our relationship with the media.

Yesterday, in his address on Northern Ireland, Dr Michael McKinley made reference to a 'mixed marriage' between a Catholic and a Protestant. In many ways the military/media relationship can be described as a mixed marriage. Like any mixed marriage, indeed any marriage, our relationship with the media can be challenging, it can be rewarding. It can be extremely frustrating – and (tongue in cheek) when that relationship breaks down – one of us invariably gets the well, and the other gets the shaft. Perhaps in the context of a marriage, Oscar Wilde is a poor choice of author, but for the military and the media, did he have it right way back in 1891 when he wrote *The Picture of Dorian Grey* and said 'a man can be happy with any woman as long as he doesn't love her'.

I must say, at the outset, that we have among the best of our journalists, some outstanding professionals. They number among them some very intelligent, dedicated and creative people; and I for one find their company stimulating and enjoyable. In Peter Young's case, and this is not meant in any derogatory way, I might well put 'provocative' in there as well. But notwithstanding some very competent people on both sides, speaker after speaker at this conference has highlighted the gladiatorial nature of our co-existennce. As the Chief of the Defence Force put it in his keynote address, the military and the media are following basically different and often contradictory agenda.

It is a trite, but sometimes necessary reminder that if history is any guide, there will, regrettably, always be wars. It matters not that many of us who have fought in one will be the first to argue that the military should be used only as a last resort. In fact, we in the military are the largest contingent of peace activists in the country. Notwithstanding that, we, like the media, are here to stay; and it is in the national interest, therefore, to find a way to co-exist in a manner that best serves our competing interests.

I am not a subscriber to the *need* for what a previous permanent secretary of the defence department, Sir Arthur Tange, referred to as 'creative tension', when describing the rift between civilians and uniformed officers in Canberra. I acknowledge that it is there but we must reduce it as far as possible – and I will cover just how I see at least the military going about that a little later. First, let me first ask what did we learn from the Fiji Crisis?

On 14 May 1987 Lieutenant Colonel Sitiveni Rambuka, supported by personnel of the Fijian military forces, entered the Fijian parliament and announced a military takeover. Prime Minister Timoci Bavadra and the members of his government were taken from the chamber under armed guard and placed under close arrest. Rambuka claimed that the coup had been executed to head off an alleged plot by the anti-government Taukei movement to assassinate the Indian members of Bavarda's one-month old cabinet – Taukei being a Fijian word translating roughly as 'owners of the land'. Answering questions from the world media as to why he had conducted the coup, Rambuka said that he wanted to avert a situation where the Fijian Army might be placed in a position where the newly-elected government might order the army to take action against the government's Fijian opponents.

It was soon to become clear, however, that the major aim of the coup was to achieve constitutional changes to ensure that there could be no future threat to traditional Fijian land ownership and to ensure that political power would remain in the hands of ethnic Fijians.

The day before the coup I and a number of other senior officers had lunched in Canberra with Brigadier Nailatikau, the commander of the Fijian military forces, and the Fijian minister for home affairs. Rambuka had timed this coup impeccably. As the news reached Australia I was sitting in the normal Thursday morning briefing in HQADF. The Chief of Operations poked his head around the door, beckoned me into the corridor and said 'There's been a coup in Fiji'. Both the military and the media had been caught, if not with their pants down, then at least by surprise. But both reacted very quickly – one overtly, the other covertly.

Despite assurances from Rambuka that there would be 'business as usual', news was spreading of a general strike and the army was continuing to make arrests. Dawn raids were being carried out against international journalists and the *Fiji Times* was closed at gunpoint. The *Fiji Sun* was also closed and a news blackout imposed on both the Fiji Broadcasting Commission and the commercial broadcasting station. As the situation deteriorated, it was beginning to look like the military might be required to assist the Fijian authorities with the evacuation of the 5,000 or so Australian tourists and residents on some of the 800 islands which make up the Fijian archipelago.

As our plans took shape I enquired as to our stock of maps. At 2am on the Sunday following the coup a survey captain appeared in the command centre with the not so welcome news that the ADF's entire stock of maps of Fiji totalled five. I dare say that in days gone by, the finance department had reacted with less than enthusiasm to proposals by the military for exercises on Viti Levu (the main island) and there had not been much call for maps of Fiji. But whatever the reason, the printing presses in Bendigo were thrown into gear – a small but significant event which happily went undetected by the *Bendigo*

Blather. Even so, maps were not finally delivered to the task force in Townsville (North Queensland) until the day the force deployed.

Eventually though, there was speculation in the media about what the military was up to. The media wanted to know our plans and it was at this point that our relationship with the media began to deteriorate. Unless things are handled with skill on both sides, divorce is on the cards. Those in the military who are less than educated in the ways of the media would, at this point, undoubtedly take heart from P. G. Wodehouse's *Jeeves in the Offing* when he wrote: 'I was in rare fettle and the heart had touched a new high. I don't know anything that braces one up like finding out that you haven't got to get married after all!'

As I previously indicated, during the Fiji Crisis I served as General Gration's Director of Joint Operations. At the joint planning committee meeting on 19 May which considered plans for Fiji, the question of media involvement in the operation was broadly addressed. Although no decision was reached at the time, the attachment to participating units of accredited correspondents selected by the Defence Media Advisory Group was discussed. In the event, accredited correspondents were not attached to the force and this caused some difficulty for the Defence Force as a whole. In particular, defence planning was tightly held in order to protect possible government intentions and decisions which had not yet been made, and this situation highlighted the difficulty of managing media releases during a military operation.

Media speculation on the possibility of a military option was heavy. Front page headlines such as 'Bavadra's Note Plea for Our Soldiers', 'Task Force Set to Pull Aussies Out' and 'Dunkirk Fleet Sails for Fiji' were common, particularly among the 'tabloid' press, which made it very difficult for the military to prepare covertly, prior to an official government announcement, for any possible deployment.

I think the major lesson that comes out of this is that, with hindsight, we would be wrong to place too much blame on the media. In my view, if the military neglects to brief the media then the 'Dunkirk Fleet Sails' speculation is going to be an inevitable result. Of course, the difficulty is compounded where a government may be, quite rightly, giving due consideration to a very significant but as yet unannounced cabinet decision. Notwithstanding, the only sure way to ensure accurate reporting is to give the media those facts which you are able; and while an early press conference may not be all that journalists desire, it will at least be able to dispel the wild speculation which inevitably accompanies this type of operation.

Operation 'Morrisdance', as the military assistance operation for the Fiji Crisis had become known, taught us many valuable operational lessons, not least of which was yet another pointer on our relationship with the media. As Jim Backus puts it 'Many a man owes his success to his first wife and his second wife to his success'.

On the media's side, as I have already indicated, one of the more serious problems is that many in the media have not the vaguest notion of the extraordinary complexities and sensitivities involved in military planning. Generously, there can be fewer than 25 journalists in the entire country who could legitimately claim to be a 'defence correspondent'. To be fair, I acknowledge the military's responsibility to assist in overcoming that problem. Education is vital and to take up Ken Llewelyn's suggestion on training – we need to look at expanding the activities of our media support unit. But it is sometimes very difficult to interest the media in the military, particularly in time of negligible threat. And then when something like Fiji or the Gulf pops up, Joe Shagnasty, who normally writes the weekly gardening column for the *Gulargambone Daily Astonisher*, is summoned by the editor and appointed as the defence correspondent.

During the Gulf Crisis, I was rung by a journalist on a Sunday tabloid. No doubt there are quite a few competent Sunday tabloid journalists but, in the time I have been director general, that has not been my overwhelming impression. This particular chap informed me that he knew we were training F-111 pilots for carrier operations in the Gulf – and would we like to come clean. I spent 20 minutes explaining, that among other things, this was likely to be a fairly dodgy proposition, particularly for F-111s on carriers. This did not deter him one iota! His editor, obliged with most of the front page and there I was on Monday, in it up to my eyeballs under a heading of 'More Aussie Pilots for the Gulf!' Across the way the opposition was demanding to know what was going on.

One of the mechanisms for controlling that sort of excess is the facsimile machine. In this particular case, I have now insisted that any further dialogue is by question and answer in writing. Incompetence or ignorance is not the exclusive preserve of the tabloids. It can also be found in the major networks. One producer was most put out when I refused to allow his camera crew into the command centre to cover the progress of the war – they would film around the secrets, he said. But just in case there are some of us in uniform who are getting a warm feeling of smugness and complacency, I would suggest that there are many, many officers and NCOs who do not understand the needs of the media and the immediacy of the news; and the very real pressures under which our colleagues in the media operate.

So what is to be done?

For our part, we are putting a number of initiatives in train. Because some of these will need to go to the Chiefs of Staff, I would ask you to treat them as 'off the record' – a background briefing – because in this relationship of ours, I trust you!

- Press conferences – the Chief of Defence Force (CDF) has indicated to me that we should do more in this area.
- Our people – we have some excellent talent in public relations. Regrettably others are less well suited and should be replaced progressively. We need to send more of our public relations personnel to military courses to broaden their knowledge. Conversely, we need to employ more 'line officers' and train them in public relations as a specialist stream. We are investigating degrees in communications through the ADF Academy whereby a graduate can, for example, serve aboard a patrol boat and then, instead of coming back into, say, the victualling area, can serve in the PR stream.
- We need to broaden the impact of our Senior Officers Media Awareness Course (SOMAC) – education is the key and I'm investigating means of putting a SOMAC 'on the road' – where formations can be lectured and trained in dealing with the media.
- At a DMAG meeting the other day we resolved to include the ministers' press secretaries in order that we might better include them in the advisory loop.
- The media ops room is now central to the way in which we function and is capable of moving to 24-hour operations in a very short space of time. A standing invitation exists for any journalist to call or visit us.
- Internally, we need to look at the conduct of our on-air interviews with the media and their impact on the troops. The media, more often than not, will focus on negatives. Let me illustrate what I mean. We have right now, in defence,

one of the best, if not the best working relationships between a CDF and secretary of defence in the history of the department. Where so often in the past we have had divisiveness between the civil and the military sides, we now have a fiercely effective, positive combination. Try putting that forward as a story – very un-newsworthy. But a public rift between two service chiefs – that's a negative – that is news! And we in PR better move to contain it. Sometimes, however, we in the military and in public relations in particular, *are* guilty of not at least acknowledging the negatives. It makes little sense, particularly to the soldier in the field who knows, for example, that the resignation rate is appalling, for me to come out the front door and tell the world we are in great shape while people are marching out the back. The media and the public will not buy it and far more importantly – you lose the confidence of your troops.

- We need to maintain our credibility at all costs. And if we can move back on the record, (I trust you!), our final initiative, which is actually one of Walter Pearson's, is to educate our own officers via the SOMAC, as to just what our policy for public information in conflict really is. For example, they need to know that through the media support unit, at the working level, where possible, the ADF provides accredited correspondents, or ACCOR, with transport and subsistence support to, from and within an area of operations. Where possible, they are provided with access to commanders and their units; detailed briefs; freedom of movement without PR minders, (which is in stark contrast to policy in the Gulf); and assistance in sending news material back to parent media organisations from even the remotest parts of Australia. They need to be aware that in return for this, the ADF asks that all news copy and material be reviewed for any possible compromises of operational security against guidelines which have been agreed to by the ACCOR. And they need to know that this review is not censorship. News copy is not reviewed for style, taste or criticism but only for security breaches. Regrettably, not every cub journalist has the depth of experience which might be attributed to David Hackworth.

Well, so much for what is on the drawing board. In closing, I would be most remiss if I didn't take issue with at least one major point from Peter Young's thesis. I have, in a way, agreed with him when I admit that we have to acknowledge our negatives – in a way which rams home just what we are doing about them. But I cannot accept his *criticism* that we are politicised, another arm of government, simply because that's exactly what we are! Albeit to be used as a last resort.

Now, of course, in one way, we are quite apolitical, in that we will serve, to the very best of our capabilities, whichever party is in power. Political parties with their ministers and Shadow ministers have a right to expect that. So I am somewhat bemused by all these calls yesterday 'to step out on our own' – tell it like it is – and get out from underneath the ministers' umbrella'. I do not know Peter Young very well but I do acknowledge his wide experience and were it not for the many many years that he has devoted to the defence debate in this country, if this were someone else urging us to expose any weaknesses we might have – I would call him naive – for the moment, I simply find it puzzling.

Finally, let me reaffirm that we in the military accept the principle of the Freedom of the Press without reservation, just as we accept that the public do need to be kept informed. In wartime, however, where lives are at risk, the Freedom of the Press and the public's right to know does not translate into the press being able to operate with complete independence.

With goodwill on both sides I think we can reduce the friction – there is a common ground. My staff will tell you that if I have had a particularly bad day at the hands of some pinko radical Sunday journal, I am prone to mutter through my teeth – 'I love the media' – and just before I left to come up here, the computer on my desk started to make a strange ticking noise. A bouncing ball had appeared on the screen and had started to write 'I love the media – one hundred times'. It won't ever come to that – but I will settle for mutual respect for each other's profession and the different tasks that we each must accomplish – together.

Index

Note: Chapter entries are in bold type